ASSOCIATION OF BUSINESS PROCESS MANAGEMENT PROFESSIONALS

Guide to the Business Process Management Common Body of Knowledge

ABPMP BPM CBOK®

Knowledge Areas

Business Process Management

| Process Modeling | Process Analysis | Process Design | Process Performance Management | Process Transformation |

Process Management Organization

Enterprise Process Management

Business Process Management Technologies

Version 2.0 – Second Release

© 2009 Association of Business Process Management Professionals
All rights Reserved

Cover designed by Jim Stuart, PMP, Business Process Management Professional, Terre Haute, Indiana, USA

© 2009 Association of Business Process Management Professionals All rights reserved.

"ABPMP", the ABPMP logo, "BPM CBOK" and "CBPP" are registered marks of the Association of Business Process Management Professionals. For a comprehensive list of ABPMP marks please contact the ABPMP legal department.

Contents

Preface		11
1	Introduction	18
2	Business Process Management	23
3	Process Modeling	37
4	Process Analysis	58
5	Process Design	86
6	Process Performance Measurement	102
7	Process Transformation	117
8	Process Organization	140
9	Enterprise Process Management	154
10	BPM Technology	175
Appendix A – References		196
Appendix B - BPM Community		200
Appendix C - Toward a BPM Model Curriculum		201
Appendix D - Certification Program		224
Appendix E – Maintenance of the BPM CBOK®		226
Appendix F – Contributors		228
Appendix G - Summary of Changes		234

Detailed Table of Contents

- Preface 11
  - Defining a Business Process Management Professional 11
  - Background on ABPMP 13
  - Core Mission/Values/Operation 14
  - Code of Ethics 15
  - Standards of Conduct 16
- 1 Introduction 18
  - 1.1 What is the Guide to the BPM CBOK®? 18
  - 1.2 Purpose of the Guide to the BPM CBOK® 18
  - 1.3 Status and Feedback 19
  - 1.4 CBOK® Organization/Summary of Chapters 20
    - 1.4.1 Values, Beliefs, Leadership, and Culture 20
    - 1.4.2 Business Process Management 21
    - 1.4.3 Process Modeling 21
    - 1.4.4 Process Analysis 21
    - 1.4.5 Process Design 21
    - 1.4.6 Process Performance Measurement 21
    - 1.4.7 Process Transformation 22
    - 1.4.8 Process Organization 22
    - 1.4.9 Enterprise Process Management 22
    - 1.4.10 BPM Technology 22
- 2 Business Process Management 23
  - 2.1 Introduction 23
    - 2.1.1 What is Business (context definition)? 23
    - 2.1.2 What is Process? 23
    - 2.1.3 What is business process management? 23
  - 2.2 Core Concepts of Business Process Management 23
    - 2.2.1 Management Discipline and Enabling Technologies 24
    - 2.2.2 Process vs. Function (end-to-end work) 25
    - 2.2.3 *Ongoing Management of Process* 25
    - 2.2.4 Process Performance and Measurement 26
    - 2.2.5 Organizational Commitment 26
  - 2.3 BPM Lifecycle 27
    - 2.3.1 Planning and Strategy 27
    - 2.3.2 Analysis 28
    - 2.3.3 Design 28
    - 2.3.4 Modeling 28
    - 2.3.5 Measuring and Monitoring 28
    - 2.3.6 Transformation 28
  - 2.4 Types of Processes 29
    - 2.4.1 Primary Processes 29
    - 2.4.2 Support Processes 29
    - 2.4.3 Management Processes 30
  - 2.5 Types of Activities 30

	2.5.1	Value Added	30
	2.5.2	Handoff	30
	2.5.3	Controls and Control Activities	30
2.6		BPM Critical Success Factors	31
	2.6.1	Alignment of Strategy, Value Chain and Business Process	32
	2.6.2	Goals	32
	2.6.3	Executive Sponsorship/Governance	32
	2.6.4	Process Ownership	32
	2.6.5	Metrics, Measures and Monitoring	32
	2.6.6	Institution Practices	33
2.7		BPM Professional Space	33
2.8		Key Concepts	35
3	Process Modeling		37
3.1		Business Process Modeling	37
	3.1.1	Diagram vs. Map vs. Model (more precision, simulate)	37
	3.1.2	Process Attributes and Characteristics	38
3.2		Purpose of Modeling	38
3.3		Benefits of Modeling	39
3.4		Modeling Standards and Notations	39
	3.4.1	Business Process Modeling Notation (BPMN)	40
	3.4.2	Flow Charting	43
	3.4.3	Swim Lanes	44
	3.4.4	Event Process Chain (EPC)	44
	3.4.5	Value Chain	45
	3.4.6	Unified Modeling Language (UML)	45
	3.4.7	IDEF-0	45
	3.4.8	LOVEM-E	45
	3.4.9	SIPOC	45
	3.4.10	Systems Dynamics	46
	3.4.11	Value Stream Mapping	46
3.5		Process Modeling Quality	46
	3.5.1	Model Validation and Simulation	49
3.6		Modeling Perspectives	49
	3.6.1	Enterprise Domain	50
	3.6.2	Business Domain	50
	3.6.3	Operations Domain	50
	3.6.4	Systems Domain	50
	3.6.5	Builder and Operator	50
3.7		Levels of models	50
	3.7.1	Enterprise	51
	3.7.2	Business Models	52
	3.7.3	Operations and Work Flow	52
	3.7.4	System	52
	3.7.5	Measurement and Control	52
3.8		Modeling Approaches	52
3.9		Capturing Information	53

- 3.9.1 Direct Observation ... 53
- 3.9.2 Interviews ... 53
- 3.9.3 Survey/Written Feedback ... 54
- 3.9.4 Structured workshops ... 54
- 3.9.5 Web-Based Conferencing ... 54
- 3.10 Modeling Participants ... 54
- 3.11 Modeling Techniques and Tools ... 55
  - 3.11.1 White Boarding and Flip Charts ... 55
  - 3.11.2 Butcher Paper and Sticky-notes ... 55
  - 3.11.3 Drawing Tools and Reports ... 55
  - 3.11.4 Electronic Modeling and Projection ... 55
- 3.12 Process Simulation ... 56
  - 3.12.1 Overview ... 56
  - 3.12.2 Mock Trials ... 56
  - 3.12.3 Technical Simulation/Load analysis ... 56
- 3.13 Key Concepts ... 57
- 4 Process Analysis ... 58
  - 4.1 What is Process Analysis? ... 58
  - 4.2 Why do Process Analysis? ... 58
  - 4.3 When to Perform Analysis ... 60
    - 4.3.1 Continuous Monitoring ... 60
    - 4.3.2 Event-Triggered Analysis ... 60
  - 4.4 Process Analysis Roles ... 61
    - 4.4.1 Optimal Team Attributes ... 61
    - 4.4.2 Responsibilities of Analysis Roles ... 62
  - 4.5 Preparing to Analyze Process ... 63
    - 4.5.1 Choose the Process ... 63
    - 4.5.2 Scope the Depth of Analysis ... 64
    - 4.5.3 Choose Analytical Frameworks ... 64
  - 4.6 Performing the Analysis ... 65
    - 4.6.1 Understanding the Unknown ... 65
    - 4.6.2 Business Environment ... 65
    - 4.6.3 Organizational Culture/Context ... 65
    - 4.6.4 Performance Metrics ... 66
    - 4.6.5 Customer Interactions ... 66
    - 4.6.6 Handoffs ... 67
    - 4.6.7 Business Rules ... 67
    - 4.6.8 Capacity ... 68
    - 4.6.9 Bottlenecks ... 68
    - 4.6.10 Variation ... 68
    - 4.6.11 Cost ... 69
    - 4.6.12 Human Involvement ... 69
    - 4.6.13 Process controls ... 69
    - 4.6.14 Other factors ... 70
    - 4.6.15 Gathering Information ... 70
    - 4.6.16 Analyzing the Business Environment ... 71

- 4.6.17 Analyzing Information Systems ... 73
- 4.6.18 Analyzing the Process ... 74
- 4.6.19 Analyzing Human Interactions ... 76
- 4.7 Document the Analysis ... 79
- 4.8 Considerations ... 80
- 4.9 Conclusion ... 84
- 4.10 Key Concepts ... 85
- 5 Process Design ... 86
  - 5.1 What is Process Design ... 86
  - 5.2 Why do Process Design? ... 86
  - 5.3 Process Design Roles ... 86
    - 5.3.1 Executive Leadership ... 87
    - 5.3.2 Process Design Team ... 87
    - 5.3.3 Subject Matter Experts ... 87
    - 5.3.4 Participants/Stakeholders ... 87
    - 5.3.5 Customer ... 87
    - 5.3.6 Project Manager ... 87
    - 5.3.7 Facilitator ... 88
    - 5.3.8 Process Owners ... 88
  - 5.4 Preparing for Process Design ... 88
    - 5.4.1 Key Activities/Roadmap for Design ... 88
    - 5.4.2 Designing the New Process ... 89
    - 5.4.3 Defining Activities within the New Process ... 89
    - 5.4.4 Comparison to Existing Process ... 90
    - 5.4.5 Creating a Physical Design ... 90
    - 5.4.6 IT Infrastructure Analysis and Design ... 91
    - 5.4.7 Creating an Implementation Plan ... 91
    - 5.4.8 Model Simulation and Testing ... 91
  - 5.5 Process Design Principles ... 93
    - 5.5.1 Design around Customer Interactions ... 93
    - 5.5.2 *Design around Value-Adding Activities* ... 93
    - 5.5.3 Minimize Handoffs ... 94
    - 5.5.4 Work is Performed Where it Makes the Most Sense ... 94
    - 5.5.5 Provide a Single Point of Contact ... 95
    - 5.5.6 Create a Separate Process for Each Cluster ... 95
    - 5.5.7 Ensure a Continuous Flow ... 95
    - 5.5.8 Reduce Batch Size ... 95
    - 5.5.9 Bring Downstream Information Needs Upstream ... 95
    - 5.5.10 Capture Information Once at the Source and Share It ... 96
    - 5.5.11 Involve as few as possible ... 96
    - 5.5.12 Redesign, then Automate ... 96
    - 5.5.13 Ensure Quality at the Beginning ... 97
    - 5.5.14 Standardize Processes ... 97
    - 5.5.15 Use Co-located or Networked Teams for Complex Issues ... 97
    - 5.5.16 Consider Outsourcing Business Processes ... 97
  - 5.6 Process Rules ... 98

- 5.7 Process Compliance 98
- 5.8 Considerations 98
  - 5.8.1 Executive Leadership 98
  - 5.8.2 Process Ownership 99
  - 5.8.3 Incentive and Rewards 99
  - 5.8.4 Cross-Functional Teams 99
  - 5.8.5 Continuous Improvement 99
  - 5.8.6 Commitment to Investment 100
  - 5.8.7 Alignment with Strategy 100
- 5.9 Conclusions 100
- 5.10 Key Concepts 101

6 Process Performance Measurement 102
- 6.1 Importance and benefits of performance measurement 102
- 6.2 Key process performance definitions 103
- 6.3 Monitoring and controlling operations 106
- 6.4 Alignment of business process and enterprise performance 106
- 6.5 What to measure 108
- 6.6 Measurement methods 109
- 6.7 Modeling and Simulation 111
- 6.8 Decision support for process owners and managers 113
- 6.9 Considerations for success 114
- 6.10 Key Concepts 116

7 Process Transformation 117
- 7.1 What is process transformation? 117
- 7.2 Improvement Methodologies 117
  - 7.2.1 Six Sigma 117
  - 7.2.2 Lean 117
  - 7.2.3 TQM 118
  - 7.2.4 Activity based costing and activity based management 119
  - 7.2.5 Performance improvement model 119
- 7.3 Redesign 120
- 7.4 Reengineering 120
- 7.5 Implementation 121
  - 7.5.1 Implementation phase 122
  - 7.5.2 Implementation activities 124
  - 7.5.3 Evaluation 135
  - 7.5.4 Quality control 135
- 7.6 Implementation roles 136
- 7.7 Sustaining the BPM Lifecycle 136
- 7.8 Organizational Change Management 138
- 7.9 Key Concepts 139

8 Process Organization 140
- 8.1 The Process Enterprise 140
  - Process Culture 141
- 8.2 Process Management Roles 141
  - 8.2.1 Process Owner 142

- 8.2.2 Process Manager 144
- 8.2.3 Process Analyst 144
- 8.2.4 Process Designer 144
- 8.2.5 Process Architects 144
- 8.2.6 Other Key Roles 145
- 8.3 Organizational Structures 147
  - 8.3.1 Process Governance 147
  - 8.3.2 Process Council 148
  - 8.3.3 BPM Office/BPM Center of Excellence 149
  - 8.3.4 Functional Centers of Excellence 150
- 8.4 Team Based Performance 152
- 8.5 Summary/Conclusions 152
- 8.6 Key Concepts 153

9 Enterprise Process Management 154
- 9.1 Definition of Enterprise Process Management 154
- 9.2 Benefits of EPM 155
- 9.3 Requirements of EPM 157
  - 9.3.1 Customer Centric Measurement Framework 159
  - 9.3.2 Process Portfolio Management 159
  - 9.3.3 Enterprise Process Improvement & Management Planning 159
- 9.4 Process Frameworks (Schematics) 161
  - 9.4.1 MIT Process Handbook Business Activity Model 162
  - 9.4.2 American Productivity and Quality Council (APQC) 163
  - 9.4.3 Value Chain Group – Value Chain Reference Model (VRM) 165
  - 9.4.4 SCOR – Supply Chain Operations Reference 167
- 9.5 Process Repository Management 168
  - 9.5.1 Why is repository administration important to EPM? 168
- 9.6 Process Management Maturity levels 168
- 9.7 EPM "Best Practices" 171
- 9.8 From Planning to Action 172
- 9.9 Key Concepts 174

10 BPM Technology 175
- 10.1 Why is technology important? 175
- 10.2 What's involved in BMP technology? 176
- 10.3 Modeling, analysis, design 177
- 10.4 Technologies that support implementation 179
- 10.5 Advantages and risks of process automation 184
- 10.6 Types of technologies available 185
  - 10.6.1 BPMS Suites 185
- 10.7 Standards 190
- 10.8 Who participates in BPM technology? 191
- 10.9 Trends and convergence of systems 191
- 10.10 Implications of BPM Technology 193
- 10.11 Key Concepts 195

Appendix A – References 196
Appendix B - BPM Community 200

Appendix C - Toward a BPM Model Curriculum ... 201
The Need for a BPM Curriculum ... 201
Contributors ... 202
Intended Users ... 202
Who would the curriculum benefit? ... 202
What type of programs would be beneficial? ... 203
The role of the model curriculum ... 203
Model Curricula ... 203
Undergraduate BPM Program ... 203
Master's Degree in BPM Program ... 205
MBA Concentration in BPM ... 208
Common Business Process Management Courses ... 209
Course Descriptions ... 210
Detailed Course Descriptions ... 211
Appendix D - Certification Program ... 224
Program Components and Qualifications ... 224
Experience ... 224
Examination ... 224
Professional Code of Ethics and Good Conduct ... 225
Recertification ... 225
Continuing Education Activities ... 225
Appendix E – Maintenance of the BPM CBOK® ... 226
Managing Future Releases and Versions ... 226
Background ... 226
Sub-Committee Structure: ... 226
Sub-Committee Mandate ... 226
Change Categories ... 227
Major changes would include ... 227
Minor changes would include ... 227
Handling Feedback ... 227
Appendix F – Contributors ... 228
Appendix G - Summary of Changes ... 234

Preface

Defining a Business Process Management Professional

The following is an excerpt from an article written for BPM Strategies October 2006 edition by Brett Champlin, President of the Association of Business Process Management Professionals (ABPMP).

Business Process Management Professionals

At several recent BPM conferences, I have asked audiences of several hundred attendees to see a show of hands, first for "Who is from IT?" generally about 30-45% of the hands go up, then, "Who is from the Business side?" another 30-45%, then, "Who here is like me, stuck in the middle?" Nearly the entire group raises their hands, generally emphatically. This is telling. Many of us, who work in process management, process redesign, process performance analysis, process automation, and the like, are conflicted. Are we business practitioners who have to understand how to leverage IT to manage by process or are we IT practitioners who have to understand the business in order to fully utilize the capabilities of new IT solutions?

BPM is both a management discipline and a set of technologies that supports managing by process. A convergence of technologies for workflow, enterprise application integration (EAI), document and content management, business rules management, performance management and analytics among other have been brought to bear with a focus on supporting process based management. A few years ago BPM software vendors were focused on the execution layer of the technology stack. Today they are delivering BPM Suites with a full range of features and functions to support process managers and analysts as well as technology developers.

Recent research studies confirm that Business Process Management (BPM) is rapidly evolving as the dominant management paradigm of the 21st Century. An April 2005 BPMG study found that "…the practice of BPM as a primary means to manage business has already gained substantial adoption" and "…more than 80% of the world's leading organizations are actively engaged in BPM programs, many of these on a global scale". An APQC benchmarking study completed in March 2005 found that "BPM is the way best-practice organizations conduct business." That study also examined proven strategies, approaches, tools and techniques (including business process frameworks and maturity models) employed by world-class, process-focused enterprises and found that while "technology, by itself, does not constitute Business Process Management, much of the promise of BPM initiatives will not be realized without powerful, flexible and user-friendly IT solutions to support them."

Business Process Management and Performance Management are merging as more and more process management groups begin to recognize the organization as a system of interacting processes whose performance must be balanced and that must be the focus of fulfilling strategies. Conversely, more and more of those engaged in enterprise performance management are realizing that it is the performance of the business processes, not the organizational functional units or a set of assets, that has to be their central focus in order to gain the true benefits of a performance management initiative. Sophisticated and powerful new technologies are central to successful and sustainable programs for both of these disciplines, and integrating the information delivery capabilities as well as management methods is critical to moving up the scale of maturity in deploying these practices.

Along with this business process management revolution, new organizational structures and roles are emerging and a new genre of professionals is emerging to support these practices. Yet, business schools don't teach us how to manage by process. No textbooks tell us what roles and responsibilities we need to put in place in order to do this kind of work. There is no authoritative research to indicate exactly how we should structure our governance and operations to do this kind of work. In fact, what research there is indicates that there is no "one-size-fits-all" solution. Various models and roles have proven successful in various industries, none showing any clear advantage over the other. One thing that is clear is that managing by process and adapting new information systems tools to support those activities is a successful strategy that brings tremendous advantage to those businesses that adopt it. And, it seems that the broader based the process management initiative is in the organization, the more effective it is and more value it adds.

There seem to be as many companies whose BPM efforts are driven by their IT organizations as there are those whose BPM programs are being led by core business areas. Likewise there seems to be two major approaches: those that are more project-oriented versus those that view BPM as a continuous process improvement and transformation effort. These different models generate roles and responsibilities with widely varying titles and alignments of responsibilities, yet all are process management focused.

Within the Association of BPM Professionals, our membership shows a diversity of titles that reflect these divergent approaches to process management. We have well over 150 different titles represented in our database, although there are clusters around some of the titles like Manager, Director, VP, Analyst, Consultant, Architect usually preceded or followed by Process, BPM, Process Improvement, Process Innovation, and the like.

One role that is particularly significant in BPM programs is that of the Process Owner. Depending on whether the organization restructures around cross-functional business processes, creates a matrix managed organization, appoints functional managers to take on a dual role, or relies on a cross-functional council of managers to oversee core business processes, they all show contain some title that ensures that someone take on the responsibilities of a "Process Owner" for each of the organization's key operational processes. This role seems to be one of the critical success factors in effective process oriented organizations.

An organizational factor that seems to reflect the evolution or maturity in organizations implementing BPM is the existence of a specialized group that is recognized as the process specialists. Many begin with a BPM "Center of Excellence" or similar group that provides to the organization process modeling, analysis, design, and project expertise along with standard tools, methods and techniques and acts as an internal consulting group. A more mature or experienced process oriented organization will have a process management governance group or "Process Management Office" that oversees the organization's portfolio of processes, and aligns, prioritizes, and authorizes transformation efforts. And, some companies may have both types of groups working together. These groups are staffed with process management professionals with a wide range of titles and alignment of responsibilities.

While there seem to be many successful models for implementing BPM in organizations, one thing they all have in common is the many new roles with new sets of skills and responsibilities all centered on BPM. This is an emerging group of professionals whose work is essential to 21st century business, the business process professional. Judging from the members of ABPMP, they are generally highly educated (67% have a bachelor or advanced degree) and have a significant amount of experience (9.9 years average) working in process improvement and redesign.

Some of the more common roles are:

- Business Process Analyst
- Business Process Engineer
- Business Process Architect
- Business Process Manager
- Business Process Consultant
- Business Process Manager
- Business Process Owner
- Business Analyst
- Business Systems Analyst
- Manager or Director of Business Performance Improvement
- Manager or Director of Business Process Innovation

- *Process Owner*
- *Process Officer*

These titles and their variants cover the majority of the new roles and responsibilities in process managed organizations. Regardless of the roles or organizational structure, they generally are responsible for the same sets of activities: Process Modeling, Process Analysis, Process Design, Process Change and Transformation, Process Implementation, Process Monitoring and Control, and Process Performance Improvement. Some of these roles may be staffed in IT organizations and some in business disciplines. Many organizations are staffing cross-discipline groups combining both IT and business knowledge or with people who have served in both IT and business units and bring a depth of knowledge and range of skills that transcend traditional boundaries. Many have found that combining people who have general consulting type knowledge and skills with those who have a depth of business specific knowledge is a successful strategy for BPM efforts.

There is a new professional in the business world today, the business process professional. The work they do is critical to the future of competitive organizations today. And, even though there is no single or clear model that one can adopt, it doesn't diminish the need for more skilled and motivated people to do this work. Eventually, universities will come out with well researched and structured models based on some of the most visible success stories. In the meantime, business can't wait for someone to tell them the "best" way to do this, they have to do this work today and there just aren't enough knowledgeable skilled people to go around. Successful organizations are finding that to staff these groups, they have to invest in training and development. Some are building their own curricula and training programs and bringing entry level people on board to work closely with the few talented BPM professionals they do have. Others are sending managers, project leaders, and systems analysts to training like the BPM-Institute certificate program to begin to build the requisite knowledge and skills. This situation will likely continue to be the most viable approach to building process organizations for the near future.

The mission of ABPMP is to engage in activities that promote the practice of business process management, to develop a common body of knowledge in this field, and to contribute to the advancement and skill development of professionals who work in this discipline. ABPMP's local chapters produce periodic events featuring case studies and presentations about BPM topics that provide an inexpensive continuing education program for their members. ABPMP has an education committee that is developing a BPM Common Body of Knowledge. Following that we will produce recommended curricula for academic and training programs. We intend to create a set of criteria to evaluate training programs and a formal endorsement process for training providers and academic programs. Following that we will develop a professional certification program to certify practitioners and expert business process management professionals.

I think working in BPM at this time is the most exciting and valuable business experience managers and professionals can get today. I see Business Process Management professionals as the new training background for future business leaders today, much as project management was 15 years ago. However, we need to develop some baseline standards, minimum qualifications, and some reasonable path for becoming a professional in this area. If you are working in process management, join others in developing the profession – join ABPMP today. Together we can build a new professional discipline that will create the future

Background on ABPMP

The Association of Business Process Management Professionals (ABPMP) is a non-profit, vendor independent, professional organization dedicated to the advancement of business process management concepts and its practices.

ABPMP is practitioner-oriented and practitioner-led.

ABPMP has local chapters in several US areas and has many more forming in the US and internationally. Individuals wishing to participate who are not located near an existing local chapter are urged to investigate the feasibility of starting a chapter where they are located. While they are not affiliated with a local operating chapter, members will be part of the Members At-Large chapter which has its own elected officers and participates in ABPMP activities as any other chapter would.

ABPMP is governed by an elected Board of Directors. Each chapter president is an ex-officio and voting member of the International Board of Directors. ABPMP also has a Board of Advisors made up of some of the most well-known authors, practitioners and thought-leaders in the field. They are also volunteers and periodically offer the Board of Directors and Chapters advice on the industry and how ABPMP can best serve its members.

ABPMP also has a number of affiliations with other professional organizations, including the International Association of Business Process Management (IABPM) who administrates the ABPMP certification process and translates the BPM CBOK® into the French and German languages. Additional affiliations are described in the Appendix labeled "Reference Disciplines."

For more information on ABPMP, please see our website at www.abpmp.org.

Core Mission/Values/Operation

The Association of Business Process Management Professionals is a non-profit, vendor-neutral, professional organization dedicated to the advancement of business process management concepts and its practices. ABPMP is practitioner-oriented and practitioner-led.

Vision
The vision of the ABPMP is to:

- Be the center for the community of practice in business process management
- Provide the leading professional society for business process management professionals
- Define the discipline and practice of business process management
- Recognize, acknowledge and honor those who make outstanding contributions to the business process management discipline

Mission
The mission of ABPMP is:

- To engage in activities that promote the practice of business process management,
- To develop a Common Body of Knowledge for BPM, and

- To contribute to the advancement and skill development of professionals who work in the BPM discipline.

Operation

The ABPMP produces educational and networking events for continuing education and sharing of best practices, new ideas, and experiences of its members and professional colleagues. Information on these events can be found on the ABPMP website at www.abpmp.org.

Code of Ethics

ABPMP is committed to the highest standard of professional ethics and believes that Business Process Management Professionals should:

- Conduct their professional and personal lives and activities in an ethical manner
- Recognize a standard of ethics founded on honesty, justice and courtesy as principles guiding their conduct and way of life
- There is an obligation to practice their profession according to this code of ethics and standards of conduct

All ABPMP members must agree to and sign the following code of ethics and statement of professional conduct.

The keystone of professional conduct is integrity. Business Process Management Professionals will discharge their duties with fidelity to the public, their employers, and clients with fairness and impartiality to all. It is their duty to interest themselves in public welfare, and be ready to apply their special knowledge for the benefit of humankind and the environment.

I acknowledge that:

I have an obligation to society and will participate to the best of my ability in the dissemination of knowledge pertaining to the general development and understanding of business process management. Further, I shall not use knowledge of a confidential nature to further my personal interest, nor shall I violate the privacy and confidentiality of information entrusted to me or to which I may gain access.

I have an obligation to my employer/client whose trust I hold. Therefore, I shall endeavor to discharge this obligation to the best of my ability, to guard my employer/client's interests, and provide advice wisely and honestly. I shall promote the understanding of business process management methods and procedures using every resource available to me.

I have an obligation to my fellow members and professional colleagues. Therefore, I shall uphold the high ideals of ABPMP as outlined in the Association Bylaws. Further, I shall cooperate with my fellow members and shall treat them with honesty and respect at all times.

I accept these obligations as a personal responsibility and as a member of this Association. I shall actively discharge these obligations and I dedicate myself to that end.

Standards of Conduct

These standards expand on the Code of Ethics by providing specific statements of behavior in support of the Code of Ethics. They are not objectives to be strived for; they are rules that no true professional will violate. The following standards address tenets that apply to the profession.

In recognition of my professional obligations I shall:

- Avoid conflict of interest and make known any potential conflicts
- Protect the privacy and confidentiality of all information entrusted to me
- Accept full responsibility for work that I perform
- Insure that the products of my work are used in a socially responsible way, to the best of my ability
- Support, respect, and abide by the appropriate local, national, and international laws
- Make every effort to ensure that I have the most current knowledge and that the proper expertise is available when needed
- Share my knowledge with others and present factual and objective information to the best of my ability
- Be fair, honest, and objective in all professional relationships
- Cooperate with others in achieving understanding and in identifying problems
- Protect the proper interests of my employer and my clients at all times
- Take appropriate action in regard to any illegal or unethical practices that come to my attention; I will bring charges against any person only when I have reasonable basis for believing in the truth of the allegations and without any regard to personal interest
- Not use knowledge of a confidential or personal nature in any unauthorized manner or to achieve personal gain
- Never misrepresent or withhold information that is germane to a problem or situation of public concern nor will I allow any such known information to remain unchallenged
- Not take advantage of the lack of knowledge or inexperience on the part of others
- Not use or take credit for the work of others without specific acknowledgement and authorization
- Not misuse authority entrusted to me

I acknowledge that I have read, understand, and will uphold these professional ethics and standards of conduct.

Signed: _____

Date: _____

1 Introduction

1.1 What is the Guide to the BPM CBOK®?

As BPM business practices, management discipline, and enabling technologies mature, our understanding of BPM also matures. There is a tremendous body of knowledge on BPM, including dozens of books, articles, presentations, process models and best practices which are based upon practice experience, academic study and lessons learned. The trend in BPM today focuses on enterprise-wide, cross-functional processes that add value for customers (both internal and external). Business processes define how enterprises perform work to deliver value to their customers. The purposeful management of these processes creates stronger business practices that lead to more effective processes, greater efficiencies, more agility, and ultimately higher returns on stakeholders' investments.

It would be impossible to collect and present all of the knowledge on the practice of BPM available in a single volume. This guide to the BPM Common Body of Knowledge is designed to assist BPM professionals by providing a comprehensive overview of the issues, best practices and lessons learned commonly practiced as collected by the ABPMP. BPM is a constantly evolving discipline. This initial release of the ABPMP BPM CBOK® provides a basic understanding of BPM practice along with references to the BPM community and other valuable sources of information. BPM professionals are encouraged to use this guide in conjunction with a variety of other sources of information, be involved in the BPM community, and expand and share their knowledge on the practice of BPM.

1.2 Purpose of the Guide to the BPM CBOK®

This Guide to the BPM CBOK® provides a basic reference document for all practitioners. The primary purpose of this guide is to identify and provide an overview of the Knowledge Areas that are generally recognized and accepted as good practice. The Guide provides a general overview of each Knowledge Area and provides a list of common activities and tasks associated with each Knowledge Area. It also provides links and references to other sources of information which are part of the broader BPM Common Body of Knowledge.

As this is the first time a formal guide to the practice of business process management has been published, the Guide is also intended as a spring board for discussions amongst BPM professionals. Often, an emerging discipline such as BPM finds different groups using language in different ways resulting in conflicting definitions for terms which can confuse discussions on the topic. This Guide to the BPM CBOK® encourages the use of a common, agreed upon vocabulary for the BPM discipline.

In addition, the Guide reflects the fundamental knowledge required of a BPM professional. Any assessment or professional certification in the field would require a demonstration of understanding of the core BPM concepts outlined in the knowledge areas, as well as the ability to perform the activities and tasks identified within it. This

Guide to the BPM CBOK® is the basis for developing examination questions for the exam that individuals must pass to become certified by the ABPMP as a Certified Business Process Professional (CBPP™). In addition to a variety of other requirements, applicants for the CBPP™ designation will be tested on their knowledge in each area in a rigorous and psychometrically sound examination. This examination is being developed by the ABPMP as the BPM CBOK® is constructed and with the aid of a professional certification and licensure testing company. ABPMP is following the International Standard ANSI/ISO 17024 and ACE (American Council on Education) General Requirements for Bodies Operating Certification of Persons in the creation of the certification and examination processes.

1.3 Status and Feedback

The development of the Common Body of Knowledge in BPM is evolving and will expand as information and experience is added, and so too will this Guide to the BPM CBOK®. The purpose of this second release of the Guide is to further define the scope and structure of the Guide. Several sections still have content under development which will be updated in subsequent releases.

The development and management of the Guide to the BPM CBOK® is the responsibility of the Education Committee within the ABPMP. The Education Committee feels that this release should be made available not only to ABPMP members but also to a broader audience in order to solicit feedback and gauge acceptance by the Community of BPM professionals. Background and contact information for the Contributors and Education Committee can be found in Appendix F - Contributors and on the ABPMP website at www.abpmp.org.

Membership support and enthusiasm are critical to the success of this Guide, the development of the Certification process, and the promulgation of knowledge on BPM topics. To support membership involvement in the evolution of the BPM CBOK® the education committee has formed a subcommittee which focuses on the support and maintenance of this Guide. This subcommittee has published procedures for soliciting and providing feedback, as well as policies for how this Guide will be periodically updated. These policies and procedures are found in Appendix E - Maintenance of the BPM CBOK® at the end of this Guide and are updated periodically on the ABPMP website at www.abpmp.org.

Additional comments are encouraged, and ABPMP members are invited to email the Education Committee at education@abpmp.org.

1.4 CBOK® Organization/Summary of Chapters

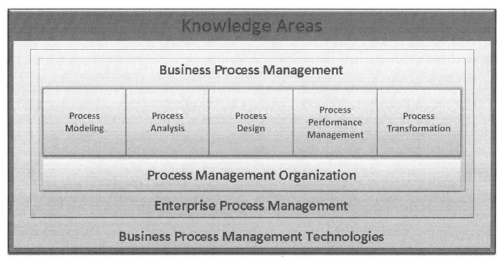

Figure 1-1 BPM CBOK® Organization

This Guide to the BPM CBOK® is organized in nine knowledge areas or chapters as outlined in Figure 1-1. Core BPM concepts are covered in the Business Process Management chapter which overlays and sets the stage for all of the subsequent Knowledge Areas. The Process Modeling, Analysis, Design, Performance Management, and Transformation Knowledge Areas cover critical BPM activities and skill sets. The larger BPM environmental issues and how the practice of BPM relates to other organizational dimensions, such as governance and strategic planning, are addressed in the Process Management Organization and Enterprise Process Management chapters. All of the BPM practices are enabled and supported by BPM Technologies.

1.4.1 Values, Beliefs, Leadership, and Culture

The practice of BPM is defined by a set of values, beliefs, leadership and culture which form the foundation of the environment in which an organization operates. They influence and guide organizational behavior and structure. The organization provides its employees opportunities for open discussion, personal and professional growth, and forms the basis for external relationships with their customers, suppliers and the community at-large. These values, beliefs, culture and leadership styles determine the success or failure of the Enterprise both from organizational and financial perspectives.

BPM focuses on end-to-end business processes which deliver value to customers. A commitment to process and customer value is a cornerstone to the practice of BPM. As a cornerstone, a discussion of the values, beliefs, leadership and culture which support and enable BPM is weaved throughout the Knowledge Areas within this Guide to the BPM CBOK®.

1.4.2 Business Process Management

The Business Process Management knowledge area focuses on the core concepts of BPM, such as key definitions, end-to-end process, customer value, and the nature of cross-functional work. Process types, process components, the BPM lifecycle, along with critical skills and success factors are introduced and explored. This Knowledge Area defines BPM and provides the fundamental foundation for exploring the remaining Knowledge Areas.

1.4.3 Process Modeling

Process Modeling includes a critical set of skills and processes which enable people to understand, communicate, measure, and manage the primary components of business processes. The Process Modeling Knowledge Area provides an overview of these skills, activities and key definitions, along with an understanding of the purpose and benefits of process modeling, a discussion of the types and uses of process models, and the tools, techniques, and modeling standards.

1.4.4 Process Analysis

Process Analysis involves an understanding of business processes, including the efficiency and effectiveness of business processes. The purpose and activities for process analysis are explored. A decomposition of process components and attributes, analytical techniques, and process patterns are also covered. The use of process models and other process documentation to validate and understand both current and future state processes is explored. A variety of process analysis types, tools and techniques are included within this Knowledge Area.

1.4.5 Process Design

Process design involves creating the specifications for business processes within the context of business goals and process performance objectives. It provides the plans and guidelines for how work flows, how rules are applied and how business applications, technology platforms, data resources, financial and operational controls interact with other internal and external processes. Process design is the intentional and thoughtful planning for how business processes function and are measured, governed and managed. This Knowledge Area explores process design roles, techniques, and principles of good design along with an exploration of common process design patterns and considerations such as compliance, executive leadership and strategic alignment.

1.4.6 Process Performance Measurement

Process performance measurement is the formal, planned monitoring of process execution and the tracking of results to determine the effectiveness and efficiency of the process. This information is used to make decisions for improving or retiring existing processes and/or introducing new processes in order to meet the strategic objectives of the organization. Topics covered include key process performance definitions, importance and benefits of performance measurement, monitoring and controlling operations, alignment of business process and enterprise performance, what to measure, measurement methods, modeling and simulation, decision support for process owners and managers and considerations for success.

1.4.7 Process Transformation

Process transformation addresses process change. Process changes are discussed in the context of a business process lifecycle. Various process improvement, redesign and reengineering methodologies are explored, along with the tasks associated with implementing process change. The topic of organizational change management, which is critical to successful process transformation, is discussed including a number of organizational change management methodologies, techniques and best practices.

1.4.8 Process Organization

The process management organization knowledge area addresses the roles, responsibilities and reporting structure to support process-driven organizations. A discussion of what defines a process driven enterprise, along with cultural considerations and cross-functional, team-based performance is provided. The importance of business process governance is explored, along with a variety of governance structures and the notion of a BPM Center of Expertise/Excellence (COE).

1.4.9 Enterprise Process Management

Enterprise process management is driven by the need to maximize the results of business processes consistent with well-defined business strategies and functional goals based on these strategies. Process portfolio management ensures that the process portfolio supports corporate or business unit strategies and provides a method to manage and evaluate initiatives. The Enterprise Process Management Knowledge Area identifies tools and methods to assess process management maturity levels, along with required BPM practice areas which can improve their BPM organization state. A number of Business Process Frameworks are discussed, along with the notion of process integration, i.e., interaction of various processes with each other and models which tie performance, goals, technologies, people, and controls (both financial and operational) to business strategy and performance objectives. The topics of process architecture and enterprise process management best practices are explored.

1.4.10 BPM Technology

BPM is a technology enabled and supported management discipline. This chapter discusses the wide range of technologies available to support the planning, design, analysis, operation, and monitoring of business processes. These technologies include the set of application packages, development tools, infrastructure technologies, and data and information stores that provide support to BPM professionals and workers in BPM related activities. Integrated Business Process Management System (BPMS), process repositories and stand-alone tools for modeling, analysis, design, execution and monitoring are discussed. BPM standards, methodologies and emerging trends are also covered.

2 Business Process Management

2.1 Introduction

This Chapter introduces the concepts and strategies required to successfully manage your business processes from a holistic end-to-end perspective. In this Knowledge Area we focus on the core concepts of BPM, such as key definitions, end-to-end process, customer value, and the nature of cross-functional work. We explore process types, process components, the BPM lifecycle, along with critical skills and success factors. This knowledge area defines BPM and provides the fundamental foundation for exploring the remaining knowledge areas.

2.1.1 What is Business (context definition)?

The term "business" as used here refers to individuals, interacting together, to perform a set of activities to deliver value to customers and a return on investment to the stakeholders. In this Guide to the BPM CBOK® "business" refers to all types of for-profit, not-for-profit, and government organizations.

2.1.2 What is Process?

In order to understand BPM, it is necessary to understand business process. A "process", in this context, is a defined set of activities or behaviors performed by humans or machines to achieve one or more goal. Processes are triggered by specific events and have one or more outcome that may result in the termination of the process or a handoff to another process. Processes are composed of a collection of interrelated tasks or activities which solve a particular issue. In the context of business process management, a "business process" is defined as end-to-end work which delivers value to customers. The notion of end-to-end work is critical as it involves all of the work, crossing any functional boundaries, necessary to completely deliver customer value.

2.1.3 What is business process management?

"Business Process Management" (BPM) is a disciplined approach to identify, design, execute, document, measure, monitor, and control both automated and non-automated business processes to achieve consistent, targeted results aligned with an organization's strategic goals. BPM involves the deliberate, collaborative and increasingly technology-aided definition, improvement, innovation, and management of end-to-end business processes that drive business results, create value, and enable an organization to meet its business objectives with more agility. BPM enables an enterprise to align its business processes to its business strategy, leading to effective overall company performance through improvements of specific work activities either within a specific department, across the enterprise, or between organizations.

2.2 Core Concepts of Business Process Management

There are a number of fundamental, core concepts which define BPM, including the notions that:

- BPM is a management discipline and a set of enabling technologies
- BPM addresses end-to-end work and distinguishes between sets of sub-processes, tasks, activities and functions
- BPM is a continuous, ongoing set of processes focused on managing an organizations end-to-end business processes
- BPM includes the modeling, analysis, design and measurement of an organization's business processes
- BPM requires a significant organizational commitment, often introducing new roles, responsibilities, and structures to traditional functionally oriented organizations
- BPM is technology enabled with tools for visual modeling, simulation, automation, integration, control and monitoring of business processes and the information systems which support these processes

2.2.1 Management Discipline and Enabling Technologies

The BPM acronym has been used loosely and its meaning often varied depending upon the context. Software companies often refer to BPM to describe the capabilities of a particular product or technology, while practitioners, management consultants, and academics typically discuss the process and management discipline of BPM.

First and foremost, BPM is a management discipline and process for managing an organization's business processes. Enabling technology is meaningless without the management disciplines and processes for exploiting the technology; the tools for managing an organization's business processes. BPM involves managing the end-to-end work organizations perform to create value for their customers. The performance of this work is essentially how organizations fulfill their mission.

Many technology vendors have created application suites which help enable organizations to better manage their business processes. These technologies typically involve tools to visually design and model business processes; simulate and test business processes, automate, control and measure business processes, and provide feedback and reporting on process performance. Some vendors have combined these functions into business process management suites that provide a complete integrated BPM platform, commonly referred to as a Business Process Management Systems (BPMS).

Most large organizations have a significant investment into a number of legacy systems. These systems are typically designed to support specific functions such as manufacturing or sales. In order to manage the end-to-end work involved in business processes, a BPMS must be able to integrate with legacy systems across the organization in order to control work, get information, or measure performance. A variety of new technologies have emerged to simplify integration efforts. A common framework for how these technologies are deployed is also being adopted and is most often referred to as a Service Oriented Architecture (SOA). The technology industry appears to be standardizing on a specific set of open technologies commonly referred to as "web services." By leveraging web services in a SOA, organizations can build and manage end-to-end business processes across organizational silos and their legacy systems. Many modern BPM technology solutions include the capability to integrate legacy systems through standards based interfaces while providing the tools to automate and orchestrate work across the entire organization.

The acronym BPM will continue to be used to describe technology products which support and enable BPM. However, BPM is first and foremost a management discipline and set of processes for managing an organization's business processes.

2.2.2 Process vs. Function (end-to-end work)

"Business functions" are typically defined by a group of activities related by a particular skill or goal, i.e., sales, finance or manufacturing. Functional organization dates back to Adam Smith's *Wealth of Nations* where he describes the notion of task specialization. By using highly skilled workers performing individual tasks, organizations could achieve huge economies of scale allowing them to increase market share and profit margins. Functions focus on these individual tasks where business processes focus on the end-to-end work, i.e., tasks and activities, across all functional boundaries to deliver customer value. Functions are ongoing where business processes have defined inputs and outputs. For example, a typical accounting department focuses on tasks associated with tracking, measuring and reporting financial transactions within an organization. The work is continuous and ongoing. Business processes, however, focus on end-to-end transactions which deliver value to customers. These end-to-end processes often include tasks associated with customer engagement through customer request through fulfillment. The functional accounting department supports these business processes by performing specific tasks. However, the accounting department is not typically responsible for the end-to-end work associated with the larger business process.

2.2.3 Ongoing Management of Process

Many people confuse Business Process Management (BPM) with Business Process Improvement (BPI) initiatives. BPI initiatives typically imply projects or a set of one-time unique improvements in redesigning or otherwise fixing a process. Common BPI methodologies include six sigma, lean, total quality management (TQM) or reengineering efforts (a la Michael Hammer). BPM, on the other hand, implies a permanent ongoing organizational commitment to managing the organizations processes. It includes a set of activities, such as modeling, analysis, a thoughtful and intentional process design, performance measurement and process transformation. It involves a continuous, never- ending feedback loop to ensure the organization's business processes are aligned to its strategy and performing to expectations. The BPM knowledge area of transformation deals with business process changes where common BPI methodologies may be applied. BPI typically addresses a specific improvement or set of process improvements. However, the use of these BPI methodologies does not imply that the organization is committed to the practice of BPM.

2.2.4 Process Performance and Measurement

The practice of BPM requires the measurement and supervision of process performance. This typically includes setting process performance goals, measuring actual performance, and reviewing the effectiveness of business processes. Process performance and measurement is a critical element in the BPM lifecycle, providing valuable information, insight and feedback to other primary activities such as process analysis, design and transformation.

Many organizations define and measure business process performance across two primary dimensions: (1) the extent to which process goals are attained; and (2) the efficiency and effectiveness of process activities. Performance measures may be available to management through reports based on information gathered at key points in a process. Measures of costs, time to completion of tasks, financial conditions and a myriad of other metrics may be developed and used to support decisions by management. The use of BPM technologies provides information systems which assist in measuring and monitoring process performance. Some sophisticated BPM systems send alerts to management of processes performance variances from designated targets. Some even automatically adjust process conditions to realign activities with process goals based upon performance objectives, i.e., moving work between work queues based upon an unsatisfactory bottleneck or backlog.

2.2.5 Organizational Commitment

The practice of BPM requires a significant organizational commitment. Traditional organizations are centered on functional areas such as sales, marketing, finance and manufacturing. The management of end-to-end business process crosses organizational boundaries. New roles and responsibilities are introduced, such as process owners, designers and architects. Individuals responsible for end-to-end process design must interact with traditional functionally based managers and new governance structures are introduced which may change the way organizations make decisions and allocate resources. BPM requires a top to bottom commitment from the organization, from executive leadership who define and support the practice of BPM, through line and functional managers who must collaborate with process owners on the design and execution of business processes, to individuals who often must often work in teams to execute processes on behalf of customers.

Experience has shown that without organizational commitment, the practice and benefits of BPM is unlikely to mature within an organization. Individuals may possess BPM skills and organizations may possess BPM technologies. Yet, without supporting leadership, values, beliefs, and culture, BPM is unlikely to successfully take hold within an organization. Strong leadership is perhaps most critical since it is the organization's leaders who most influence culture, set the structures, goals, and incentives for the organization, and have the necessary authority to make changes in order to create an environment for success.

2.3 BPM Lifecycle

The management practice of BPM may be characterized as a continuous lifecycle (process) of integrated BPM activities. While several variations of BPM lifecycles are recognized,[1] most lifecycles can be summarized by an iterative, phased set of activities including: (1) Planning; (2) Analysis; (3) Design and Modeling; (4) Implementation; (5) Monitoring and Control; and (6) Refinement. As business processes move through the lifecycle, they are enabled or constrained by a variety of factors including the four primary factors of Leadership, Values, Culture and Beliefs as illustrated in Figure 2-1.

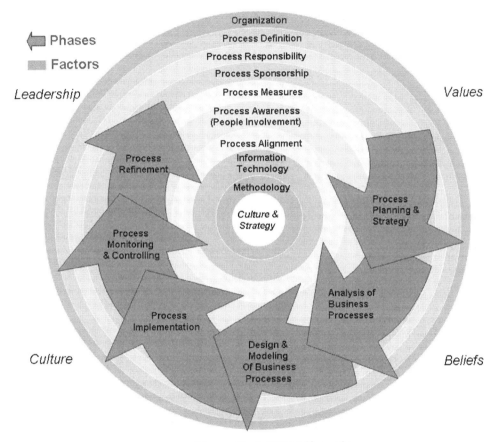

Figure 2 - 1 BPM Lifecycle

2.3.1 Planning and Strategy

In this model the BPM lifecycle begins with developing a process driven strategy and plan for the organization. The plan starts with an understanding of organizational strategies and goals designed to ensure a compelling value proposition for customers. The plan provides structure and direction for continued customer centric process management. It lays a foundation for a holistic BPM approach to ensure the alignment with organizational strategy and the integration of strategy, people, processes, and

---

[1] zur Muehlen, 2004; Scheer, et. al. 2004

systems across functional boundaries. This phase sets the strategy and direction for the BPM process. It also identifies appropriate BPM organizational roles and responsibilities, executive sponsorship, goals, and expected performances measures and methodologies. If significant transformation activities are expected to occur, organizational changes in management strategies are examined.

2.3.2 Analysis

The analysis of business processes incorporates several methodologies with the goal of understanding the current organizational processes in the context of the desired goals and objectives. Analysis assimilates information from strategic plans, process models, performance measurements, changes in the environment, and other factors in order to fully understand the business processes in the context of the overall organization.

2.3.3 Design

Process design activities focus on the intentional, thoughtful design of how end-to-end work occurs in order to deliver value to customers. The sequence of activities, including the design of what work is performed, at what time, in what location, by what process actors using what methodology is documented. Design defines what the organization wants the process to be and answers the what, when, where, who and how questions of how end-to-end work is executed. An important component of design is also ensuring that the proper management controls and metrics are in place for compliance and performance measurement. In an iterative BPM lifecycle, initial design activities may look at standardizing or automating current ad hoc activities, while more mature design activities may look at redesign or radically reminding a process, or incremental improvements designed for optimization.

2.3.4 Modeling

Understanding the process typically involves process modeling and an assessment of the environmental factors which enable and constrain the process. For organizations that are less mature in the practice of BPM, it may be the first time the entire end-to-end business process has been documented. More mature organizations may focus more on environmental factors, nuances, and exceptions to the business processes.

2.3.5 Measuring and Monitoring

Continuous measuring and monitoring of business processes provides the information necessary for process managers to adjust resources in order to meet process objectives. In the context of the BPM lifecycle, measuring and monitoring also provides critical process performance information through key measurements related to goals and value to the organization. The analysis of process performance information may result in improvement, redesign or reengineering activates.

2.3.6 Transformation

Process transformation implements the output of the iterative analysis and design cycle. It addresses organizational change management challenges and is aimed at continuous improvement and process optimization. In this context, "optimized processes" are those that consistently achieve predefined goals in terms of both efficiency and effectiveness. They are managed in such a way that they are able to respond to environmental changes for consistent results.

2.4 Types of Processes

There are three different types of end-to-end business processes:

- Primary processes (often referred to as core processes)
- Support processes
- Management processes

2.4.1 Primary Processes

Primary processes are end-to-end, cross-functional processes which directly deliver value to customers. Primary processes are often referred to as "core" processes as they represent the essential activities an organization performs to fulfill its mission. These processes make up the value chain where each step adds value to the preceding step as measured by its contribution to the creation or delivery of a product or service, ultimately delivering value to customers.

Value chains are comprised of what Michael Porter (1985) described as "primary" activities and "supporting" activities. The Enterprise-wide Business Process Value Chain describes a way of looking at the chain of activities (processes) that provides value to the customer. Each of these activities has its own performance objectives linked to its parent business process. Primary processes can move across functional organizations, across departments, or even between enterprises and provide a complete end-to-end view of value creation. Primary activities are those involved in the physical creation of the product or service, marketing and transfer to the buyer, and after-sale support, referred to as value-adding.

2.4.2 Support Processes

Support processes are designed to support primary processes, often by managing resources and/or infrastructure required by primary processes. The primary differentiator of support and primary processes is that support processes do not directly deliver value to customers, while primary processes do. Common examples of support processes include information technology management, facilities or capacity management, and human resource management. Each of these support processes may involve a resource lifecycle, and are often tightly associated with functional areas. However, support processes can and often do cross functional boundaries. For example, capacity management, the process of managing capacity, does not directly deliver value to customers but supports an organizations ability to deliver products and services. Capacity management often involves a number of cross-functional activities, from planning to procurement, engineering and design, construction, and the process of putting capacity into production. Each of these activities could include cross-functional teams with representatives from finance, procurement, engineering, manufacturing, information technology, and other functional organizations.

The fact that support processes do not directly deliver value to customers does not mean that they are unimportant to an organization. Support processes can be critical and strategic to organizations as they directly inelegance the ability of an organization to effectively execute primary processes.

2.4.3 Management Processes

Management processes are used to measure, monitor, and control business activities. Management processes ensure that a primary or supporting process meets operational, financial, regulatory, and legal goals. Management processes do not directly add value to customers, but are necessary in order to ensure the organization operates effectively and efficiently.

2.5 Types of Activities

2.5.1 Value Added

Value adding activities are those that contribute to the process output in a positive way. For example, contacting the customer several days after servicing their car to check that they are satisfied, adds value to the Service Vehicle process both by measuring customer satisfaction and by enhancing the company image as a caring and concerned service provider.

2.5.2 Handoff

Handoff activities pass control of the process to another department or organization. Transferring a customer to another department after determining the appropriate group to resolve their issue is an example of a handoff activity.

2.5.3 Controls and Control Activities

Control activities assure that the processes behave within desired tolerances. Controls help ensure processes achieve desired goals and adhere to standards, legal, and/or regulatory requirements. Controls identify exceptions and can trigger exception processes. They can even identify dangerous conditions so they can be addressed through intervention.

A "control activity" is a specific validity checkpoint in a process. Control activities can prevent, detect or correct undesirable conditions or change the flow of a process to ensure that process goals are met. Control activities typically involve the application of rules and measures of conditions that will call for automated or manual intervention.

The design and application of control activities has been applied extensively to finance, accounting, manufacturing, operations, and virtually all important aspects of an enterprise. A key element of process management is the identification and definition of computing financial and operational controls. Achieving successful adherence to these controls requires the design, testing, implementation, and monitoring of control activities.

Understanding the need for controls and those activities within the process that support and enforce controls is an important contribution of the logic and methods of process management. Quite often management and auditors design controls to address legal and regulatory requirements without a complete understanding of the end-to-end processes being controlled. Without a process management framework, the list of potential controls designed for risk reduction can be excessive and very difficult if not impossible to manage.

2.6 BPM Critical Success Factors

Successful BPM efforts typically involve the consideration of a number of factors including organizational, management, process, and technology practices. While the Guide to the BPM CBOK® covers many BPM success factors throughout, Figure 2-2 highlights and summarizes some of the more critical success factors for enterprise-wide BPM initiatives.

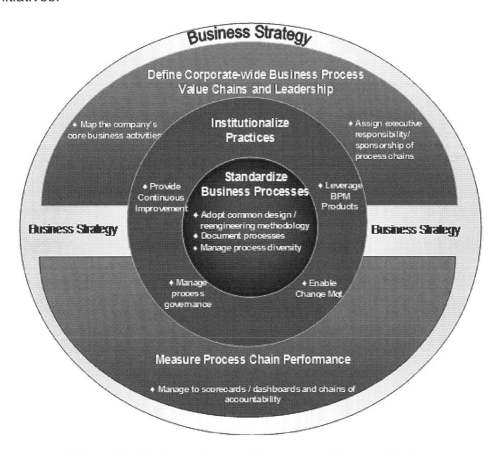

Figure 2-2: Business Process Management Success Factors

2.6.1 Alignment of Strategy, Value Chain and Business Process

Experience has shown that the most successful organizations implementing BPM pay particular attention to the alignment of business strategy, value-chain definitions, and business processes. BPM relies on key business strategies that set the primary direction of the enterprise, usually in terms of value propositions for goods and services delivered to customers. The business strategy then leads to enterprise and business unit goals as the basis for action plans and business tactics. These goals are often stated in terms of operational objectives and financial goals.

2.6.2 Goals

Business goals are most often an output of an organizations strategic planning efforts, and are typically decomposed to include functional goals which align an organizations functional areas to overall strategy. For example, sales, marketing, and financial goals would typically align with overall strategic goals and objectives. In a similar manor, process goals would align business processes with overall organization strategy.

2.6.3 Executive Sponsorship/Governance

Enterprises that are mature in their approach to BPM typically assign executive leadership responsibility to oversee the performance of key processes. The performance of a process is measured with accountability falling under the executive leadership and reported throughout the enterprise. In order to discover and manage key processes, it is important to have organizational discipline to utilize methodologies to document, store, manage and continuously improve the business processes, particularly those that make up the value chains. This would include governance mechanisms to support BPM with all its tools and institutionalized across all functional areas in order to optimize the impact on value chain performance.

2.6.4 Process Ownership

Organizations who successfully implement BPM recognize that the role of a process owner is critical. A process owner is responsible for the entire end-to-end process across functional departments. The success of this role depends on the authority the individual has to control the budget and make decisions that effect the development, maintenance, and improvement of the business process.

2.6.5 Metrics, Measures and Monitoring

To manage one must measure. Business process measurement and monitoring provides critical feedback on process design, performance, and compliance. It is necessary to measure process performance in terms of a variety of possible metrics related to how well the process meets its stated goals. Metrics may include sales growth, cost reduction or containment, cycle time, and customer satisfaction or retention.

2.6.6 Institution Practices

The effective attainment of these BPM success factors to create value for an enterprise and its customers is dependent upon both organizational practices and mastery of concepts and skills by individuals with accountability for managing business processes.

2.7 BPM Professional Space

From the perspective of BPM practitioners, the BPM "professional space" can be characterized by nine components as shown in Figure 2-3 below. The first three components exist within the External Environment: the Enterprise's Relevant Environment, i.e., competitors, industry associations, and regulators; BPM Practice Influencers, i.e., professional associations, rule-making institutions, and technology vendors; and BPM Professional Development Programs, i.e., Common Body of Knowledge publications, research projects, education programs, and professional certification. The ABPMP is strongly committed to supporting programs that promote BPM professional practices and professional development.

The next five components exist within the Enterprise: Business Strategy and Governance, BPM Professional Practices, i.e., the management of the organization's business processes (Process Management) utilizing the BPM sub-disciplines described in the following section, Business Processes (both internal and extended), Applications, Data, and IT platform, and the Values, Beliefs, Leadership and Culture of the Enterprise.

The last component exists within the Extended Enterprise. These are business processes that are outsourced. Although executed in an external environment, they are also extensions of the Enterprise's business processes and therefore are shown as a separate box on the diagram.

The key message here is that the impact and influences to BPM extends outside the Organization and need to be considered if there is to be a holistic view of its business processes.

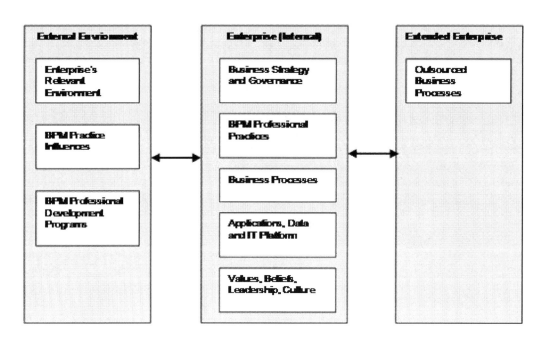

Figure 2-3 BPM Professional Space

2.8 Key Concepts

BUSINESS PROCESS MANAGEMENT - KEY CONCEPTS

1. Business Process Management (BPM) is a disciplined approach to identify, design, execute, document, measure, monitor, and control both automated and non-automated business processes to achieve consistent, targeted results consistent with an organization's strategic goals.
2. BPM involves the deliberate, collaborative and increasingly technology-aided definition, improvement, innovation, and management of end-to-end business processes that drive business results, create value, and enable an organization to meet its business objectives with more agility.
3. It enables an enterprise to align its business processes to its business strategy leading to effective overall company performance through improvements of specific work activities either within a specific department, across the enterprise, or between organizations.
4. A process is a defined set of activities or behaviors performed by humans or machines to achieve one or more goals.
5. There are three types of business processes: primary, support and management.
   - Primary processes are cross-functional in nature and make up the value chain.
   - Support processes such as human resources and IT enable other processes.
   - Management processes are used to measure, monitor and control business activities. Management processes ensure that primary and supporting processes meet operational, financial, regulatory, and legal goals.
6. BPM Critical Success Factors include the following:
   - alignment of business strategy, value-chain definitions, and business processes
   - establishment of enterprise and business unit goals to meet business strategy
   - development of action plans and business tactics to successfully meet the organization's goals
   - assignment of executive sponsorship, responsibility, authority and accountability for processes leading to attainment of goals
   - assignment of clear process ownership along with authority to engineer change
   - establish metrics, measure, and monitor process
   - institutionalize practices such as continuous improvement investigations, change management, change controls, and proper leverage of BPM products and tools that lead to improvements and change
   - standardize and automate business processes and related methodologies

BUSINESS PROCESS MANAGEMENT - KEY CONCEPTS

    across the enterprise
7. BPM is a professional discipline made up of eight sub-disciplines: Modeling, Analysis, Design, Performance Measurement, Transformation, Organization, Enterprise Process Management and Technology.
8. The four cornerstones of BPM are Values, Beliefs, Leadership, and Culture.
9. The BPM lifecycle includes Planning and Strategy followed by Analysis, Design and Modeling, Implementation, Monitoring, and Controlling thereby leading to Refinement.
10. Key factors impacting the BPM lifecycle are organization, process definition, responsibility, sponsorship, measurement, awareness, alignment, information technology, and BPM methodology.
11. A key element of BPM is the identification and definition of computing financial and operational controls. Achieving successful adherence to these controls requires the design, testing, implementation, and monitoring of control activities.

3 Process Modeling

Process modeling combines a set of processes and skills which provide insight and understanding of business process and enable analysis, design and performance measurements.

3.1 Business Process Modeling

"Business Process Modeling" is the set of activities involved in creating representations of an existing or proposed business process. Business process modeling provides an end-to-end perspective of an organizations primary, supporting and management processes.

A "model" is a simplified representation that supports the study and design of some aspect of some thing, concept, or activity. Models may be mathematical, graphical, physical, or narrative in form or some combination of these. Models have a wide range of application that include: Organizing (structuring), Heuristics (discovery, learning), Forecasting (predicting), Measuring (quantifying), Explaining (teaching, demonstration), Verification (experimentation, validation), and Control (constraints, objectives).

"Process" in this context means a business process and can be expressed at various levels of detail from a highly abstracted contextual view showing the process within its environment to a highly detailed internal operational view that can be simulated to evaluate various characteristics of its performance and behavior. Because business processes are carried out by people interacting with others, people interacting with information systems, and/or completely automated information systems functions, a fully developed business process model will typically represent several perspectives serving different purposes.

A process model may contain one or more diagrams, information about the objects on the diagram, information about the relationships between the objects, information about the relationships between the objects and their environment, and information about how the objects represented behave or perform.

3.1.1 Diagram vs. Map vs. Model (more precision, simulate)

The terms, process diagram, process map, and process model are often used interchangeably or synonymously. However, process diagrams, maps, and models have different purposes and useful application. In practice it is more often the case that diagram, map, and model are different stages of development, each adding more information, utility and capability in understanding, analyzing and designing processes.

A process diagram often depicts simple notation of the basic workflow of a process. The diagram depicts the major elements of a process flow, but omits the minor details which are not necessary for understanding the overall flow of work. An analogy can be made to a simple diagram which may be used to show the route to a store location; it may depict things like landmarks and distances in an exaggerated or simplified format, but still serve to help find the store. In a similar manor, a simple process diagram helps us quickly identify and understand the major activities of the process.

Mapping implies more precision than a diagram and will tend to add more detail about not only the process, but also some of the more important relationships to other things such as performers (actors), events, results, etc. Process maps typically provide a comprehensive view of all of the major components of the process, but vary from higher levels to lower levels of detail. Most process mapping tools allow one to capture these attributes and relationships in extensions of the diagram.

Modeling implies that the representation can be used to represent the performance of what is being modeled and therefore more precision, more data about the process, and more data about the factors that affect its performance. Modeling is often done using tools that provide simulation and reporting capability which is helpful to analyze and understand the process.

3.1.2 Process Attributes and Characteristics

Processes have attributes and characteristics which describe the properties, behavior, purpose, or other elements of the process. Often, process attributes are captured in a tool in order to organize, analyze, and manage an organization's portfolio of processes. Depending on the techniques and the capabilities of the tools used, there are many attributes that can be modeled in a process flow. Capturing these characteristics enable various analyses of the process performance. A sample of some of the data that can be useful to capture in process models includes the following:

Inputs/Outputs	Arrival Patterns/Distributions
Events/Results	Costs (indirect and direct)
Value Add	Entry Rules
Roles/Organizations	Exit Rules
Data/Information	Branching Rules
Probabilities	Join Rules
Queuing	Work/Handling Time
Transmission Time	Batching
Wait Time	Servers (number of people available to perform tasks)

3.2　Purpose of Modeling

The objective of process modeling is to create a representation of the process that describes it accurately and sufficiently for the task at hand. By definition, a model will never be a complete and full representation of the actual process, but will focus on representing those attributes of the process that support continued analysis from one or more perspectives. So a simple diagram may suffice for one purpose while a fully quantitative model may be required for another.

Process models have many benefits in managing business operations such as understanding the business process, enhancing communications by creating a visible representation, and establishing a commonly shared perspective. In business process management, the models are the means for managing the organization's processes, analyzing process performance, and defining changes. They are the expression of the target business state and specify the requirements for the supporting resources that enable effective business operations: people, information, facilities, automation, finance, energy, etc.

Some of the most common reasons for creating process models are as follows:
- To document an existing process clearly
- To use as a training aide
- To use as an assessment against standards and compliance requirements
- To understand how a process will perform under varying loads or in response to some anticipated change
- As the basis for analysis in identifying opportunities for improvement
- To design a new process or new approach for an existing process
- To provide a basis for communication and discussion
- To describe requirements for a new business operation

3.3 Benefits of Modeling

In a process managed business, process models are the primary means for measuring performance against standards, determining opportunities for change, and expressing the desired end state preceding a change effort.

Models are, by definition, simplified representations that facilitate understanding of that which is being studied and making decisions about it. Process modeling is an essential mechanism for understanding, documenting, analyzing, designing, automating, and measuring business activity as well as measuring the resources that support the activity and the interactions between the business activity and its environment. As such, it has a broad extent of application, and, therefore, can be addressed from a variety of viewpoints or needs within the organization.

These are some benefits of modeling:
- Models are relatively fast, easy and inexpensive to complete
- Models are easy to understand (when compared to other forms of documentation)
- Models provide a baseline for measurement
- Models facilitate process simulation and impact analysis
- Models leverage various standards and a common set of techniques

3.4 Modeling Standards and Notations

There are a number of modeling and notational standards and techniques in use today. Some of the benefits of using a standards based approach include the following:

- A common symbology, language, and technique which facilitate communication and understanding
- Standards-based models provide common and consistently defined processes definitions which eases the process of design, analysis and measurement and facilitates model reuse
- An ability to leverage modeling tools based on common standards and notations
- An ability to import and export models created in various tools for reuse in other tools
- Some tool vendors are leveraging standards and notations for developing the ability to be exported from a modeling notation to an execution language (for example BPMN to BPEL)

Many of standards and notations have been developed as part of a larger business process improvement methodology. The next section provides a brief description of some of the most commonly encountered model notations.

3.4.1 Business Process Modeling Notation (BPMN)

Business Process Model Notation is a relatively new standard created by the Business Process Management Initiative, a consortium of tool vendors in the BPM market that is now merged with the Object Management Group (OMG), an information systems standards setting group. BPMN appears to be emerging as the largest, most widely accepted business process modeling notation in the industry. It provides a simple, yet robust, symbology for modeling all aspects of business processes. More information on BPMN can be found at: www.bpmn.org/

The following are examples of process flow diagrams using BPMN:

- Simple task flow diagram

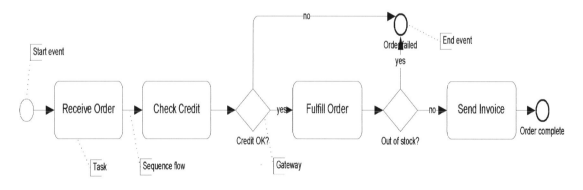

Diagrams from BPMN Method and Style, courtesy of Bruce Silver, reproduced with permission of the publisher

- More detailed and complex task flow diagram

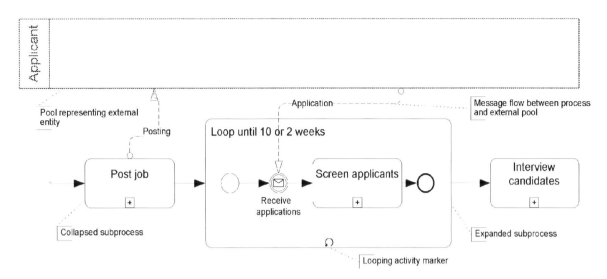

Diagrams from BPMN Method and Style, courtesy of Bruce Silver, reproduced with permission of the publisher

- Traditional swim lane diagram

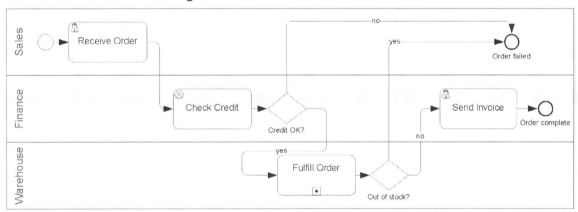

Diagrams from BPMN Method and Style, courtesy of Bruce Silver, reproduced with permission of the publisher

- Collaboration diagram (use of pools, artifacts and messaging)

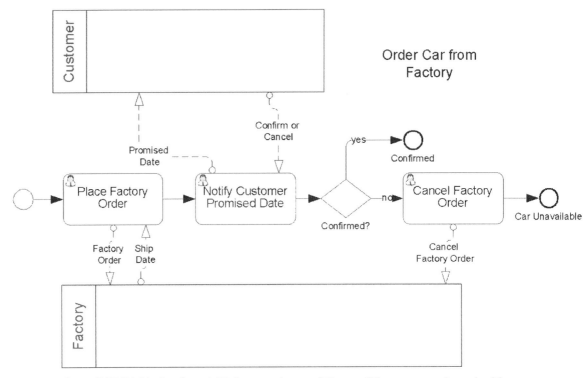

Diagrams from BPMN Method and Style, courtesy of Bruce Silver, reproduced with permission of the publisher

- High level business process diagram

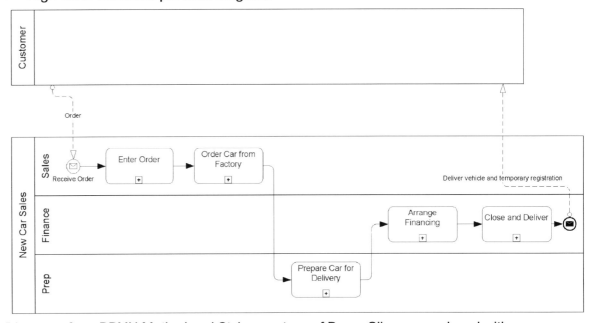

Diagrams from BPMN Method and Style, courtesy of Bruce Silver, reproduced with permission of the publisher

- Lower level business process diagram

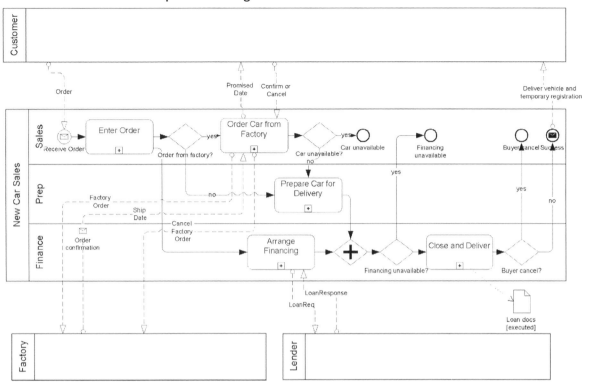

Diagrams from BPMN Method and Style, courtesy of Bruce Silver, reproduced with permission of the publisher

3.4.2 Flow Charting

Flow charting is widely used and is based upon a simple set of symbology for tasks, decisions, and other primary process elements. Many credit the Total Quality Management (TQM) movement, which originated in the early 1950's and gained popularity throughout the 1970's, for the adoption of flow charting techniques in modeling business processes. The notation for the most common flow charting was approved as an ANSI standard in 1970 for representing systems flows. Other flow charting notations have been used by industrial engineers for decades and utilize different symbols and layouts for specific industrial mappings to describe the flow of materials, roles and work, or placement of machinery, analysis of egress and ingress in dispatch centers, etc.

A typical flow chart may have the following kinds of symbols:

- Start and end symbols represented as lozenges, ovals, or rounded rectangles usually containing the word "Start" or "End", or another phrase signaling the start or end of a process such as "submit enquiry" or "receive product."

- Arrows coming from one symbol and ending at another indicate that control passes from one symbol to the next.
- Processing steps are represented as rectangles.
- Input/Output is represented as a parallelogram.
- Condition (or decision) is represented as a diamond (rhombus). These typically contain a Yes/No question or True/False test. This symbol is unique in that it has two arrows coming out of it, usually from the bottom point and right point, one corresponding to Yes or True, and one corresponding to No or False. The arrows should always be labeled. More than two arrows can be used, but this is normally a clear indicator that a complex decision is being taken, in which case it may need to be broken down further or replaced with the "pre-defined process" symbol.
- There are also a number of other symbols that have less universal currency.

Flow charts may contain other symbols such as connectors, usually represented as circles, to represent converging paths in the flow chart. Circles will have more than one arrow coming into them but only one going out. Some flow charts may just have an arrow point to another arrow instead. These are useful to represent an iterative process (in computer science this is called a loop). Off-page connectors are often used to signify a connection to part of another process held on another sheet or screen. It is important to remember to keep these connections logical in order. All processes should flow from top to bottom and left to right.

3.4.3 Swim Lanes

Introduced in the book *Managing Organizational Performance* by Rummler and Brache, swim lanes are an addition to the "boxes and arrows" process flow view of flow-charting that show how the work flows across organizational units or is handed-off from one role to another. This is accomplished by the use of horizontally or vertically arranged rows (swim lanes) representing an organizational unit, role, or in some instances, external organization. These rows resemble the channel or lane markings in swimming competitions. By arranging the flow of activities and tasks across these rows, it is easy to visualize handoffs in the work; a critical aspect of the Rummler-Brache process analysis which is focused on minimizing and managing handoffs.

3.4.4 Event Process Chain (EPC)

Event Process Chains are very similar to activity diagrams regarding the addition of events or outcomes of tasks. An EPC is an ordered graph of events and functions. It provides various connectors that allow alternative and parallel execution of processes. The tasks (activities) are followed by outcomes (events) of the task, developing a very detailed process model. Furthermore it is specified by the usages of logical operators such as OR, AND, and XOR. A major strength of EPC is claimed to be its simplicity and easy-to-understand notation. This makes EPC a widely acceptable technique to denote business processes. Event Process Chains are typically used to help transition processes towards machine automation or simulation.

The EPC method was developed within the framework of ARIS by Prof. Wilhelm-August Scheer at the Institut für Wirtschaftsinformatik at the Universität des Saarlandes in the early 1990s. It is used by many companies for modeling, analyzing, and redesigning business processes.

Unfortunately, neither the syntax nor the semantics of EPC are well-defined and can very from tool to tool. EPC requires non-local semantics, so that the meaning of any portion of the diagram may depend on other portions arbitrarily far away.

3.4.5 Value Chain

Value chain notation is used to demonstrate a single continuous flow from left to right of the sub-processes that directly contribute to producing value for the organization's customers (clients/constituents). This notation was introduced by Michael Porter in his works on corporate strategy and is typically applied at the enterprise planning level. SCOR, the consortium that defined the Supply Chain Reference Model used a value chain notation to describe the high level process flow supporting supply chain management and its sub-processes. Recently, a Value Chain Reference Model has been proposed by another group, VRM.

3.4.6 Unified Modeling Language (UML)

UML provides a standard set of nine or more diagramming techniques and notations primarily for describing information systems requirements. While UML is primarily used for systems analysis and design, a limited number of organizations also use UML activity diagrams for business process modeling. UML is maintained by the Object Management Group (OMG), a standards setting body for the information systems field. Additional information on UML can be found at the website www.uml.org.

3.4.7 IDEF-0

IDEF-0 is a Federal Information Processing Standard (FIPS) that was developed by the US Air Force for documenting manufacturing processes. It is a notation and technique that is one part of a methodology for defining the work processes and information systems in manufacturing environments. It was widely used and available in many diagramming tools for many years and is now in the public domain.

3.4.8 LOVEM-E

LOVEM-E (Line of Visibility Engineering Method - Enhanced) is a notation set and a modeling technique that was developed as part of IBM's Business Process Reengineering Methodology. What is unique about LOVEM-E is that it adds to flow charting with swim lanes, a concept of the customer encounter and the collaborative nature of work between external and internal parties, and the supporting information systems. BPMN also supports these concepts.

3.4.9 SIPOC

SIPOC stands for Supplier, Input, Process, Output, and Customer. It is a style of process documentation used in Six Sigma. There is no standard or preferred notation set and this technique may be satisfied by completing a table with those headings.

3.4.10 Systems Dynamics

More than just a different notation, Systems Dynamics models are "activity on arrow" diagrams rather than "activity on node" diagrams like most of the other notations listed. Systems dynamics models are especially useful in developing dynamic lifecycle type models that focus on the overall business system's performance and the impact of changing the key variables that affect overall performance. These are more often used to model an entire enterprise or line of business rather than lower level workflow type models. System Dynamics models are often used to describe the enterprise business "architecture" from a dynamic behavioral perspective rather than a static structural perspective.

3.4.11 Value Stream Mapping

Value Stream Mapping is a technique used in Lean Manufacturing. Not to be confused with value chain notation, Value Stream Mapping expresses the physical environment and flow of materials and products in a manufacturing environment. At Toyota, where the technique originated, it is known as "Material and Information Flow Mapping."

3.5 Process Modeling Quality

It is useful to have some standards and measures of quality as it relates to process modeling. Typically, the accuracy, amount of detail, and completeness of the model define the models quality. It is common that multiple versions or iterations of models are created over time to capture more detail and improve the quality of the model.

Most process analysis and design efforts require the use of models to describe what is happening during the process. These models are often called "as is" models. The models that are created are based on the decisions made previously regarding which methodologies and techniques to use. They can be as simple as drawings on a white board, to very complex using sophisticated business process modeling tools. The model created should have sufficient detail to explain these following attributes and workflow within and about the process:

- The business environment including the customers, suppliers, external events or market pressures that effect or interact with the process
- The organizational structure which includes the hierarchical or functional view of the organization and how the people work together (this information helps understand who the key decision makers are within the process)
- The functional or departmental structure of the organization which explains how the functions or departments work together in the process
- The business rules which control the decisions that are made during the process and workflow
- The activities or actions that take place within the process and who does those actions

During the modeling of a process, several disconnections, restrictions, and/or barriers may become apparent. Those items should also be noted on the model as well as any other information discovered that will help create a common understanding of the current state.

Some organizations use numeric scoring to assess model quality. The following is part of an example model quality standard. It is used to assess models for completeness and adherence to standards. Typically this is linked to some point-value system to track the overall quality of the models that have been captured in an enterprise model management environment.

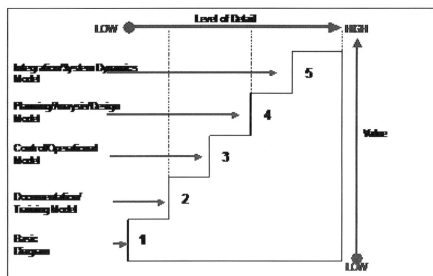

Figure x – Process Model Levels of Completeness

Level 1 - Basic Diagram

- One or more graphical depictions – diagrams
- May be process flows or a hierarchy of activities or both
- Cannot deviate too radically from BPMN notation standards
- May be in either drawing tool (using the company BPMN stencil) or Company Standard Tool

Level 2 - Documentation/Training

The model:
- Must follow company naming standards
- May be in either accepted drawing tool or Company Standard Tool
- Should have at least one process flow diagram at the activity or task level

All diagrams must:
- Have a diagram title at the top of the page
- Contain the date, version, and other document control information
- Adhere to company minimum standards
  - A unique title that follows the company process naming standards
  - use the BPMN notation

All process objects:
- Major Processes down through Activities require a Description – a clear description explaining of what work is done
- Tasks require procedural documentation

Level 3 - Control/Operational

All Documentation/Training standards plus:

All diagrams:
- Are assigned to a subject area

All process objects on the diagrams have:
- Defined purpose and description

Figure 3-1 an example quality matrix for process models

3.5.1 Model Validation and Simulation

It may be useful or necessary to validate the model through simulation before finalizing the analysis. One method of validating the model through simulation is to compare simulated outputs to real-world results. Any salient differences should be understood and corrected before the model is used for detailed analysis. Another way to validate a model is to collect a group of people who work in the process and simulate the process by having one person in the group describe each activity and its product(s). Real-world participants may be able to tell if the model is accurate.

3.6 Modeling Perspectives

Processes can be modeled from many perspectives. Process modeling has been used for strategic planning, improving operations, and specifying information and applications system requirements for many years. However, it was the advent of process-focused management disciplines that created a need to develop models that integrated these different perspectives. In a BPM environment an organization's strategy is enacted through process performance, which is linked to the operations model that must be supported by the information technology platform. To keep these aligned, there needs to be a line of visibility from one perspective to the other in a coherent framework, typically maintained in a process repository. Figure 3-2 is an example representation of the different perspectives which may need to be maintained.

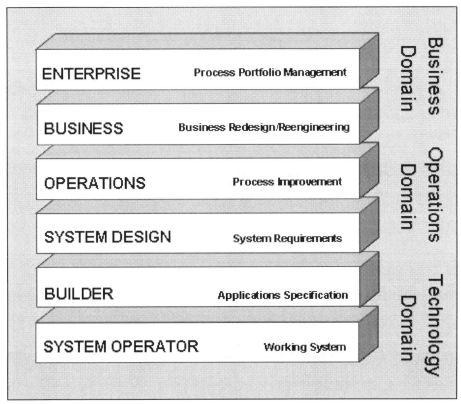

Figure 3-2 Modeling Perspectives

3.6.1 Enterprise Domain

The top perspective is for those who need to see how the enterprise operates overall and that the primary processes are arranged in some category that gives a sense of their interaction. This view supports those who must align overall enterprise strategy with aggregated process performance.

3.6.2 Business Domain

A business view supports each of the process owners who is accountable for and has the authority to address overall process performance. This business view is also required as the business context that describes each major business process and defines the scope and reach of major transformation efforts.

3.6.3 Operations Domain

More detailed models support the perspectives of those managers who are responsible for monitoring performance and look for ways to continuously improve operational performance.

3.6.4 Systems Domain

A perspective that identifies how work gets done and how the systems support that work is the systems perspective. It is a view that describes requirements for systems support and performance in support of tasks and procedures.

3.6.5 Builder and Operator

The lowest level models support the individuals who have to build all of the support systems to enable work and to operate the systems that are required to continue to perform that work.

3.7 Levels of models

Models supporting these perspectives or views of an enterprise's processes can be developed and maintained for different audiences or purposes. These models are explained in Figure 3-3.

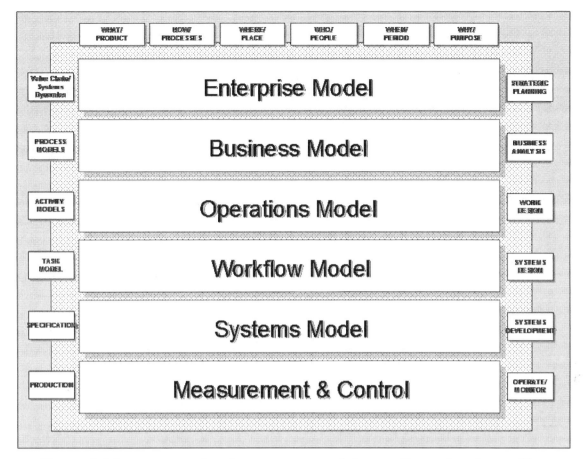

Figure 3-3 is an example of a process model repository structure with example labels for the types of models and their usage.

3.7.1 Enterprise

An enterprise view model is typically a highly abstracted business classification model that is used to describe the focus of the organization and to organize the business' processes in an overall "business architecture." Some examples of this type of model are the APQC Process Classification Framework, Porter's value chain, and industry specific frameworks such as those in the energy distribution, oil and gas production, telecommunications, and insurance industries.

These models typically organize processes into categories such as primary, support, and management. Each of these categories may be used to group the major processes of the business. Here are some examples:

- In Porter's value chain, the primary processes are Inbound Logistics, Operations, Outbound Logistics, Marketing and Sales, and After-Sales Service.
- In the APQC Process Classification Framework, the primary (Operations) processes are Develop Vision and Strategy (1.0), Design & Develop Products and Services (2.0), Market and Sell Products and Services (3.0), Deliver Products & Services (4.0), and Manage Customer Service (5.0).

- In a more customer oriented services model, the primary categories might be Engage Customers, Transact Business, Fulfill Customer Expectations, and Service Customers within which the various major business processes are grouped.

Generally each of the high level business processes are then described in more detail by their major components (sub-processes). An enterprise model will typically have two or more levels of detail and serve as a high level business "blueprint" or business architecture. They may or may not include support and management processes.

These models have uses other than as a general classification and communications tool. The processes may be mapped to Key Performance Indicators (KPIs) and strategic goals in a process portfolio and used to prioritize resources and project efforts. They may be mapped into a System Dynamics type model to formulate strategies for alternate future scenarios or to develop high level estimates and forecasts.

3.7.2 Business Models

Business models depict the major events, activities, and results that describe each of the major end-to-end processes, their sub-processes, and their interactions with their environment. Business models also typically describe the support and management processes as well and how they interact with or support the primary processes.

3.7.3 Operations and Work Flow

Operations level models typically describe how the business model is carried out. These are detailed models mapped down to activity, task, and procedural level details and describe the physical implementation details of the operating processes.

3.7.4 System

Systems models depict the triggering events, software processes, data flows, and system outputs required to support business operations.

3.7.5 Measurement and Control

Measurement and control models indicate points in the operation where key performance measure and control points are monitored.

3.8 Modeling Approaches

There are a number of approaches to process modeling: top-down, middle-out, or bottom-up. Some process model development methods call for an iterative process approach where it is expected that several successive passes to developing the model are required. The approach used varies depending on the purpose and the scope of the effort.

Traditionally, process models were generally created for the purpose of improving narrowly focused functions within a single department or operation. Often, the process has not been documented and the first step is to attempt to discover what is actually occurring. Bottom-up approaches, centered on very detailed activity and task oriented work flows, work best for these kinds of projects.

It is now becoming more common to find process modeling applied to improving and innovating large scale, end-to-end, cross-functional business processes and as a means to manage performance of these business processes. Some process transformation efforts begin with developing a new business model first and then determining what needs to be done to be capable of its implementation. A more holistic business process management approach utilizing enterprise-wide process models (or "architectures") as a mechanism to align business processes with business strategies are also becoming more common. These types of modeling efforts are best developed with top-down methods.

The key is to determine the purpose of the modeling effort and then apply the best approach for that purpose.

3.9   Capturing Information

There are several different ways to capture information for process modeling. Direct observation, one-on-one interviews, structured workshops, web conferencing, written feedback, or some combination of these techniques can all be used to gather descriptions of a process.

3.9.1 Direct Observation
Direct observation is a good way to document current procedural detail. It may uncover activities and tasks that might not be otherwise recognized and can be effective in identifying variations and deviations that occur in day-to-day work. However, because it is necessarily limited to a relatively small sample size, it may not capture the range of variations across groups and locations. Direct observation also entails the risk of the performers doing what they think you want to see rather than what they normally do.

3.9.2 Interviews
Interviews can create a sense of ownership and participation in the process of modeling and documenting business processes. This approach requires minimal time and disruption of normal duties from the participants. However it may take more overall elapsed time to schedule and conduct the interviews than other methods. It may be difficult afterward to build a cohesive process flow and to map the different views into a single view. This technique generally requires follow up and sometimes doesn't uncover all of the activities to completely describe the process.

3.9.3 Survey/Written Feedback

Written feedback also requires minimal time and disruption of duties. Generally, data may be collected in this fashion. Though, it is often prone to the same problems as are encountered with one-on-one interviews such as taking more time, missing some information, time spent reconciling differences of opinion or where the same work has just been described differently by different people, it may require follow up.

3.9.4 Structured workshops

Structured workshops are focused, facilitated meetings where enough subject matter experts and stakeholders are brought together to create the model interactively. This offers the advantage of shortening the elapsed calendar time required to develop the models and gives a stronger sense of ownership to the workshop participants than other techniques. Structured workshops can also have the advantage of a facilitator who may be skilled in modeling techniques not commonly known by process participants. However, due to the potential travel and expense that may be required, workshops may be more costly than other methods. Generally, models produced in workshops require less follow up and generate a commonly agreed upon description of a process faster and with higher quality than other techniques.

3.9.5 Web-Based Conferencing

Web-based conferencing can be employed to gain much the same benefits as face-to-face workshops, but work best with smaller groups. Web-based conferencing can be more convenient and less expensive when the participants are widely distributed. Using this kind of technology effectively depends on having facilitators who are skilled in the use of these techniques. In workshops done this way it can be more difficult to monitor and manage individual participation in the group work.

3.10 Modeling Participants

There are a number of roles involved in developing process models due to the wide range of applicability. The development of process models may involve many people to create a set of models that fully represent the process. Business strategists, business managers, financial analysts, auditors, and compliance analysts, process performance analysts, requirements analysts, systems analysts, or others may create different process models for their particular purposes. Models can be created by individuals expressing their personal knowledge or models can be created by groups outlining the scope and depth of the business they are addressing. In a more structured approach, typically there will be a facilitator, a modeler, and several subject matter experts involved.

The subject matter experts may be executives expressing high level business dynamics, mid-level managers defining monitoring and control mechanisms, or workers who actually perform the work being modeled. For redesign efforts, information systems personnel who develop the requirements for IT support must consider organizational design personnel who determining roles, responsibilities and reporting structures, or financial personnel who are measuring cost and value options.

3.11 Modeling Techniques and Tools

There are many modeling tools and techniques available ranging from the use of simple white boards, butcher paper or sticky-notes to sophisticated and specialized BPM tools that include modeling and data stores for those models and processes. Process analysis can be done effectively and efficiently using any type of tool. The focus of the analysis or design, however, should be on the process and not on the tool itself.

None of these techniques is necessarily exclusive of the others and all can be employed in a process redesign or improvement project with different groups or in differing circumstances.

3.11.1 White Boarding and Flip Charts

Using a white board with erasable markers to draw the process flows and flip charts to capture other information and then later transcribing the results into drawing or modeling and reporting tools is a common method used in workshops, interviews or structured/facilitated modeling sessions.

3.11.2 Butcher Paper and Sticky-notes

Another common workshop technique is to cover the walls of a room with taped up Butcher paper and have the workshop participants put removable sticky-notes on the paper until they have arranged the activities into the sequence on which they agree. Sometimes this is done with the participants directing the facilitator in the placement of these activities, and other times the participants place the notes depicting activities. The resulting model must then be transcribed into a drawing or modeling and reporting tool later.

3.11.3 Drawing Tools and Reports

During or after interviews and workshops, participants capture the process flows and notes using inexpensive drawing tools, such as Visio, PowerPoint or any other electronic drawing tool. Often, these drawings are inserted into Word documents or PowerPoint presentations as a means of reporting findings and sharing the results. This is a common means of process modeling used in organizations today.

3.11.4 Electronic Modeling and Projection

Utilizing electronic drawing or modeling tools and projecting the images to large screens to capture and view the developing models has become a common practice today. This technique has several benefits. The model is visible and can be modified during the workshop. When the session is completed, there is no transfer to another toolset required. Many tools allow the resulting models to be quickly and easily shared via email immediately or shortly after the session. Adding web-based conferencing tools, remotely located stakeholders can also participate in the sessions. In addition, several current modeling tools are repository-based which allows the reuse of objects or patterns that have already been defined in previous efforts.

3.12 Process Simulation

3.12.1 Overview

Process simulations are a form of models which provide valuable insight to process dynamics. Simulations require sufficient data which typically allows the process to be mathematically simulated under various scenarios, loads, etc. Simulation can be used to achieve the following:

- Validate a model by demonstrating that real transaction sets, when run through the model exhibit, produce the same performance characteristics as those in the actual process
- Predict the process design's performance under differing scenarios (vary the number of transactions over time, the number of workers, etc.)
- Determine which variables have the greatest affect on process performance
- Compare performance of different process designs under the same sets of circumstances

Simulations can be manual or electronic using process simulation tools. Process laboratories are often used as part of a process improvement, redesign, or reengineering effort. A process laboratory can perform simulation by developing mock transactions which can be manually executed through an end-to-end business process by a small cross functional team. Simulation can be run against "as is" processes or designed as "to be" processes. Process laboratories often identify exceptions and handoffs while providing important insights on existing and required communication between tasks, functional areas, teams, and systems. Some organizations require a successful process demonstration in a laboratory setting prior to piloting or rolling out new processes or changes to process design.

3.12.2 Mock Trials

Mock trials can be similar to events run in a process laboratory. However, mock trials are typically one-off testing events versus the ongoing study and simulation often found in laboratories. Mock trials include running test transactions based on actual or sample data from real processes on an end-to-end basis.

3.12.3 Technical Simulation/Load analysis

Some process simulation tools provide the ability to perform load analysis. For example, simulating peak, average, and valley transaction loads predict impact on cycle time, resource requirements, bottlenecks, etc. Simulation generates data sets that allow many different types of process analysis. Some of the typical analyses are resource utilization, distribution analysis, cycle time analysis, and cost analysis. Some process simulation tools can also present animations of the simulations. Animations may be helpful in visually identifying phenomena during performance that may not be readily apparent in typical analysis of simulation data sets.

3.13 Key Concepts

PROCESS MODELING - KEY CONCEPTS

1. Process models are simplified representations of some business activity.
2. A process model serves as a means to communicate several different aspects of a business process.
3. Process models are used to document, analyze or design a business model
4. Process models are useful as documentation, a means for communication and alignment, design and requirements, or a means to analyze aspects of the process, training, and explanation.
5. Different levels or perspectives of business processes are expressed by models showing different scopes and levels of detail for different audiences and purposes.
6. There are many different styles of process modeling notation and ways to develop process models.

4 Process Analysis

The first step in establishing a new process or updating an existing process is creating a common understanding of the current state of the process and its alignment with the business objectives. The creation of this common understanding is process analysis.

This chapter explores the how and why of process analysis. After reviewing why a process must be analyzed and who is involved in the analysis stage, the specifics of how to analyze a process will be explored in detail followed by discussions about the techniques, tools, methodologies, and frameworks that can be used. Finally, a discussion concerning the suggested practices will be presented to ensure a complete understanding of what is necessary for a successful analysis of process.

4.1 What is Process Analysis?

A process is a defined set of sequential or parallel activities or behaviors to achieve a goal. Process analysis is creating an understanding of the activities of the process and measures the success of those activities in meeting the goals.

Process analysis is accomplished through various techniques including mapping, interviewing, simulations and various other analytical techniques and methodologies. It often includes a study of the business environment and factors that contribute to or interact with the environment such as government or industry regulations, market pressures, and competition. Other factors also considered include the context of the business, its strategy, the supply chain (the inputs and outputs of the process), customer needs, organizational culture, business values and how the process will perform to achieve business goals.

The information gained through the analysis should be agreed upon by all those that interact with the process. It should represent what is actually happening and not what is thought or wished to be happening. It should also be an unbiased view without placing blame for existing inefficiencies. The result of this analysis forms the foundation for process design and is addressed in the following chapter.

4.2 Why do Process Analysis?

An analysis generates the information necessary for the organization to make informed decisions assessing the activities of the business. Without it, decisions are made based on opinion or intuition rather than documented, validated facts.

In addition, as business cycles fluctuate and customer needs change, the products and services offered also change. When combined with changes in government regulations, economic conditions, marketing strategies, advancing technology and internal leadership changes the processes of an organization can quickly become inconsistent to their original design and no longer meet the needs of the business.

The process analysis, therefore, becomes an essential tool to show how well the business is meeting its objectives. It does so by creating an understanding of how work (the transformation of inputs to outputs) happens in the organization.

Specifically, the analysis will generate an understanding and measurement of process effectiveness and its efficiency. The effectiveness of a process is a measurement of achieving the purpose or need for the process whether the process meets the needs of the customer, satisfies the objectives of the business or is the right process for the current business environment or context.

Measuring the efficiency of the process indicates the degree of resources utilized in performing the activities of the process. It measures whether the process is costly, slow, wasteful, or has other deficiencies and is a measurement of the performance of the process.

An analysis of these measurements helps uncover important facts about how work flows in the organization. They then help in the design and/or redesign of processes to better meet the goals of the business.

The information generated from this analysis will include the following:

- Strategy, culture, and environment of the organization that uses the process (why the process exists)
- Inputs and outputs of the process
- Stakeholders, both internal and external, including suppliers, customers and their needs and expectations
- Inefficiencies within the current process
- Scalability of the process to meet customer demands
- Business rules that control the process and why they must exist
- What performance metrics should monitor the process, who is interested in those metrics and what they mean
- What activities make up the process and their dependencies across departments and business functions
- Improved resource utilization
- Opportunities to reduce constraints and increase capacity

This information becomes a valuable resource to management and leadership to understand how the business is functioning and will help them to make informed decisions on how to adapt to a changing environment and ensure that the processes running the business are optimal for attaining business objectives.

4.3 When to Perform Analysis

The need to analyze a process can be the result of continuous monitoring of processes or can be triggered by specific events. This section discusses the impact of each.

4.3.1 Continuous Monitoring

Business Process Management is a long-term commitment as part of the business strategy rather than a single activity that is completed and then forgotten. Managing the business by process implies not only that there are regular and consistent performance metrics that monitor the processes of the organization, but also that these metrics are routinely reviewed and steps are taken to ensure process performance meets the pre-determined goals of the organization. As such, the eventual goal of any organization should be the ability to continuously analyze processes as they are performed through the use of monitoring tools and techniques. When this is in place, timely decisions can be made.

This continuous analysis benefits the organization in numerous ways. First, it alerts management to potential poor performance of the process and can help point to the cause of the poor performance such as system deviations, competition, environmental factors, etc. If the process is not performing, immediate action can be taken to resolve the cause. Next, the real-time feedback through continuous analysis provides a measurement for the human performance and reward systems. Finally, it reduces the number of process improvement projects performed, thus saving time and cost associated with those efforts.

4.3.2 Event-Triggered Analysis

Much of the discussion in this chapter is centered on event-triggered analysis since this is the most common reason that process analysis is performed. The following are just a few of the events that may trigger a process analysis.

Strategic Planning

Regularly, most companies review and update their strategic plans. They survey the market and competitive landscape for new opportunities and establish new goals. Process analysis may need to occur following an update to the strategic plan to re-align the processes to meet the new organization's objectives.

Performance Issues

Current performance may be declared inadequate for a variety of reasons, i.e., product quality is not acceptable, scrap rates are increasing, production rates are not keeping up with demand, etc. Process analysis can assist in determining the reasons for the inadequacies and identify changes that may improve performance.

New Technologies

Advancing technologies can improve process performance and an analysis will help create an understanding of how they should be adopted. New technologies, however, must be applied deliberately to avoid unintended consequences. For example, inserting a faster machine in the middle of a process without increasing the production at preceding and subsequent steps can lead to starvation of the machine at the input point or inventory buildup at the output point. Process analysis will help the organization understand how and where new technologies should be applied to gain the maximum benefit to the organization.

Startup Venture

When new ventures or businesses are anticipated, managers and leaders should be concerned about identifying the processes that will be required to successfully deliver the new products and services.

Merger/Acquisition

Business mergers and acquisitions often result in the joining of production and service processes. A process analysis should be performed before the merging of processes to ensure that the combined outcome meets the combined business objectives.

Regulatory Requirements

Often regulatory bodies governing businesses will create or change regulations that require the business to modify its processes. Performing a process analysis as part of meeting these requirements will ensure the business is able to meet the requirement change with as little impact to the business as possible.

4.4 Process Analysis Roles

A successful process analysis will involve a variety of individuals within the organization. Examples of the roles involved in process management are defined in the chapter "Process Organization" (Chapter 8) of the CBOK®.

Several additional roles are also necessary to perform a process analysis and are defined below. One of the first steps in a process analysis is to establish and assign those roles. The individual or group ultimately responsible for the performance of the process, whether it is the process owner or the executive leadership team, should carefully select those who will lead and manage the team in the various roles to ensure successful completion of the project and that the analysis is comprehensive and accurately represents the state of the process.

4.4.1 Optimal Team Attributes

Process analysis can be performed by a single individual but best practice shows that, for larger organizations, it is most successfully performed by a cross-functional team. This cross-functional team will provide a variety of experiences and views of the current state of the process and ultimately result in a better understanding of both the process and the organization. This team should include subject matter experts, stakeholders, functional business leaders, and others that have an interest in the performance of the process and also have the authority to make decisions about the process.

It is also important to make sure that enough time has been allocation for these resources to function properly in the assignment. As in any project, process improvement projects often fail because of a lack of importance and priority placed on the project. When the same people responsible for the process improvement project are caught between the competing priorities of their primary responsibility, the process improvement project is usually what will suffer.

The analyst or a member of the analysis team should have competencies in the process management frameworks, methodologies, and tools or techniques used in process management as described later in this chapter. Often, outside consultants with expertise in process management are used if the analysis team lacks the adequate knowledge of process management frameworks.

Once the process improvement team is in place, the next step would be to communicate to the team their responsibilities according to the role that each will play in the process. They should have a thorough understanding of the expectations of each member and agree to commit the time and effort required to make the project a success.

4.4.2 Responsibilities of Analysis Roles

The following describes the responsibilities of each role within process analysis.

Analyst

The analyst has the responsibility to decide the depth and scope of the analysis, how it is analyzed, and then proceeds to perform the analysis. Often, members of an analysis team will take on responsibilities of project management or facilitation to help project advancement. Once the analysis is complete the analyst or analysis team has the responsibility to provide documentation and final reports to the stakeholders and executive leadership.

Facilitator

Facilitators are often used to lead process analysis teams. Regardless of whether the facilitator is from inside the organization or is an external consultant, the facilitator must approach the responsibility with an unbiased view. Objectivity is critical to ensure the analysis truly represents the current state. A good facilitator will not steer the group down a particular path but rather let the group discover the path through the analytical techniques chosen and through proper management of group dynamics.

Subject Matter Experts

The analysis of a process is best done using the knowledge and expertise of the individuals closest to the process. Subject Matter Experts (SMEs) include not only experts in the business process but also those that are familiar with both the business and technical infrastructure that supports the process.

4.5 Preparing to Analyze Process

Before beginning an analysis project the scope of the project and the frameworks and tools to be used should be determined. The following sections will discuss these decisions.

4.5.1 Choose the Process

Although most often the process to be analyzed has been previously selected, there may be instances of competing priorities and several processes that need to be analyzed. One method of choosing which process should receive priority is through examining the critical business goals of the organization.

A critical business goal for an organization defines why the organization exists and what controls the success of the organization. An airline, for example, exists to put people on planes. That is how they make their money. The more people they can put on planes, the more planes they can fly and the more money they make. All functions, departments, and other processes of that company exist only to support that one process: putting people on planes.

A business may have one or more critical business goals. Once critical business goals have been identified the processes supporting those goals should be identified. These processes should be governed by performance metrics and monitored closely. The performance can then be analyzed and ranked to understand where the effort for process analysis should be placed.

One process ranking method involves scoring each process by assigning a severity number between 1 and 10 with 10 being the most severe. Once each member of the team has scored each process, the results are averaged and the process with the highest score is the first to be improved.

Another ranking method involves creating a 2 x 2 matrix as in the following.

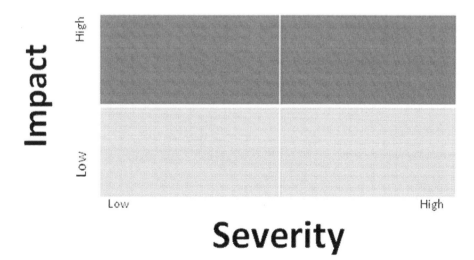

Each process is listed somewhere within the matrix based on its severity and impact to the organization. Those processes that scored a high in both impact and severity are the processes that need the most attention first.

Whatever method is chosen to rank processes for analysis, the processes chosen should directly meet the goals of the organization and have a positive impact to the critical business result.

4.5.2 Scope the Depth of Analysis

Scoping the depth of the process that is to be analyzed is one of the first actions of the analyst or analysis team. The depth of the analysis is the beginning and end of the analysis. Scoping is critical to decide how far the project will reach, how much of the organization it will involve and the impact any changes will have upstream and downstream of the process analyzed.

As an example, suppose that the analysis team has been assigned to analyze an invoicing process. Since receiving checks paid on invoices must also interact with the invoice process, the analysis team would need to decide if that is also an activity that should be analyzed as part of the project or if it should be analyzed as part of a payment received process and separate from the current project.

It may be necessary to interview a variety of individuals in various business functions before making this decision. An important consideration is that the more business functions and activities included in the analysis project, the more complicated the analysis and the longer it is likely to take. The analyst or team may wish to break down larger processes and analyze sub-processes in order to optimize time but before doing so must consider the impact of future process improvement projects.

4.5.3 Choose Analytical Frameworks

There is no single right way to perform a business process analysis. Topics to be studied, methods for studying them, tools to be used, etc. are all dependent on the nature of the process and the information available at the time the analysis begins. Some projects may start with a completed, verified model that can be used for analysis while others may require the development of a model (or at least its validation for use in the analysis), or development of a simulation based on the model.

The analyst or analysis team should review and decide which of the methodologies, frameworks or tools should be used. A discussion of the various common frameworks can be found in the chapter "Enterprise Process Management" (Chapter 9) of the CBOK®.

Once the framework or methodology has been agreed, the analysis team decides what techniques and tools to use in addition to or as part of that framework. Although it may be tempting to use all of the known or available techniques, it is best to only use those that make the most sense for the process being analyzed and for the organization. As will be described further as a critical success factor, too much analysis can also hinder the process of creating or re-designing a new process.

4.6 Performing the Analysis

Although there are several well recognized and published methodologies for process analysis it is beyond the scope of the CBOK® to describe or promote them. The following sections, therefore, describe common activities that are typically followed during a process analysis. These activities apply whether the process is an established or a new process regardless of the size of the process.

4.6.1 Understanding the Unknown

The process of analysis is a process of discovery involving finding answers to a series of questions about the process and generating data to ensure that any conclusions are based on facts extrapolated from the data and not on hearsay or generalizations. Developing an understanding of what is happening with the process, its strengths, weaknesses, and results achieved can be facilitated by considering the following discussion topics and questions.

4.6.2 Business Environment

A general understanding of the reason for the process to exist within the business environment can be determined by answering these questions:

- What is the process trying to accomplish?
- Why has it been created?
- What triggered the analysis?
- What are the systems required to support or enable the process and how sustainable are those systems?
- Where does it fit into the value chain of the organization?
- Is the process in alignment with the strategic objectives of the organization?
- Does it provide value to the organization and how critical is it?
- How well does it function in the current business environment and how well could it adapt if the environment were to change?
- What are the risks to the process (external, environmental or internal) and can the process adapt to survive those risks?

4.6.3 Organizational Culture/Context

Every organization has a culture that impacts and is impacted by the internal and external processes of that organization. That culture includes how work is performed and what motivates the members of the organization to do the work. By changing the process by which they work, the culture may also change. This may lead to unintended consequences as new processes are put into place. Part of the analysis process is to ask questions that will help the analysis team understand the culture of the organization and those unwritten rules that determine how and by who work is really accomplished. The goal of these discussions is to understand what will happen to the organization when the process is changed. Inquire of the following:

- Who in the organization are the leaders (or those that seem to have the most influential power) of the organization? Are they in positions of authority? If they do not agree with the process improvements, will the improvement be successful?
- What kind of social networks exist in the organization? How will any changes affect those social networks? If individuals will be displaced as a result of a process change, what would be the anticipated result of these networks?
- Will individuals voluntarily leave the company as a result of the process change? If so, how will this disrupt the process?
- What is the motivating factor for production? If the workers are not self-motivated how does work get done? What are the incentives that reward work output? If the success of a process has been measured on quantity as opposed to quality, what will happen if the measurement is shifted to quality? Will the organization stop producing to ensure quality?
- How will the change affect the leadership training in the organization? What is the motivating factor for promotion? Will the goals for measuring leadership change?
- How will the reason for the process change be interpreted by the individuals effected or responsible for the process? Is it a sign of weakness in the organization or strategy?

4.6.4 Performance Metrics

Performance issues can be defined as gaps between how a process is currently performing in relation to how it should be performing to meet the organization's objectives. A methodical analysis can help to understand the nature of the gaps, why they exist, and how the situation can be rectified. A key element of this understanding is the identification of actionable and auditable metrics that accurately indicate process performance. These metrics will provide indicators as to where and how a process should be adjusted. Key questions to ask during this discussion include the following:

- Is the process meeting its performance goals?
- Does the process take too long and if so, why and what is the measurement of "too long"?
- What could happen to make it worse?
- How would we know if the process has improved, i.e., if time is the measurement of the process, can cost be ignored or if cost is the measurement of the process, can time be ignored?
- How is data reported about the process, who views this data, and what do they do with it?
- Where should performance points be recorded so the process is accurately measured and monitored?
- Would entering these performance points affect the performance of the process?

4.6.5 Customer Interactions

Understanding the customer interactions with the process is critical to understanding whether the process is a positive factor in the success of the organization's value chain. Generally, the fewer the number of required interactions between the customer and a given service, the more satisfied the customer. Typical discussions could revolve around the following questions:

- Who is the customer, what is his need, why does he choose to participate in the process and could he go elsewhere instead of using this process?
- Do customers complain about the process?
- How many times does a customer interact with the process? Is it too many? Are there redundancies in the interactions?
- How do we know if they are satisfied?
- What is the customer's expectation or objective with the process and why does he need the process?
- How does the customer want to interact with the process?
- If the process supports internal activities, what is the impact or indirect effects to the customer?

4.6.6 Handoffs

Any point in a process where work or information passes from one system, person or group to another is a handoff for that process. Handoffs are very vulnerable to process disconnections and should be analyzed closely. Typically, the fewer number of handoffs, the more successful the process. After identifying each handoff, the following questions might be used to guide this discussion:

- Which of the handoffs are most likely to break down the process?
- Are there any bottlenecks of information or services as a result of handoffs happening too quickly?
- Can any handoff be eliminated?
- Where do streams of information come together and is the timing accurate?

4.6.7 Business Rules

Business rules create constraints that impact the nature and performance of the process. They help define the performance expectations and create clear guidelines around these expectations. Often business rules are created without an understanding of why they exist or are so outdated that they no longer apply but because of organizational culture they still are being followed. When analyzing the business rules of the process, consider the following:

- Do the current business rules cause obstacles by requiring unnecessary approvals, steps, or other constraints that should be eliminated?
- Are the business rules in alignment with the objectives of the organization?
- Who created the business rules and upon what were they based?
- When were the rules created and does their need exist?
- If the rules were eliminated, what would be the result?
- How flexible is the process to accommodate changes in the business rules?

4.6.8 Capacity

Analyzing the capacity of the process tests upper and lower limits and determines whether the resources (machine or human) can appropriately scale to meet the demands. When analyzing the capacity of a process, consider the following:

- Is the process scalable and if inputs were increased, at what point will the process break down?
- What would happen if the process slowed down and what is the cost of the idle time of the process? If idle, can those resources be put to work on other processes?
- What happens when the process cannot get supplies and materials quickly enough to meet demand?
- If the process speeds up can the consumer of the process handle the increase in production?

4.6.9 Bottlenecks

A bottleneck is a constraint in the process that creates a backlog of work to be done. These are typically not good in any process. The following questions may help the team understand the nature of the bottlenecks:

- What is being constrained: information, product, service?
- Why does the bottleneck exist, what are the factors contributing to the bottleneck, and are these factors people, systems, or organizational?
- Is it the bottleneck the result of handoffs or lack of information?
- Is the bottleneck the result of a resource constraint and what type of resource: human, system, or machinery?
- Are there unnecessary check points that create the bottleneck that can be eliminated?
- If multiple streams are processing information in parallel, do the streams come together at the same time or is one waiting for the other?
- Does the process create a backlog upstream or downstream from the process?

4.6.10 Variation

Although especially true in the manufacturing industry, variation in any mass production industry is not good. Variation inevitably slows down the process and requires more resources to properly scale. If the nature of the business requires variation as its core business strategy then look for places where some of the variation can be reduced which could save on the overall cycle time of the process. Discussion topics could include the following:

- How much variation is tolerable for the process?
- Is variation necessary or desirable?
- Where are the points where variation is most likely to occur? Can they be eliminated and if so, what are some recommendations?
- Can automation help eliminate variation?

4.6.11 Cost

Understanding the cost of the process helps the team understand the value of the process in real dollars to the organization. Some of the discussions might revolve around the following:

- What is the total cost of the process?
- Can the process be broken up into small cost allocations?
- Is the cost in line with industry best practices?
- Is the cost absorbed by the customer directly or is it a cost of business?
- Can the cost be reduced through automation or technology improvements? If so, how and by what extent?

4.6.12 Human Involvement

Processes involve either automated activities or activities performed by real people. Automated activities generally run consistently, and when they don't it is possible to find and correct the situation that is causing the problem. Activities performed by real people are more complex as they involve judgment and skill that cannot be automated. People do not always do the same task in the same way. The following questions can help guide the discussion around this important analysis.

- How much variability is introduced by the human element? Is the variability tolerable?
- Can the action be automated? What would be the result to the process? What would be the result to the human element and to the culture of the organization?
- How complex is the task? What are the skill sets required? How are performers trained for the task?
- How do the performers of the task respond to external events during the task?
- How does the performer know when the task is done well? What feedback systems are in place to guide the performer? What can the performer do with this feed back – what can he or she change with this knowledge?
- Does the performer know where the task lies in the process and what the results of the actions are downstream? Does he /she know what happens before the task? What does the performer do with variations in the inputs for the task?
- Can the performer identify variations before the task is completed?
- What is the motivation for performing the task or performing the task well?
- How much knowledge is available to the performer to accomplish this task? Is it sufficient?

4.6.13 Process controls

Process controls are put in place to ensure adherence to legal, regulatory or financial constraints or obligations. Process controls are different from control processes in that the former defines the control while the latter defines the steps to achieve that control. For example, the requirement to obtain a signature is a process control while the steps that must be performed to obtain that signature is a control process. The following questions may assist in understanding what process controls are in place.

- Are there any legal controls that must be considered in relation to the process?

- What are the environmental impacts of the process and do those impacts need to be controlled?
- Who are the regulatory or governing agencies that will regulate the process and do they need to be informed of the process change?

4.6.14 Other factors

The purpose of the discussion topics described above is to spark discussion about the process. Other discussion topics not mentioned above will naturally arise during the process analysis and should equally be explored. Conversely, some of the topics noted above might not apply to the process being analyzed. The key point to remember is that the analysis must encompass a variety of techniques and topics to achieve a complete and well rounded understanding of the process.

4.6.15 Gathering Information

The next step in the analysis would be for the analyst or team to gather as much relevant information about the process and business environment as possible. The types of information gathered depend on the business and process being analyzed and can include any or all of the following information:

- The strategic information about the company such as long term strategy, markets, threats, opportunities, etc.
- A company's performance in comparison to its peers, or benchmarked to other related industries
- The rationale for the process analysis and at who's request
- The fit of the process into the organization
- The people who should be involved in the process analysis project

This information may be found through various methods as follows:

- Interviews with individuals involved in the process.
- Performance records/transaction reviews on the process (although this data may or may not substantiate the information learned in the stakeholder interviews) and perhaps walkthroughs of the process.
- Audit reports (identify anomalies and soft spots in organizational performance.)

Interviewing

An important method of gathering information and preparing for the process analysis is to interview those who have activities in or are somehow associated with the process. Those who are interviewed may include process owners, internal or external stakeholders (vendors, customers, or partners), those who work the process and those who pass inputs to or receive outputs from the process. These interviews can be in a formal face-to-face setting or can be conducted via phone or e-mail. Typically, the formal face-to-face setting is more productive as they allow for greater dialog and discussion about what is or was actually happening. A group interview performed by a facilitator can also be effective in generating discussion about processes.

Observing

Another important method of gathering information, and similar to interviewing, is through direct observation of the process. Either through directly observing the systems or observing the human interactions with the process, observing the process will help create an understanding of what the process is actually doing.

Often analysts find that during an analytical observation of a process, further questions and interviews need to be conducted to better understand a certain point. Interviews and fact finding should take place throughout the analysis process and it is quite appropriate to call interviews during any part of the analysis process.

Researching

A final method for gathering information includes researching any documentation or notes regarding the existing process. This could include any written documentation created when the process was created, transaction or audit logs, process diagrams, etc. Should this information not be available the analyst may wish to request a written descriptions of the process from the key stakeholders and actors in the process.

4.6.16   Analyzing the Business Environment

Before understanding a business process, the analyst must also understand how the business and the business environment interact. A business environment analysis includes understanding the market, the external factors affecting that market, the customer's demographics and needs, business strategy, the suppliers, and how work transforms to meet the needs of the customers.

As the business environment changes over time, so must the organization's processes. The business analysis helps understand those environmental changes that took place since the process was first created and can help explain the reasons for poor performance of a process. Increased crude oil prices, for example, lead to increased gasoline prices which lead to people being less inclined to drive long distances which lead people to stay home instead of vacationing. Understanding these relationships is important to understand how processes might need to change.

There are as many methods to analyze the business environment as there are researchers and consultants within the field of business management. The following are a few common techniques used that help analyze the business environment.

Value Chain Analysis

Originally identified in his book *Competitive Advantage*[2] (1985), Michael Porter introduced a generic value chain model that introduced a sequence of five primary and several support activities that are fairly common through most organizations. Since his introduction of these concepts they have become adaptable to all organizations. To the

---

8   Porter, Michael, Competitive Advantage, 1985

process analysis professional it is easy to see the relationship of the value chain to standard process management principles:

- Inbound logistics (inputs)
- Operations (acting on inputs to create value)
- Output and distribution logistics (outputs)
- Sales, marketing, etc.
- Service and support

Porter further defined several common supporting activities that influence the value chain such as:

- Infrastructure (organizational structure, culture, etc.)
- Human Resources
- Procurement
- Technology

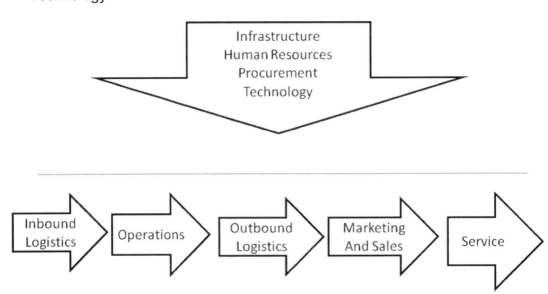

A value chain analysis enables the process analyst to look at the process from a macro view that includes suppliers, vendors, customers, etc. This view helps identify weaknesses in the process that might occur upstream or downstream from the actual process itself. Examples of this in the manufacturing industry are clear. If a manufacturer cannot get materials from a supplier routinely on time, it does not matter how good the process is; the outcome will always be late. Looking at this view enables the analyst to understand these relationships on the performance of the process.

S.W.O.T.

Although typically used in marketing and other strategic alignments, an S.W.O.T. analysis can assist the analyst team in understanding the customer or their target market and what tolerances for process inefficiencies exist for the customer within their market. If the market provides a highly specialized or customized product that is focused completely on quality at whatever cost (custom built furniture for example) then the market probably has a very high degree of tolerance for process inefficiency since cost is secondary to quality. Most markets, however, do not have a high degree of tolerance for process inefficiency and, therefore, should be considered volatile and highly effected by the process of the organization.

This analysis will help the process professional understand those relationships and know the degree of importance to place on rooting out inefficiencies within the process.

4.6.17 Analyzing Information Systems

An information systems analysis is possibly the easiest type of analysis to perform as it requires fewer individuals and is easier to base upon fact and not opinion. A few common analytical techniques are described below.

Information Flow Analysis

Information flow analysis (or data flow analysis) seeks to understand how data flows through a system and to understand how those points interact with that data through the process. This analysis is usually done during the modeling of the analysis and allows a unique view of what happens to the data during the process.

Several disciplines have complex variations of information flow analysis based on the view of data. For example, a simple analogy would be to follow an envelope through the process of being mailed and examine the systems and people that handle that envelope along the way.

The data or information followed can be from any number of sources such as the envelope to customer information saved from a web site and stored in a relational database. The interactions with that data, be it system or human, are charted from the beginning point to the end point.

This type of analysis helps the analyst uncover bottlenecks, unneeded queues or batches, and non-value-added interactions to the data. It also assists to uncover business rules that should or should not be applied based on the data. Such business rules might include how long the data should be in a valid state before it is archived or destroyed, who is able to see the data, how secure data should be, or the reporting processes that need to interact with the data.

Discrete Event Simulation

A discrete event simulation is used to record the time of an event or a change in the state of an event. An event can include the time a customer order was received and when the order was actually shipped. The data derived from this analysis can assist the analyst in discovering bottlenecks and isolating event or activity specific breakdowns. Discrete event simulation can be used when simulating new processes during the design stage of the process improvement project.

4.6.18 Analyzing the Process

The following analytical instruments are often used to extract information about a process such as how long the process takes, the quantity of product through the process, the cost of the process, etc. The process analyst team should look for those instruments that will best extract and explain the type of data desired for the process being analyzed.

This is not an exhaustive list but it does contain the more common techniques and will provide a broad spectrum of the types of analytical techniques that could be performed. The analyst or analysis team will rarely use more than a few of these for any one initiative and it is the job of the team to determine which ones are applicable to achieve the desired objective.

Creating Models

Process models are often used to show processes and the various interactions with the process. An entire chapter in the CBOK® is devoted to various techniques that can be used to create process models.

Cost Analysis

Also known as activity based costing; this analysis is a simple list of the cost per activity totaled to comprise the cost of the process. This analytical technique is used frequently by businesses to gain an understanding and appreciation of the true cost associated with a product or service. This type of analysis is often used in conjunction with other analytical tools and techniques discussed in this section.

This analysis is important to the process analyst in order to understand the real dollar cost spent on the process so it can be compared to the dollar value in the new process. The goal being decreased costs, or if increased efficiency, than the value of the increase in production compared against the cost.

Transaction Cost Analysis

A transaction cost analysis (TCA) is also used often in software application design to analyze how much time and computing resources are used for each transaction processed by the application. The TCA is usually accomplished through specialized tools that monitor different aspects of the software within all tiers of the application including client, web server, database server, application servers, etc.

This type of analysis can quickly uncover bottlenecks in the application as well as bottlenecks in business processes as they interact with the system. As most processes are dependent on some sort of automated system, the interaction and cost per transaction of the system is critical to understanding the system.

Cycle-Time Analysis

A cycle-time analysis (also known as a duration analysis) looks at the time each activity takes within the process. Each activity is measured from the time the input begins the activity until the activity creates the desired output including the time any subsequent activity begins. The total time to complete all activities is the time the process takes to complete.

The purpose of this analysis is to analyze the process in terms of the time the process takes to complete with the goal of reducing that time. It is also very useful to uncover bottlenecks and potential bottlenecks within the process that prevent the process from performing correctly. This analysis assists the analyst in discovering non value added activities that do not contribute to the process output.

Pattern Analysis

A pattern analysis looks for patterns within the process that can be streamlined into a single sub-process to obtain efficiencies. Through the process of discovery the analyst might uncover that the same set of activities happen at one or more stages of the process. By recognizing this pattern the analyst can look for ways to combine these activities (or systems) together to achieve a more efficient process, thus saving resources and time.

Further, systems and activities within organizations tend to mimic themselves within the same organization. By recognizing these patterns in the organization it is possible to find duplications. By combining these patterns together in a single process throughout several organizations it is possible to gain an economy of scale in the organization. An example would be combining the billing process from two separate organizations into a single process.

Decision Analysis

Decision analysis uses a structured method of considering the outcome of a decision. These types of analytical tools include a wide variety of well known practices such as tree diagrams, probability analysis, cause and effect diagrams, etc. The common thread among all of these analytical methods is to examine the relationship between the decision and the outcome. All of these are to aid the process analyst to not only discover why a process has taken shape over time but also to assist in creating a new process.

Distribution Analysis

Although the term "distribution analysis" means different things in different disciplines, the term generally applies to a comparison of attribute-based data. This comparison would be plotted on a chart to show the comparisons of the data points. The shape of the distribution (curve or straight line) can help the process analyst identify the biggest population of data affected by a particular attribute in the data, or assist in predicting the probability of an outcome, or assist in understanding the degree of variation that exists within the data.

An example would be a comparison of the age distribution of a customer base. By plotting the ages of each customer one might find most of the customer base is centered on a particular age group. This might assist the analyst in understanding why a process may or may not work for that customer base.

Root-cause Analysis

A root-cause analysis is a 'post-mortem' technique used to discover what truly caused a given outcome. The intent of the analysis is to prevent the outcome from happening again.

Finding the root cause for an outcome is not always as easy as it may seem as there may be many contributing factors. The process of finding the root cause includes data gathering, investigation, and cause and effect relationship diagramming to eliminate outcomes. This process is much easier when the outcome is isolated and can be easily reproduced.

Sensitivity Analysis

A sensitivity analysis (also known as a "what if" analysis) tries to determine the outcome of changes to the parameters or to the activities in a process. This type of analysis will help the process analyst understand the quality of the process as defined below.

- The responsiveness of the process. This is a measurement of how well the process will handle changes to the various parameters of the process. Such parameters would include an increase or decrease of certain inputs, increasing or decreasing the arrival time of certain inputs. This will enable the analyst to know how quickly the process will flow, how much work the process can handle and where the bottlenecks will occur given any set of parameters.
- The variability in the process. This is a measurement of how the output of the process changes through the varying of parameters in the process. Often, one of the goals in performance improvement is to eliminate variability in the outcome. Knowing how variability in the parameters affects the outcome is an important step to understanding the process.

The sensitivity analysis is instrumental in understanding the optimal performance and scalability of the process and the effects of any variations in the parameters.

Risk Analysis

Similar to the sensitivity analysis, the risk analysis examines the effects of the process under external pressures. Examples of these external pressures include foreign currency fluctuations, civil wars, or natural disasters affecting the supply chain, thereby having an adverse effect upon the process designed. The risk analysis aims to consider what would happen to the process should any of these scenarios happen and ultimately what the outcome would be to the organization.

4.6.19   Analyzing Human Interactions

Many processes require some type of direct human involvement to ensure progression of the process. It is these processes that usually require the most analysis to attain an understanding of the process. The following are techniques that can be used to assist the analyst in creating that understanding.

Direct Observation

One technique is to directly observe those performing the process. Much can be learned by just watching process performers in action. They are the experts and generally have found efficient ways to do what they have been asked to do within the constraints that have been imposed on them. After the analyst feels he understands the basics of what the performer is doing, it may be helpful to ask a few questions about actions that are not understood.

The primary advantage of direct observation is that the analyst can see the current process firsthand. An analyst's presence, however, can be a disadvantage causing a slightly altered behavior by the performer. Sufficient observation time should be allowed for the performer to become comfortable with someone (a stranger, in many cases) who is watching and taking notes on the action being performed. Care should be taken to ensure the act of observation does not change the behavior of the performer thus skewing the analytical results. Changes to the process should be done after the analysis is complete.

Specific things to learn from this kind of analysis are:

- Does the performer know how what he does impacts the results of the overall process and customer of that process?
- Does the performer know what happens in the overall process or is he simply working in a black box.
- What criteria does he use to know whether at the end of each performance cycle he has done a good job? Could he change anything with that knowledge? Would he want to?

As a worker may work seamlessly from "transactional based" to "knowledge based" work it may be difficult to observe and document all of the actions and knowledge required for the human interaction. In addition it may also be difficult to match the processes to the type of worker required within the industry of the organization. The analyst should also demonstrate how the actions performed by the human interaction impact the outcome of the process.

Apprentice Learning

To watch someone do something versus learning what is being done offers different levels of comprehension of a performed action. When possible and useful, the performer may teach the analyst the job which can yield additional detail about the process. By teaching, the performer has cause to think about aspects of the process that might occur subconsciously.

This method is usually performed on repetitive tasks such as order fulfillment. By performing the process, the analyst has a greater appreciation for the physical aspects of the activity and can better assess the details of the operation.

During the apprentice learning period, it is useful to have a second analyst observe the learning process and the initial actions of the apprentice.

Participatory Video Analysis

Another variant of direct observation is to record with video the actions of the performer. This overcomes the stigma of having someone watching and noting every move that is made. Sometimes a performer adapts to the recording equipment faster than to having someone watching. Note that there may be liability and personal intrusion issues with taping the actions of anyone. Care should be taken to ensure proper releases from those involved.

An advantage of having video recordings of performer actions is that the performer can be asked at a later time to narrate the recording, providing additional information about the actions. Sometimes things occur out of camera view that the performer can explain.

Activity Simulation

One method of analyzing human performance is through a simulation of the activities involved in a process. The activity walk-through can be accomplished in a variety of ways:

- An individual analysis may carefully step through each activity, observing its inputs, outputs, and the business rules that govern its behavior.
- A group of process participants might sit in a conference room, each taking the role of a process participant, and talk through the process. At each activity, the person representing the performer discusses in detail what is done, how actions are governed, what will be produced, and how long it will take. Handoffs from one performer to the next can be observed to ensure all needed inputs are available for the next activity and from what source. It is advantageous to have the process model available, preferably in a format that all can see, so those who are not directly involved in an activity can follow the process in the model and note any deviations. Deviations are then discussed to determine if the model requires correcting or if the work description is incorrect.
- A final variation is to video record the group walk-through for later analysis and discussion to ensure nothing important has been omitted.

The latter two variations involve participants in the real process who are the real experts and offer the best means for improvement.

Workplace Layout Analysis

A workplace layout analysis is mostly a physical analysis of a work place, assembly line, or manufacturing floor space. This type of analysis can quickly uncover queuing or batch related bottlenecks, disconnections, and duplicated efforts as work items are transferred from one physical location to another.

This analysis can be useful for any process that involves a physical space where activities are performed and handed off between individuals, groups, machines, etc.

Resource Allocation Analysis

Very similar to the cycle-time analysis explained below is a study of the resources required to complete each task. This analysis takes into perspective the skills of the resources and abilities of tools or other automated systems in meeting the needs that a process demands. It generally seeks to determine why an activity takes a given amount of time from these following perspectives:

- Capability of the resource. This analysis considers what the resource is capable of accomplishing and asks whether the skills and training are sufficient to perform the activity adequately. Comparisons can be made to similar resources doing similar tasks to validate whether the resource in question will accomplish what could be accomplished in the same amount of time. This analysis might also include the capabilities of a piece of machinery to meet the demands of the process.
- Quantity of resources. This analysis examines whether the resource is constrained. For non-human resources such as a piece of equipment the analysis examines the specifications of the equipment to ensure that it is being used within the tolerances given by the manufacture. For human resources the analysis examines whether the resource simply has too much work to do and thereby has become a bottleneck.

Often, companies working through a process improvement initiative, undergo a resource allocation analysis only to discover it is not the process but the resources that are inefficient in working through the process. By performing this type of analysis, the analyst can often uncover several bottlenecks that can be improved with little cost or change in infrastructure given the organization's ability to manage human resource issues.

Motivation and Reward Analysis

One commonly overlooked analytical technique is the examination of the human motivational and reward systems in place for the process. Activities that include human intervention have an associated reward system in place. The reward system could include any number of rewards such as a paycheck, bonuses, emotional satisfaction, etc. Understanding those motivations and rewards as a process is analyzed will help uncover unseen disconnects and bottlenecks in the process.

For example, if a worker is rewarded for the number of widgets produced and not rewarded for quality, than quality will ultimately suffer. The reverse is also true. Further, the motivation and reward analysis should also consider what rewards should be in place to positively affect any new process or activity that is introduced.

4.7 Document the Analysis

The final step in an analysis is the generation of the reports and other documentation. The documentation of the analysis serves several purposes. It acts as a formal agreement among those that participated as to the accuracy of the analysis. Next, it forms the basis to present the results of the analysis to Management.

This documentation could include any of the following items as appropriate for the process that was analyzed:

- Overview of the business environment wherein the process lives
- Purpose of the process (why it exists)
- Process model (what it does) including inputs to the process and outputs
- Gaps in performance of the process (why it needs to be re-engineered)
- Reasons and causes for the gaps in the process performance
- Redundancies in the process that could be eliminated and the expected savings as a result
- Recommended solutions

Methods for documenting the results may take on many forms. An example would be the use of digital pictures of any models created on a white board as opposed to models created with modeling tools.

The documentation should clearly present an understanding of the current state but does not and should not need to do more than that.

4.8 Considerations

The following section outlines several of the critical success factors, suggested practices and some of the pitfalls that should be avoided during a process analysis.

Executive Leadership

One of the most important factors to ensure success during any stage in a process improvement project is the support and direct encouragement of the executive leadership team. Ideally, executive leadership should be the primary driver behind the process improvement project. When not, however, the executive leadership team should be made aware of and provide full support to the process engineering or improvement project.

If the executive team is not in full support of the process engineering or improvement project getting the proper funding and necessary resources for the duration of the project will be difficult.

Often it becomes necessary to convince the leadership team of the benefits of a process improvement project through the completion of a few small projects that show the gains in real dollars to the organization through effective process reengineering. Once these small gains have been proven and sustained over time it is easier to gain support for larger process improvement projects for the eventual goal of managing the entire business through process management.

Organizational Process Maturity

Before beginning the analysis process, it is important to understand the maturity of the organization in relation to the Business Process Maturity scale that is defined in the chapter "Enterprise Process Management (Chapter 9) of the CBOK®. Understanding the maturity of the organization in process management will help define the level of analysis preparation needed.

An organization that is relatively new to the idea of process management will need, first, to be briefed on the concepts of process management that are described in the CBOK®. They will need to understand the purpose of process management and the benefits it will provide the organization. Alternatively, an organization that already manages their business by process knows the benefits and simply needs to analyze a process in question.

Avoid Designing Solutions

Although mentioned previously in this document it deserves repeating at this time. Often during the analysis process solutions to process problems will arise. Members of the analysis team will want to explore these solutions and sometimes begin work immediately on designing that solution. This practice may be unwise since creating a design before completing the analysis is analogous to beginning construction on a building with only part of the blueprint.

At the same time it is important not to discourage suggestions for solving process problems that are uncovered during the analysis process. One practice is to create a 'parking lot' of suggestions based on the items discovered. When it becomes time to design the new process, those items on the list can then be addressed as part of the larger true process design.

Paralysis from Analysis

Experience has shown that it is possible to do too much analysis. Some members of the analysis team will want to document each trifle detail about each activity that happens in a process. Such detail can quickly become tedious and those involved in the process improvement team can lose interest. Further, if the analysis is prolonged, members assigned to the project may not have the time necessary to remain dedicated to the project due to other commitments.

If it appears that the analysis team is getting too focused in a particular part of the analysis and cannot seem to move on to the next step, it is time for the team to step back and take another look at the goals of the project and to simplify the analysis. Often taking on small chunks of a bigger project is another way to avoid becoming stagnant in the process.

In order to be effective, the progress of the analysis should be quick and readily visible to all members of the team and the leadership team supporting the project. A good consultant or facilitator can also assist in moving the team forward and should be considered should progress be slow.

Analyze with Metrics

The use of metrics throughout the analysis is critical to receiving the validation of the analysis from the leadership or sponsors of the analysis. Merely stating that "the process did not meet the performance goals" only sparks further questions such as "by how much?" Where ever possible validate the results of the analysis with appropriate metrics, such as cost, time, etc, related back to the objective of the process.

Proper Time & Resource Allocation

Often, resources assigned to improvement projects also have mission-critical responsibilities in the organization. Although it is wise to get the most knowledgeable individuals on the process improvement team, it is usually those same individuals who are critical to running the business. The problem therein becomes that these individuals cannot dedicate themselves sufficiently enough to keep the project moving forward.

Fortunately, company leaders realize this problem and decide to retain consultants or contractors to assist in the process improvement so the management team can continue running the business. If consultants cannot be retained, it is critical that those who are assigning the resources allow those resources appropriate time away from daily responsibilities to complete the project.

Customer Interaction

One of the biggest factors leading to a successful analysis is the consideration of the customer within the process. If a process appears to work within the context of the organization it may not necessarily work for the customer. Inevitably, without considering the customer in the process, customer satisfaction will be sacrificed and the process will not result in the increased performance as expected.

There is an increasing trend toward considering inter-departmental relationships as customer service oriented relationships. This type of relationship should be considered with caution. Although the same 'customer service' oriented interactions should take place within departments of the organization as the interaction toward customers, it is important to realize that transactions between departments are not customer transactions unless the departments are separate business units that also serve customers external to the business in the same way.

Customers can be defined as those that buy goods and services from a business. Community organizations that provide free services, but receive funding through benefactors, can define customers to include those that consume the community organization's services. Under this definition, very few inter-departmental relationships classify as customers. However, processes between departments should still be examined for improvement with the true customer as the focus of those improvements and how those improvements indirectly will impact the customer.

This concept can be difficult to understand when, for example, the organization is trying to improve an internal function such as payroll processing. When considering how payroll processing affects the customer the analyst will examine how the reduction of overhead expenses can be used to decrease costs for the customer. This analysis result illustrates the direct relationship between everything the organization's operations and its effect on the customer.

Benchmarking

During the analysis process it is a good practice to compare the performance of a process to similar processes in the same or similar industries. These processes also can be compared to similar processes in different industries. A baked goods process, for example could easily be compared to the automotive industry. Although at first glance they appear quite different, both have a process that must be followed exactly to be successful and both are producing a good that is packaged and sold. As such, there are many aspects about the manufacturing process that has been perfected in the automotive industry that could easily be applied to the baked goods industry.

There are three types of benchmarking techniques that can be used. The first investigates direct competitors of the subject organization. It analyzes how processes compare to competitor processes and considers competitive advantages. An S.W.O.T. (strengths, weaknesses, opportunities, threats) analysis is part of this investigation. Competitive analysis techniques include obtaining information from public sources, brokerage firms, accounting firms, industry trade associations, web sites, suppliers, customers, past employees, etc. The organization is then benchmarked against these direct competitors. Obtaining this information requires determination, but most often proves fruitful.

The second type of benchmarking analysis finds organizations in the same industry that are not direct competitors. These organizations reside in a region of the country or the world where the subject organization does not operate or are found elsewhere in the supply/value chain of the organization. Given the proper incentive, these companies are usually more than willing to assist in providing detailed information and in discussing design features of their processes.

The final type of benchmarking analysis identifies processes that are similar to the process being analyzed but exist as best practices in other industries. Consider a symphony orchestra that wants to redesign the season ticket subscription process. The process of buying a season subscription is a form of the ordering process. On-line and mail order catalog companies engage 'best practice' in order processing. The symphony orchestra is apt to discover breakthrough processing ideas since they are interviewing companies outside their industry. This analysis allows the process designers to escape the "group think" syndrome that often exists when organizations only look within their own company or industry. This type of analysis is often the catalyst to make truly transformational change possible in an organization.

Understanding and analyzing these benchmarks in relation to the processes being analyzed will help the analyst team understand the performance potential of the process and its weaknesses in achieving that performance.

Understanding Organization Culture

Stated previously in this chapter, understanding the culture of an organization is critical to the success of the analysis and ultimately the design and implementation of the new process. The following are some of the key elements that should be addressed when considering the culture of the organization. Consideration of these topics during the analysis stage will help ensure that the analysis presented not only represents the true organization but is accepted by the organization as such.

Avoiding Blame

If any change to a new process is to be successful, it is vital that the analysis avoids any accusation of problems that exist in processes toward any individual or group. By eliminating blame and simply stating the facts, the analysis will more likely be accepted as a correct understanding of the current state and avoid any finger pointing that can result.

Potential Threat

The beginning of a process analysis could be considered by the owner of that process as a threat. The process owner could potentially misinterpret the analysis as a criticism about the way the process has been managed. They could even refuse to participate and fight against the analysis and improvement effort. In instances such as these, it is vital for the leadership team to negotiate the situation and insist that the project is not a threat but a necessary part of doing business. Involving the process owner in the analysis process is a key factor in overcoming this issue.

Threat of Obsolescence

When "reengineering" began to be practiced widely among businesses, several executives began to use the term to describe the reason why layoffs had occurred in the organization. Although in reality this was not the reason for the layoffs, many in the workforce have come to mistrust the term or any related terms like "process improvement." As a result, employees who are interviewed could resent the fact that a process improvement project is beginning as they could associate that with a pending layoff as their job disappears through outsourcing, technology or any number of different reasons. It is critical for the executive leadership and the analyst to manage this situation and any rumors that may result to prevent any explosive situation from occurring.

4.9   Conclusion

Process analysis creates a common understanding of the current state of the process to show its alignment with the business environment. It is accomplished by the employment of a professional analyst or a team of individuals to perform the analysis. Using several different techniques, frameworks, methodologies, and suggested practices, the analysis team documents the business environment and creates models and other documentation to illustrate the workflow of the various activities involved of the process and the relationship to the environment where the process operates. This information is then used to discover areas of concern for the process

Process analysis is not simply an event, but a commitment that allows organizations to continuously improve the processes of the organization by monitoring the performance of these processes and thereby improving the performance of the organization.

4.10 Key Concepts

Process Analysis - Key Concepts
1. Process analysis serves to create a common understanding of the current state of a process and whether it is meeting the goals of the organization within the current business environment.
2. Process analysis can occur at any time the organization considers it necessary but the organization should have a goal to continuously monitor processes as opposed to waiting for single events to trigger a process analysis.
3. The various individuals that assist with process analysis include executive leadership and a cross-functional team including stakeholders and subject matter experts and process analysis professionals.
4. The analysis should find an explanation of the interaction of the process within the business and find any of the following disconnections: a. Performance goals not being reached b. Failing customer interactions c. Handoffs that create disconnections d. Process variations e. Bottlenecks
5. Many analysis techniques can be used during the process analysis to obtain the type of information necessary for the process being analyzed. The techniques used should consider human performance systems, technology, modeling tools, business environment, and strategy assessments.
6. Process methodologies and frameworks help guide the process analysis down a commonly accepted path to achieve best results.
7. Critical success factors for a successful process analysis include: executive leadership, considering metrics, benchmarks, customer interactions, and cultural considerations as they relate to the process.

5 Process Design

This chapter will focus on the design or redesign of the desired process state. It will discuss the key roles required, preparation for process design, key activities in process design, and key success factors for the initiative.

5.1 What is Process Design

Process design involves the creation of specifications for new and modified business processes within the context of business goals, process performance objectives, workflows, business applications, technology platforms, data resources, financial and operational controls, and integration with other internal and external processes. Both a logical design (what activities are performed) and a physical design (how the activities are performed) are included as deliverables.

5.2 Why do Process Design?

Since the purpose of business process management is to ensure that an organization's processes are effective, agile, and efficient, the importance of the design stage cannot be understated. It is during this stage that the plan for the desired state is developed whether it is for a process redesign or the development of a new process.

Bypassing this crucial stage of formal design and moving directly into implementation with preconceived assumptions will inevitably lead to problems with the process and force future re-design efforts. Just as constructing a building must begin by creating a blueprint, building a process must likewise start by creating a design.

5.3 Process Design Roles

The following are roles that play a critical part in the definition of process design. The level of involvement of each role depends on the scope of the process and the degree of the change. Transformational process changes that affect the entire enterprise must have a top-down approach involving everyone within the company and be led by the executive management team. Departmental or process specific improvements require more of a bottom-up approach to process improvement and involve only those individuals and groups necessary to effect the change within the scope of that process. An individual may assume more than a single role in the process improvement initiative. To avoid "re-inventing the wheel" with a bottom-up approach, the project manager should consult with other departments to determine if a similar business process improvement project already has been completed. If true, any lessons learned and approaches undertaken may be considered for this new project.

5.3.1 Executive Leadership

The role of executive leadership during the design of a process is to ensure that the process designed will correctly meet the needs of the organization. The executive leadership must provide support and agree to the design changes before they are implemented.

5.3.2 Process Design Team

A common practice is to select a cross-functional team of individuals that represent the stakeholders, participants, subject matter experts, and customers that interact within the process. If a cross-functional team is not created and the design work is left to an individual process designer, it is important that the designer validate the design with stakeholders, participants, and customers.

5.3.3 Subject Matter Experts

When designing the new process it is critical to involve the individuals that are closest to the process and have the expertise necessary to ensure the process is a success. Individuals from every business function that touches the process should be part of the design team. Since technology is used most often to manage the processes and interact with existing systems, the IT organization must also be engaged early in the initiative to ensure that any processes (or systems to monitor and control those processes) can be achieved through the available technology in the organization.

5.3.4 Participants/Stakeholders

A participant is anyone who participates in or has activities that affect the process. These individuals play a critical role in defining the business process through outlining the activities that comprise the new process. For larger organizations, typically one individual will represent an entire class of stakeholders, e.g., a senior sales person or sales manager representing the sales force.

Stakeholders also play a critical part in the design process and they work closely with the process owner to ensure their interests in the performance of the new process are sufficiently met.

5.3.5 Customer

As any successful process improvement revolves around customer expectations, the customer should be allowed to test the process and comment on its effectiveness. Involving the customer during the design stage increases the chances that the goals of the process and the customer's expected outcome are properly addressed.

5.3.6 Project Manager

If not managing the process improvement directly, the process owner will often assign a project manager to manage the process improvement initiative. This individual is responsible for the schedule and steps involved in achieving the stated goals of the initiative. During the design stage, the project manager is responsible for the schedule, project plan, communication plan, managing scope, and mitigating risk.

5.3.7 Facilitator

The facilitator plays a key role in the design stage of process improvement. This individual (or team of individuals) leads the team through the development of the future design of the processes. It is usually best that this individual or team be process professionals with knowledge in both business processes and the needs of the organization. When not found within the organization, professional consultants specializing in business processes can be utilized as effective facilitators to assist the organization and ensure effective process transformation.

5.3.8 Process Owners

The process owners are also part of the design team. During the design of the process, the process owners help ensure that the new design meets the required objectives while remaining within the assigned budget.

5.4   Preparing for Process Design

Before beginning any process design the process professional will review those deliverables from the analysis stage. These should include current state documentation, a clear scope statement for the design, and a list of constraints. Additionally, the methodology and modeling tools that best fit the organization and the desired goal in the process design should have been selected. A modeling tool may have already been used in the analysis phase.

During the analysis stage, the processes in the organization are listed, weighted and prioritized. This reveals a clear picture of the weaknesses of the current process or processes and helps decide which are to be redesigned and in what order. Once these processes are selected, the degree of the change can be assessed to make either incremental or large scale systemic changes. Sometimes making frequent, small changes can have an equally significant effect on process performance as large radical changes, provided there is a clear and accepted vision of the future state.

5.4.1 Key Activities/Roadmap for Design

With knowledge gained from the analysis and a study of the design principles listed above the process design can begin. Although the methodologies to design a new process may vary, there are certain key activities that take place during the design stage of process management. This section will address several of the most common of these key activities:

- Designing the new process
- Defining activities within the new process
- Defining rules that control the activities
- Defining handoffs of process between functional groups
- Defining desired metrics in the new process
- Gap and comparisons to existing analysis

- Creating the physical design
- IT infrastructure analysis and design
- Model simulation, testing and acceptance
- Creating an implementation plan

It is important to note that although these key activities listed above appear in a logical order they do not necessarily always occur in that order and many of the activities will occur simultaneously.

5.4.2 Designing the New Process

There are many ways to design the new process from using simple white boards through sophisticated software modeling tools that allow the storage and retrieval of processes. In addition, there are also many different informational gathering activities (brain storming, story creation, etc.) that can be used to facilitate the creation of the model.

A complete discussion of the tools, activities, and methodologies used to model processes is beyond the scope of the CBOK®. All of the tools or methods used have their various strengths and weaknesses. The correct tool, methodology, and activity to define the process depend on the project goal, the culture of the organization and the current infrastructure.

The importance of process modeling, however, can be found in the discipline it provides the organization in ensuring that the model created matches the expected outcome. It also serves as written documentation of the process and detailed activity descriptions, customer interactions, business rules, and outputs.

In addition, it is critical to involve as many people from the different functions that interact with the process as possible, thus utilizing the breadth of experience and knowledge of those closest to the process. This ensures that the process truly reflects what the organization can accomplish. Finally, it should be stated that the simplest designs are most often the best designs.

5.4.3 Defining Activities within the New Process

Activities are a series of steps that are performed to execute a process. During an order fulfillment process, for example, the activities would include entering the order, packing the order, shipping the order, and billing for the order. Each one must be performed for the order process to be complete and often the steps depend on one another and so must be completed in sequence.

As stated previously, there are several approaches that can be utilized to list the key activities within a process. Although to list all of these methods is beyond the scope of the CBOK®, some options to use would include sophisticated modeling tools, white boards, or even sticky-notes. Any method the organization chooses is valid as long as the activities can be placed in order and can represent the final process design when completed.

One of the keys to a successful outcome in this task is the focus on the activities, not the actors. Another key to success is to keep the process as simple as possible. The more simple a process the more likely it will be completed without error. Further, activities that can be completed in parallel with other activities help move a process along faster.

5.4.4 Comparison to Existing Process

The new processes should also be compared to the existing state. A comparison analysis allows a gap analysis to be performed which will show the level and scope of the change. This analysis provides important information that can allow the process improvement team to demonstrate the savings that can be generated by the new process once the process is implemented. This information also helps build the case for the new process which will assist in managing resistance to change. Further, through the documentation of the gap between the old and new process, the information provides weight to the need for the organization to manage by process. The gap between the old and new can also show the degree of the savings that can be achieved via process improvements in other areas of the organization.

The existing process analysis event or transaction history provides information about conditions that created variation in process execution and performance. Evaluation of this history may suggest critical factors, e.g., event frequency, event workload, or event complexity that, in turn, could offer a set of event-action scenarios that the proposed process must accommodate. These scenarios must be tested to assess the robustness of the proposed design.

Finally, a comparison analysis also allows the process design team to revisit the existing state and ensures that the new design does, in fact, meet the expected goals and resolve the issues discovered in the analysis stage.

5.4.5 Creating a Physical Design

The focus of the prior steps was to develop a coherent description of WHAT activities are to be included and their order of execution. This logical design emphasizes the expected business value, relevant performance metrics, and the delineation of the appropriate activities and tasks as well as the linkages to other internal and external business processes.

This physical design determines HOW each activity or task is to be performed—manual or automated means or a combination of each. All the resource categories for people, technology, and facilities must be considered. A tentative budget that now includes more detailed development and operating costs is evaluated for financial feasibility. Acceptance by organizational stakeholders also must be considered. The timeline for installation must be considered in relation to the original expectations for implementation.

The degree of detail to be planned, documented, and evaluated for a physical design is dependent upon the magnitude of the business process change. Small projects may only require a brief, but accurate statement for changing existing processes or activities.

The larger or more transformational projects will require significant detail before moving forward to actual implementation.

5.4.6 IT Infrastructure Analysis and Design

One of the key roles throughout the process design stage is the role of the IT groups. As most processes involve a degree of automation in information flow, technology can be the vehicle to enhance process performance. Involving the IT professionals in the design stage ensures that the process can be automated and that data can flow seamlessly between systems and activities within the process.

When involving the IT organization, here are some key concerns that should be addressed:

- What software or systems best match the needs of the process?
- Are there limitations in the current infrastructure that limit the design?
- Can the design be implemented quickly?
- What will be the impact to the organization?
- Can a staged approach be employed?
- What will the new implementation cost (including training, technology, etc.)?
- Are there vendors that can assist in the implementation?

5.4.7 Creating an Implementation Plan

Although implementing the new business process will be addressed later in the CBOK®, it is important to create an understanding of implementation concerns at all stages of the process improvement initiative, especially during the design stage. As concerns are discovered, they should be documented and referenced. Some key issues that might arise during the design stage include: defining change management techniques that ensure employee support of the new process, identifying which existing systems will be affected including how change to these systems should be accomplished (incremental shift or immediate change), and whether the new process is piloted or tested. Once the new process has been designed, the concerns can be reviewed using an implementation plan created to appropriately address those concerns.

5.4.8 Model Simulation and Testing

As a final activity in the design process, the new process should be tested. This ensures that the new process will work as intended and that the expected results are achieved. Although implementation techniques will be discussed more thoroughly in a later chapter, the following briefly reviews a number of approaches that can be used to test a new process. Options include role-play, practice, or run a simulation of the new design.

1. Role-playing, during which you send fake inputs through the process to test it, involves assigning relevant process roles to people (not necessarily team members). For example, someone might take the role of customer while another might play an order taker, and so on. The fake inputs could be orders, contracts, or requests. Try to make them as realistic as possible. Once the roles have been

assigned, each person must play his or her "part" when the new process is performed.

2. In a practice run, the new process has been designed, real inputs are used, and the people who will actually be working in the process participate. The practice run is different from role-playing in that a role player might not actually perform that step when the process is enabled.

3. Simulation involves the use of computer software and hardware. The new process flow and key performance metrics are tested under various scenarios to find bottlenecks and other problems. These types of information technology enablers are more thoroughly discussed in other sections of this book. Role-playing, practice, and simulation have multiple advantages.

First, there is no risk. The new process can be debugged without any negative consequences. In fact, it is advantageous to try and break the new design during these test runs. Try to increase the volume that goes through the process or add complexity to the inputs thereby challenging the process to identify weak spots, bottlenecks, quality, and coordination issues. The problems can be addressed and solved safely without harming customer relationships or creating negative consequences associated with actual process operation.

Second, role-playing, practice, and simulation can demonstrate to people the dependability of the new design. Once you have the role-playing, practice, or simulation operating properly, ask senior management and those resisting the new process to observe it. Encourage questions and comments. When skeptics see the new process working and have their questions and concerns addressed, they often become supporters of the new design.

The next option is to test the design in a pilot. During a pilot, the new design is run for real but the scope of the process is constrained. For instance, you might try the pilot for one customer group, one geographic area, or one product line. The pilot can be constrained by time as well; run the pilot for six months and then evaluate its effectiveness. A pilot is slightly more risky than a role-playing, practice, or simulation because it involves real products, customers, and services. Thus a problem can have negative consequences.

The advantages to a pilot are several. First, risk is constrained. Pilots are closely monitored so if a problem does occur, it can be fixed immediately. Second, the people working in the pilot can become super-trainers as you introduce to the rest of the organization. Third, the pilot is another opportunity for skeptics to visit the pilot location and learn from those working the pilot.

Finally, when testing the new design, it is important that all involved in the process from senior management to all participants be allowed to comment on the new process. This not only provides valuable information as to the effectiveness of the process but also creates organizational acceptance and enthusiasm for the change.

5.5 Process Design Principles

The following process design principles described here represent the major concepts involved in most process redesign projects. Not every design principle applies to every process. Never abandon common sense when you apply them. As a guideline, the principles should prove to be quite helpful.

5.5.1 Design around Customer Interactions

Customer interactions represent a point of contact into the organization and represent opportunities to show the success or failure in meeting the needs of the customer. Every customer interaction is an opportunity to enhance the reputation of the organization. The customer experience is the sum of the quality of each customer contact point.

When considering customer interactions during the design stage of process improvement, it is important to consider all the different opportunities where the customer could contact the organization. It is inefficient to optimize an order fulfillment process without considering the customer support process that facilitates resolving problems with that order. Although the order was processed smoothly, if the wrong item was shipped and the customer becomes frustrated trying to return the item, the outcome of the customer experience is not positive and repeat business is less likely.

The customer experience is dependent upon the primary business processes that directly interact with the customer and the internal support processes that indirectly influence customer experience quality. Thus, serious attention, perhaps with different issues, also must be directed to these support processes.

5.5.2 Design around Value-Adding Activities

This principle requires a clear understanding of what the customer of the process requires. Transforming information or material to meet customer requirements creates value-adding activities. In addition, any step the customer is willing to pay for, such as a service, is also value-adding. Study the "as-is" process flowchart and determine exactly where the value-adding activities are performed. Then, extract these activities from the "as-is" process and explore a means to enable the value-adding activities efficiently and effectively.

Do not discuss who will do any particular activity or where it will be performed at this point in the process. Combining the activity's "what" and "who" at this stage will distract the team from developing a creative, unique process solution. Your efforts to create an effective process can initiate debate about who should be responsible for the task. After an effective process flow is created, then a discussion can ensue regarding who is responsible for the work required to enable the process.

To create a new process, job descriptions, work location, and task assignment must be flexible. Team members should be aware that the existing configuration of jobs, work location, and organizational structure can be reassessed. Additionally, do not impose constraints thinking. Freedom of thought, outside of existing patterns, allows people to create a dramatically improved process.

Some redesign methods serve to explore non-value-adding activities to eliminate or reduce them. This approach may create acrimonious relationships with people involved in this work. Informing people that their work adds no value to the process may trigger animosity in defense of their positions. To circumvent this situation, look for value-adding activities to optimize instead. Simply by focusing and optimizing value-adding activities, the non-value-adding activities will dissolve thereby avoiding any potential confrontation that may create resistance to the redesign project.

5.5.3 Minimize Handoffs

As activities and rules are defined during the process definition, handoffs between functional groups become apparent. A "handoff" in business process management occurs when ownership of an activity or information is passed from one individual to another. For example, when a purchase order is transferred to invoicing, a physical handoff is created as the activity is transferred from one group (shipping) to another (billing).

Handoffs between individuals or functional groups present an opportunity for a breakdown in the process. As a transaction transfers from one group to another, data can be lost or misinterpreted. In addition, the more information transferred, and the more times the information is transferred, can further distort the information and lengthen the completion time of the process.

A key success factor is to simplify the handoffs and limit handoffs when possible. Automating handoffs through technology will also assist in reducing errors and speed up the activity between individuals and groups.

5.5.4 Work is Performed Where it Makes the Most Sense

Task assignment occurs after an effective process flow is designed. Application of the first design principle may negate some existing work, create new work, and/or may move work from one department to another.

For example, during one redesign effort, a team was challenged to decide who should be responsible for the initial review. The initial review required the expertise of an engineer with a broad background rather than a specialist. The position did not exist in the original process structure. To implement the new process, the department had to develop a job description for a generalist engineer and then hire someone for the new position. Therefore, current job titles and locations should not be constrained. Create the position(s) necessary to enable the process flow to operate with the greatest efficiency and effectiveness.

5.5.5 Provide a Single Point of Contact

A common symptom of not having a single point of contact is multiple transfers of customers' calls. Another symptom of not having a single point of contact occurs when staff is not directed who to ask for information.

A single point of contact can be a person such as a project manager, process consultant, or customer service representative. In addition, a single point of contact could be a data repository like an intranet.

5.5.6 Create a Separate Process for Each Cluster

Often a single process attempts to handle every variation. However, process inputs and outputs can often vary by complexity, type, size, and so forth. For some variations, the process might work smoothly, but for others it might be cumbersome and slow.

For example, when shopping at a grocery store a shopper has eight items to purchase and chooses to checkout in the express checkout lane. The store has two checkout processes, one for many items and one for few. The regular checkout line has a bagger, but a bagger is not needed for the express line.

If inputs naturally cluster from significant differences, then a decision diamond should be placed at the front end of the process asking which sub-process is most appropriate for this cluster. Additional resources and costs are introduced, but efficiency of throughput and greater client satisfaction should occur. The input cluster is then routed to the appropriate process.

5.5.7 Ensure a Continuous Flow

In a manufacturing process, steps that directly add value to the customer such as delivering supplies, building the product, and shipping it, represent the main sequence. In lean terminology the main sequence is the value stream. In a service process, the steps that make and deliver the service are the main sequence. The customer pays for the output of the value stream. This is a means by which an organization earns revenue.

Lean thinking recommends that nothing should impede or slow down the value stream.

5.5.8 Reduce Batch Size

Batching causes wait time for items at the end of the batch. Batching causes inventory to build as it moves through your process. As you cut batch sizes, you start creating a smoother flow through the process. Ultimately, a batch size of one or processing transactions in real-time is ideal.

5.5.9 Bring Downstream Information Needs Upstream

Explore, at each step of the process, what may cause frustration by team members. When a team member expresses frustration, i.e., it is frustrating when there is missing, incomplete and incorrect information, then the design principle should be considered.

There are two ways of implementing a design principle. If the process is routine and not complex, the upstream person should be trained or given a template or check sheet to capture what the downstream person needs. However, this solution will not work when the process is complex and/or changes frequently. For complex processes, the downstream person must be brought upstream during a redesign to receive information directly from the source.

5.5.10   Capture Information Once at the Source and Share It

If a process requires entering the same data more than once, then the design principle is appropriate. Root out data redundancy, re-keying, and reconciliation. Enterprise resource planning (ERP) software is designed to accomplish this principle. However, knowledge of the processes must be clear before installing an ERP system.

5.5.11   Involve as few as possible

The children's game, "Telephone," illustrates the importance of this design principle. In the game, ten kids line up, and the first whispers in the ear of the next child. Each child passes the message along from ear to ear. The last child announces what the message was, and everyone laughs because the relayed version differs substantially from the original.

In a relay race, the baton pass is most important. Often, a slower team will beat a faster team because the faster team had a problem with the baton pass. (During the 2004 Olympics, both the U.S. men's and women's relay teams suffered from poor baton passes and didn't win the gold medals.)

Think of the handoff of work or information as the baton pass or message in "Telephone." Every handoff offers the potential for error. Eliminating "baton passes," eliminates that potential. This is accomplished by expanding the job scope upstream and downstream so that a person "runs" with the work longer. This requires cross-training and often a change in compensation to reward knowledge or pay for new skills. There are some advantages to cross-training.

First, work often doesn't arrive at an organization in a steady, even flow. Instead there are spikes and bottlenecks in the workload. With more cross-trained workers, bottlenecks can be broken as more workers are qualified to manage them.

Second, if a person does more of the work, he or she will take increased pride in the outcome. This person can see his or her major contribution to the whole. This pride increases the desire to produce a quality product or service.

5.5.12   Redesign, then Automate

One of the worst things an organization can do is take the "as-is" flowchart and lay information technology on top of it. This is bad for two reasons. First, information technology can be expensive. There might be much less expensive but equally effective solutions, such as redesigning processes or training. Second, despite the investment, the problem might not be solved and automating it could magnify the issue. It is crucial to first employ process design principles, benchmarking, best practices, and lean thinking before automating an "as-is" process. Otherwise, a faster but much more expensive and still ineffective process may result. A clear understanding of the organization's processes is necessary. IT may not be the solution.

The process improvement team will begin to envision a new process after benchmarking best practices and using design principles. At this point, engage in conversation with IT on current and future IT capabilities, thereby conjoining innovative process ideas with enabling IT tools.

5.5.13   Ensure Quality at the Beginning

Quality problems encountered in the first several steps of a process will create exponentially negative effects downstream. The time spent to fix inefficiencies by the downstream people can be excessive. There are certain stages in a process where an investment in time and money are warranted and the beginning is one of them. Time and money spent upfront to ensure quality, also emphasized by Lean thinking, pays for itself in preventing reviews and rework later.

5.5.14   Standardize Processes

Sometimes a significant variation in output is caused by five people doing the same process five different ways. This creates three concerns. First, with this kind of variation, it's difficult to improve the process. Second, when a problem occurs, it is difficult to determine if it is a process or training problem. Third, how can there be process control when there's no standardization? It's much easier to find the root cause of a problem when people standardize their work. Even less structured processes might be de-composed into more and less structured components. The former may be amenable to standardization.

5.5.15   Use Co-located or Networked Teams for Complex Issues

Complex problems require people to pour over information and data in real time. If complex problems occur regularly, consider co-locating team members. If co-location doesn't make sense, then network the team so information can smoothly flow.

5.5.16   Consider Outsourcing Business Processes

Several organizations may decide that the best course of action is to outsource one or more processes to companies that specialize in the performance of that process. Outsourcing certain processes can free up the organization to focus on other more strategic processes that add greater value to the organization. If outsourcing is considered, it should be compared to the costs of designing the process in-house as well as compared to the risks associated with outsourcing, e.g., IP protection, quality and controls delegated to the outsourcer, and disposition of current employees.

Such risks could include the financial solvency of the outsourcer, integration of their process with your own, as well as the culture change that would result of the outsourcing. It is also important to consider how to terminate the outsourcing arrangement should you need to do so in the future. Although these risks seem great, many organizations find that outsourcing some business processes is a viable strategic model and helps the business become more agile and focus on those key activities that add the greatest value to their organization.

5.6 Process Rules

As activities are defined, the need for certain business rules will become apparent. Business rules define how or when a particular activity can be performed and help control the flow of the activity. Examples of business rules include "if a purchase order is over 50,000 USD it must be approved by finance", or "when the total sales of the customer reaches 30,000, apply a discount of 10%."

When defining business rules, the tendency for most organizations is to make them complex in order to eliminate confusion and emphasize control. Complexity in a set of business rules that govern an activity creates complexity in the process. The more complex the process is, the more opportunities for the process to fail. As a best practice, business rules should be applied when necessary, e.g., to enforce organization policies or external regulations, reduce process errors, and expedite process execution.

5.7 Process Compliance

Most industries have standards and guidelines relating to the execution of their business processes. Some of these are actual laws and non-compliance can result in stiff penalties or even jail time for company officers. Several examples are listed below:

- ANSI—American National standards Institute
- ISO—International Standards Organization
- HIPPA—Health Insurance Portability and Accountability Act
- SOX--Sarbanes – Oxley
- Others-- industry specific

5.8 Considerations

Based on the level of experience of business process management professionals, there are several critical factors to consider when creating a successful process design. These success factors, if not considered, can quickly become serious pitfalls during the design stage and can prevent a successful outcome of the new process. Therefore attention to the details of these success factors should be observed throughout the design stage.

5.8.1 Executive Leadership

The most important success factor is the direct involvement and leadership of the executive team. As a BPM initiative can have far reaching and lasting effects throughout the organization, it is vital that the executive leadership not only agree to the change but is visibly seen as the promoter, leader and champion of such change. The minute the organization senses that the leadership is distracted from the message of process management, the process change initiative will flounder and ultimately not yield the promised success that BPM can yield. One means to maintain this visible engagement is frequent communications to the organization reinforcing aspirations and reporting progress to date.

5.8.2 Process Ownership

Next to executive leadership, the next critical success factor is the ownership of the process. All too often organizations assign ownership of the process change initiative to a project manager who has little or no authority over the actual process. Those organizations that have successfully implemented process management testify that a process owner manage the change initiative.

Process ownership can take the form of a single individual responsible for the process, a cross-functional team of department directors or other type of management. When the burden of success for the initiative is placed on the process owner there is a much higher probability that the process will meet its stated expectations.

This may mean that the process owner has to delegate other responsibilities until the process change has been completed. It may also mean other disruptions to the organization. When considering the huge benefits gained from a top-down approach to managing the processes of the organization, the small disruption in daily activities is more than compensated.

5.8.3 Incentive and Rewards

A successful process management system will have incentive programs built into place and encourage the adoption of the new process and changed roles and behaviors. These incentives should be based on the goals established in the analysis and are most effective when aligned with the customer's expectations and corporate strategy.

5.8.4 Cross-Functional Teams

The true success in BPM lies in the ability to tie together seamlessly all of the functions to meet the needs of the customer. The success of these efforts depends on the degree of participation from all the functional groups that touch the process. During the design stage, key decisions makers must be present and agree on the new design.

5.8.5 Continuous Improvement

As a key success factor, continuous improvement implies that small changes that happen frequently can have a powerful cumulative effect. Ideas for improvement can come from process metrics, workers in the process, supervisors, managers, process owners, and customers or even from information technology enhancements.

In addition, it is necessary to act quickly in the process initiative. By acting quickly and making some small wins to move efforts along, participants maintain enthusiasm for the effort. One of the key benefits of a BPM system is the agility it brings to the organization and that agility should be demonstrated within the BPM change process itself.

The longer the initiative takes, the more likely those involved could be siphoned off to run other projects, lose interest or focus, or leave the organization all together. It could also be perceived that the effort was simply another effort at "management speak" to encourage shareholders but really amounts to "business as usual."

By quickly implementing a few small changes, the positive effects of those changes can be communicated to the organization and will serve as a catalyst for the larger organizational changes.

5.8.6 Commitment to Investment

Although one of the goals of business process management is to reduce cost, there are often initial financial investments that must be made before that reduction is realized. These financial investments are in the form of consultant services, new technology and possibly of additional resources. The organization's leadership must be committed to make the necessary investment to ensure the process improvement is successful before the return on the investment is achieved.

5.8.7 Alignment with Strategy

Understanding the business strategy and its relationship to the customer is critical in the design of the new process. A successful business strategy is one that is designed around the needs of the customer. Careful design considerations should be made to ensure that all activities in the process work toward the end goal of meeting that customer need and realizing the business strategy. A hard look at any activity that does not meet the needs of the customer should be considered extraneous and should be seriously considered before being included in the process.

5.9 Conclusions

The process design stage in a process improvement initiative attempts to define the new process state and outlines the steps necessary to achieve that state. Throughout this chapter the key activities, critical success factors and suggested practices for achieving a successful process design have been discussed. The next step, addressed in the following chapter, is to implement the new design.

5.10 Key Concepts

Process Design - Key Concepts

1. Process design is the creation of a new process that aligns the business around the business strategy.
2. Process design involves the executive leadership, process owners, and stakeholders in the creation of the new process.
3. The process design team should include subject matter experts, stakeholders, participants, and customers.
4. While designing a new process, consideration should include the following best practices:
    a. Design around value-added activities.
    b. Perform work where it makes the most sense.
    c. Create a single point of contact for the customer.
    d. Combine processes around clusters.
    e. Reduce handoffs.
    f. Reduce batch sizes.
    g. Put access to information where it is needed the most.
    h. Capture information once and share it with everyone.
    i. Redesign the process before considering automation.
    j. Design for desired performance metrics.
    k. Standardize processes.
    l. Consider co-located networked teams and outsourcing.
5. The activities associated with process design include the following:
    a. Design the process with modeling and other tools.
    b. Define the activities of the new process.
    c. Define the rules of the new process.
    d. Define the handoffs between activities.
    e. Define the metrics.
    f. Perform comparisons and benchmarking.
    g. Perform simulation and testing.
    h. Create the implementation plan.
6. Critical success factors include the involvement of executive leadership, process owners, and cross-functional teams.
7. Process design must be for continuous improvement as opposed to a one time event.
8. Businesses must commit to invest in process management to benefit from process efficiency.
9. All processes should be aligned to the business strategy and customer needs.

6 Process Performance Measurement

6.1 Importance and benefits of performance measurement

The importance of measuring the performance of a process can not be overstated or overestimated. Aligning process performance to organizational goals is the primary reason for undertaking process management practices. It has been said that, "if you can't measure it, you can't manage it." This statement holds true and no business should invest time and resources to improve a process if they didn't know what they had to measure to improve.

Many process improvement efforts tend to focus on one functional area, for example, manufacturing, without consideration for the enterprise context. There is nothing wrong with focusing efforts on functional process improvement and management provided that it can be linked to the overall cross functional process performance that drives enterprise level performance metrics.

Figure 6.1 below illustrates the cross functional order to cash process from an enterprise perspective

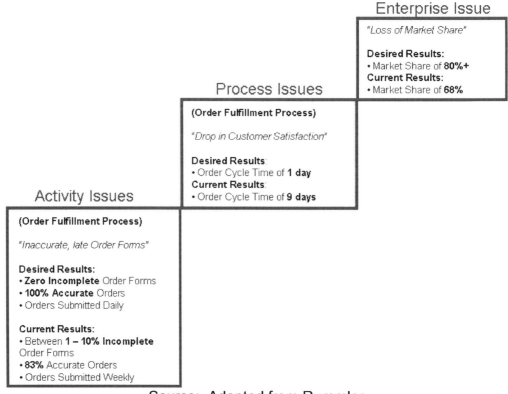

Source: Adapted from Rummler

There are countless industry examples that demonstrate how addressing the process metrics as illustrated Figure 6.1 above have dramatically improved the overall performance of companies and their competitive positions. This happens more often in those companies that put importance on process and associated process performance metrics versus just financial metrics alone.

An example will illustrate the importance of this point with an example. Assume that a company is experiencing a loss in market share. Their current market share is 68%, but their goal is to have an 80% share. For simplification, this is a mature industry and the company and its competitors are not really interested in new products, but rather in taking market share from one another. Market share is what the company uses to measure itself in terms of revenue growth, but aside from market share, what is the reason, in process terms, for why the company is having difficulty? If Order Fulfillment process is reviewed, we see that there has been a drop in customer satisfaction, but why? After some process analysis, it is discovered that the current order cycle time is 9 days, that is, it takes the company 9 days to accept and commit and order and then ship it to the customer. In this competitive global economy, in this type of industry, that type of performance is not acceptable, especially to the customer who can easily get the same product from a competitor, which is probably what is happening – hence the drop in market share. The next question is, what is causing such a delay in the order cycle time? After further analysis of the process, it is discovered that the sales staff are entering in the customer orders late and there are a lot of errors or incomplete forms for customer orders. Between 1-10% of forms are incomplete and order accuracy is only 83%. Furthermore, sales representatives are entering their orders once a week instead of daily. The desired results simply are not being achieved and it is impacting different levels of the process, but more importantly, it's impacting the customer. This is important to understand because, not everyone in the organization has the complete picture of what is happening. The Vice President of Marketing views this issue as a market share problem. The Vice President of Supply Chain views this as an order cycle time problem, and finally the Vice President of Sales views this as an issue with the accuracy and timeliness of the sales order forms. Neither understands the others perspective. The CEO only knows that revenue isn't growing, and therefore neither is profits. Each person may or may not have a metric that they are accountable to, but more importantly, they more than likely don't have an understanding of the extent of the cross functional process that links them all together from a process performance perspective. What is worse is that they are process focused, which means that they will attack the symptoms independently and most likely make things worse.

6.2 Key process performance definitions

Process performance management has many schools of thought about how best to approach and manage it. It's important to first review the definitions of process performance. All processes have a metric or measurement associated with the work or output of the process that is performed. These metrics are based on the following fundamental metric dimensions:

Time – is a measurement of process duration

- Cycle Time – measures the time it takes from the start of a process to the completion of that process in terms of the output

Cost – is a measurement of the monetary value associated with a process.
- Resource cost – is a measurement of the monetary value associated with the resources (human or non-human) required to complete a process.
- Opportunity cost – It is the value that is lost from the process by not getting the resultant output of the process. An example would be when a sales order is lost due to an error (Quality metric) in the sales order.

Capacity – this is an amount or volume of a feasible output associated with a process.
- An example would be the number of transactions associated with a process. Capacity usually has a revenue connotation associated with it. For example, if a manufacturing line of a widget manufacturer could improve the yield (reduce variation) of the line, then in essence the number of good products that could be sold to customers would increase, thereby increasing the revenue to the manufacturer.
- Capacity can also have a throughput connotation associated with it. An example of this would be when in a manual process, sales orders are manually entered into a system by sales people. The number of sales orders processes per hour would be limited by the number of people and how many orders could be processed during each hour (preferably without errors). If orders could be processes through a browser interface directly by the customer into the order management system, then the number or orders processed per hour would be limited by the number of concurrent users on the website, however, it would more than likely be more in quantity than if orders were processed by individual sales people.

Quality – is usually expressed as a percentage of actual to optimal or maximum in process terms and can take many forms.
- Satisfaction – is a measurement of customer satisfaction, which is usually associated with a service level expectation on the part of the customer.
- Variation – this is a measurement of the amount, extent, rate, or degree of change and is generally expressed as the difference between the actual and target or expected result
- Error or defect rate – is an example of variation in the measurement of errors associated with the output of a process

There are other measures, such as efficiency and effectiveness, however, these measurements are generally a function of one or more of the four fundamental metrics discussed above. Another aspect of process performance management is the concept of value added versus non-value added. This concept has its roots in Deming and Juran. However, we will not delve into those principles, but we will discuss the concept briefly. A process is value added either when it is required to generate the output required by the customer of the process or when the customer is willing to pay for the process (or activity) that generates the output; or to maintain quality and consistency of the component resources or output or to provide continuity or transport depending on circumstance. In services, it may be a value added activity if it enhances customer experience even when it does not contribute directly to the specific service, e.g., the personal greeting and attention provided in a Ritz-Carlton is value added even though it is not directly related to providing the room. Bottom line is that the activity does something that is perceived as having added value to the customer. Understanding whether a process is value added or non-value added is important when it comes time to decide whether to eliminate a step or activity of a process when doing improvements.

Effective metrics generally referred to as key performance indicators or KPIs have 12 characteristics:

Metric	Characteristic
Alignment	Key performance indicators (KPIs) are always aligned with corporate strategies and objectives
Accountability	Every KPI is "owned" by an individual or group on the business side who is accountable for its outcome
Predictive	KPIs measure drivers of business value and are leading indicators of desired performance
Actionable	KPIs are populated with timely, actionable data so users can intervene to improve performance before it's too late
Few in number	KPIs should focus users on a few high value activities, or on the overall effectiveness of the process.
Easy to understand	KPIs should be straightforward, not based on complex indexes that managers don't know how to influence directly.
Balanced and linked	KPIs should balance and reinforce each other, not compete and confuse. Otherwise, you will degrade process performance
Transformative	A KPI should trigger a chain reaction of positive changes in the organization, especially when it is monitored by the process manager or officer.
Standardized	KPIs are generally more effective when based on standard definitions, rules and calculations so they can be integrated across dashboards, throughout the organization and used for benchmarking within and across industries.
Context-driven	KPIs put performance in context by applying targets and thresholds so users can gauge their progress over time.
Reinforced	The impact of KPIs may be enhanced by attaching compensation or incentives to them.
Relevant	KPIs gradually lose their impact over time, so they must be reviewed and refreshed periodically.

Source: www.techrepublic.com

The overall purpose of understanding process metrics is so that a manager can attribute a value to improving or changing a process as part of process performance management.

6.3 Monitoring and controlling operations

Continuing with the example from above, not only is it important to measure processes, but it is even more important to continually measure, monitor and control the process in order to achieve the desired results. In that respect, basic process performance management is more of a journey and not a destination. Once the order fulfillment process is documented in its entirety, and the process metrics are identified, collected and managed, then can the company can monitor for changes that will ultimately impact the market share of their product.

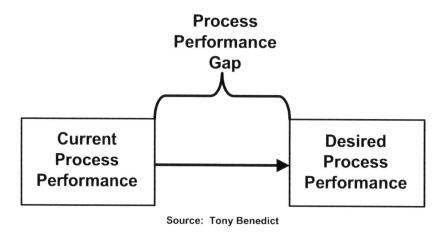

Source: Tony Benedict

While the importance of understanding the process can not be emphasized enough, monitoring and controlling performance of the process is what makes the difference in the marketplace. As business changes, so will the desired performance of the process. The process itself will have to change in order to achieve the desired performance, but this can't be determined unless the process and the performance of the process are monitored and controlled to the needs to the customer requirements.

6.4 Alignment of business process and enterprise performance

Enterprise performance and corresponding metrics are best expressed with respect to satisfying the needs of the Customer. The example discussed in Figure 6.1 was centered on the Order Fulfillment (Order to Cash) process, however, examples of enterprise performance metrics are extrapolations of the Time, Cost, Capacity and Quality foundations:

Time Dimensions:
- Delivery Performance, Request Date
- Order Fulfillment Lead Time
- Product Development Lead Time

Quality Dimensions:
- Product Launch Variance
- Forecast Accuracy

Cost Dimensions:
- Sales Cost
- Manufacturing Cost
- Logistics Cost
- Inventory Days of Supply

Capacity Dimensions:
- Customer Dollars per Order (Wallet Share)
- Customer Growth Rate
- Market Share

These examples are all Enterprise level metrics that have cross functional processes associated with them. Some examples of cross functional processes that drive enterprise level metrics are:

- Order to Cash
- Procure to Pay
- Campaign to Quote
- Plan to Fulfill
- Manufacture to Distribution
- Issue to Resolution

What's important to note is that the cross functional processes will impact more than just one enterprise level metric. For example Plan to Fulfill will impact Delivery Performance, Request Date and Order Fulfillment Lead Time.

When different process transformation methods are used, it's important to understand whether that methodology (Lean, Six Sigma, Process Reengineering/Redesign, etc.) will address the cross functional process or just a sub process within the cross functional process or even an activity within a sub process. What happens with many companies is that they settle on a process improvement methodology, like Six Sigma, and they still don't perform well at the enterprise level as a company. There are many examples of companies that have fallen victim to this way of thinking. "In fact, of 58 large companies that have announced Six Sigma programs, 91 percent have trailed the S&P 500 since, according to an analysis by Charles Holland of consulting firm Qualpro (which espouses a competing quality-improvement process)"[3]. The diagram below illustrates the point of linking the process to the enterprise level desired performance metric.

---

[3] Betsy Morris, Fortune senior writer, July 11 2006: Fortune Magazine

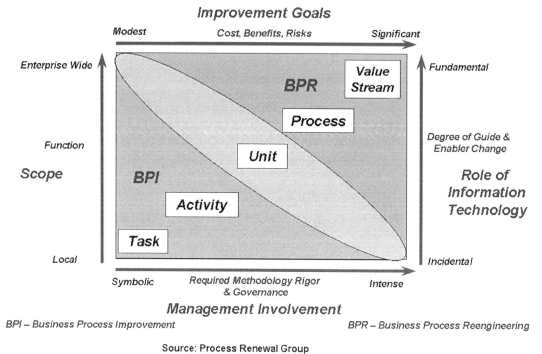

Figure 6.2 Illustration of linking the process to the enterprise level desired performance metric

Presently, there is not yet a hierarchy of metrics that link a process to enterprise level operational performance; however, there are enough linkages between the cross functional processes and enterprise level metrics to give BPM practitioners a good foundation to improving the right processes within the enterprise.

6.5 What to measure

What to measure in process performance management has been a mystery to some and a dilemma to others. The best way to understand what to measure in a process is to first understand the desired result. The foundational metric dimensions were discussed in 6.1 above.

The information required for measuring the quality dimensions of a process can be obtained at both the input and output of the process as well as the overall process when it comes to service level satisfaction. Metrics such as error and defect rates are examples of quality based metrics based on input and output information garnered from a process. Information required for measuring the cost dimension is usually based on the resources needed to perform the process itself, although the opportunity cost can also come from the output information. Capacity information comes from the output information of the process. Time based dimensional metric information is obtained from the entire process – that is from supplier to customer – but can also be broken down between supplier and input and output and customer.

6.6 Measurement methods

There are two very common methods for measuring a process. One is manual, that is collecting data by hand and either drawing it on paper or entering it into a spreadsheet or modeling tool. The other method is an automated method enabled by sophisticated software such as business process management suites or enterprise software modeling tools. There is the use of statistical methods, value stream mapping and activity-based costing. The purpose of this section is not to recommend one method (manual or automated) over another, but simply to point out that there are many methods that can be used to measure processes, each with their own pros and cons and appropriateness for each situation or process.

There are several common methodologies used by BPM practitioners and only three are mentioned here.

a. Value Stream Mapping (http://www.asq.org/glossary/v.html or http://www.leanqad.com/glossary/)
- Value Stream Definition: By locating the value creating processes next to one another and by processing one unit at a time, work flows smoothly from one step to another and finally to the customer. This chain of value-creating processes is called a value stream. A value stream is simply all the things done to create value for the customer.
- Value Stream Mapping: A Lean planning tool used to visualize the value stream of a process, department or organization. First, follow a product's production path from beginning to end and draw a visual representation of every process in the material and information flows. Second, draw a future state map of how value should flow. Below is a diagram of the 7 wastes identified in Lean Value Stream mapping.

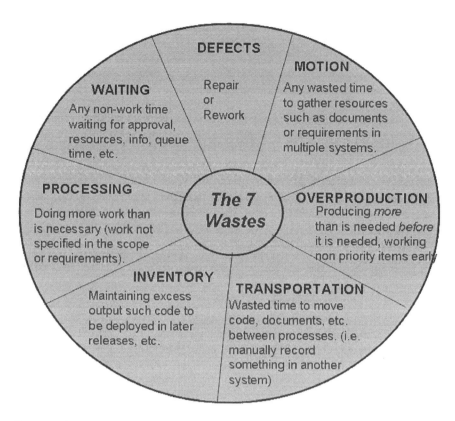

b. Activity-Based Costing
- Definition: An accounting methodology that assigns costs to activities rather than products or services. ABC doesn't eliminate or change costs, it provides data about how costs are actually consumed in a process
- Axiom:
  - Activities consume resources
  - This consumption is what drives cost or inefficiency
  - Understanding this is relationship is critical to managing overhead
- Used to discover opportunities for cost or efficiency improvement
- Focuses on overhead, traces rather than allocates each expense to a particular cost object
- Makes indirect expenses direct

- An ABC approach will account for:
  - Activities / processes (comparing before and after the re-engineering project)
  - The frequency and cost of the activity/process (comparing before and after the re-engineering project)
  - The do-nothing scenario (what would happen if we do not do the project)
  - Which processes provide value (i.e. are needed to attract and retain customers, result in operational savings)
- When to use:
  - High overhead
  - Cost of errors is high

- Inefficiency
- Competition is stiff

c. Statistical Methods
- Definition: the science of collecting, analyzing, presenting, and interpreting data.
- Axioms:
  - All work occurs in a system of interconnected processes
  - Variation exists in all processes
  - Variation may occur in at least two forms:
    - random—natural variation due to the nature of the process; may be reduced, bit not eliminated
    - systemic—variation due to some consistent cause that can be addressed and eliminated
  - Variability is what drives error rates or inefficiency
  - Understanding what reduces the variability will help improve the process
- Used to understand and then reduce or eliminate variability in processes for improvement
- Focuses on data (the X's [inputs] which drive the Y [output])
  - Determines which processes are primarily responsible for driving the X's, then focus on those processes for improvement
- When to use:
  - High rate of errors
  - Inconsistency of outputs

All of the various measurement methods used today have associated with them either software or spreadsheet based tool that can be used.

6.7 Modeling and Simulation

The measurement methods discussed in the previous section are powerful when used to measure process performance. Modeling and simulation are the next step in terms of not only measuring the current state process performance, but for developing desired future states of process performance and identifying the gaps in the current process preventing transition to the desired future state.

For the purposes of this section, modeling and simulation will be used synonymously, as process modeling has already been covered. The definition of simulation is the enactment or representation of the behavior or characteristics of one system through the use of another system. In the case of business processes, simulation is enacting the behavior of a process by use of another system, in this case software that has the capability for simulation. Most of the major enterprise-modeling vendors have simulation capabilities as part of their software. In essence, a process is modeled in the software with all the parameters associated with a process entered into the software.

An example of the cycle time parameters for each activity:
- in-queue time (before work begins)
- work delay time (from start of resource involvement until start of work)
- work time (from beginning of work to production of output)
- out-queue time (from output production to release of output)

An example of the cost parameters are:
- Labor (total staffing costs allocated by headcount)
  - the resources associated with each activity
  - the cost of each resource
- Material
  - Direct costs – material consumed each time an activity is performed
- Overhead (administrative costs allocated as a percent of labor)
  - Indirect costs – allocated to activities requiring resources that are incurred over an interval of time

Other considerations with respect to the parameters are:
- How many times the process runs per interval time (X times/hour/day)
- Decision points in process (example – 60/40 split between path A and path B)

All of the parameters of the process are finally entered into the modeled process and simulation is performed first on the current state process. Once the simulation is completed, an output is generated from the software, often in a spreadsheet type format that is easy to interpret. The output will show each activity with all of the time metric dimensions summarized per activity along with the cost metric dimensions summarized by activity. The output of the simulation allows for rapid identification of process performance problem areas that are supported by extensive data from the simulation. Once the current state performance is analyzed completely, then it is easy to then begin modeling the desired future state process. Once the future state process is modeled, then the parameters are adjusted to achieve the desired process performance and another simulation is run with a corresponding output generated for analysis and interpretation. The BPM practitioner can then adjust the parameters and continue running simulations until a desired process performance is achieved. During the simulation analysis, the process model may change with the parameters until the final model and parameters are determined. This is all done in the modeling software before a BPM practitioner embarks on the actual process improvement/reengineering effort with a team of people. This can save a tremendous amount of time because it's all done in the software before it's implemented in the organization. Modeling and Simulation provide an experimental lab to do the process reengineering efforts before actual implementation. It is not a substitute for the actual field work, nor is it a perfect method for determining the future state process, but it is a very powerful tool to help the BPM practitioner get there faster than trying to do it manually. The biggest benefit of simulation is that it will automatically calculate the benefits of the process improvement via the Time, Cost, Capacity and Quality dimensions to help build a data driven business case for process improvement/reengineering.

6.8 Decision support for process owners and managers

This section will briefly highlight the need for decision support for process management and also discuss some of the common frameworks and technologies in use today.

Decision support for process owners and managers is essential for continuously monitoring the actual process performance. Poor information about business processes can lead to poor decisions about where to invest in and how to improve company performance. Many companies use a Balanced Scorecard framework.[4] The Balanced Scorecard (BSC) is a strategic planning and management system used to align business activities to the vision and strategy of the organization, improve internal and external communications, and monitor organizational performance against strategic goals.[5] In essence, it is a dashboard to measure performance of the organization. Dashboards are a form of decision support and have been referred to as Business Intelligence & Analytics. Business intelligence generally deals with addressing process performance management and control within an enterprise context. When business intelligence is instituted at an enterprise level, it mines information about specific cross functional processes and the performance of those processes in real-time, displaying the information in a dashboard format. There are many examples of companies who have built broad capabilities for enterprise-level business analytics and intelligence, and their capability goes well beyond data and technology to address the processes, skills and cultures of their organizations[6].

The notion of decision support actually begins with the planning of the "when", "what" and "how" process performance will be measured, managed, and controlled. An analogy would be planning the maintenance schedule for one's automobile. For example, one plans for changing the oil every 3,000 or 4,000 miles, a tune up at 60,000 miles, rotating the tires every 10, 000 miles, etc. A clear maintenance plan is well thought out for automobiles by the manufacturer and put into an owner's manual. The actual following of the maintenance schedule is left to the owner of the vehicle. Process performance management generally begins with a plan for what processes will be measured, how often the processes will be measured, how decisions about process performance will be addressed when encountered, etc. Decision support frameworks, like a balanced scorecard, are useful in the planning for monitoring and controlling of business processes. Once a process performance plan is in place – the management framework and dashboard reporting – and you have identified the cross functional processes which will be monitored, the business intelligence and analytics technology will provide the insights into the performance of the business processes, usually in real time, enabling the process manager to review the performance and take the appropriate actions. The business intelligence technology is a great enabler and powerful mechanism in the hands of a process manager. The right decision support can save the process manager a lot of time in detecting process performance issues.

---

[4] http://www.balancedscorecard.org/

[5] Ibid.

[6] "Competing on Analytics: The New Science of Winning," by Thomas H. Davenport; Jeanne G. Harris (March 2007)

6.9 Considerations for success

All of the metrics, methods and tools discussed in this section make it seem like process performance management is relatively easy. One cannot forget the most important part of any BPM effort, and that is the soft skills needed to manage the people impacted by the business process change. This aspect is always grossly underestimated and is usually in the top three culprits when the effort fails. One important point is that process designs which change organizational culture and human behavior need to be aligned to the desired outcomes and working methods of the future business process. This is not as easy as it sounds.

Some considerations are:
- Competency matching – making sure that the people who will be performing the actual work in the new process actually have the competencies and skill sets to do the work effectively to achieve the desired outcomes.
- Roles and responsibilities – making sure that these are clear to people, otherwise there will be tremendous confusion accompanied by process deterioration.
- Organizational structure – structure the new organization to take advantage of the new process, but also to manage it effectively
- Empowerment with accountability – this goes double for the process managers who will own the enterprise level process performance
- Performance measures and objectives – these should be tied to roles along with the corresponding compensation and incentives to drive the desired behaviors
- Personal growth opportunities – people don't want to feel like they've been pigeon-holed into one role with the new process but want to see how they can grow within the new roles

The critical success factors for doing process performance management as part of any process improvement/reengineering effort are:
- Focus on PEOPLE as much as the process
- Education – make sure everyone knows the entire process and not just "their" part of it
- Everyone has the same understanding of what a "process" is
- Everyone understands why process is important – tie it to operational performance metrics for the company and align compensation to it.
- People who design and approve the activities are the same people who do the activities
- Attempt to "Over Communicate" the goals and objectives (performance metrics) of the process.

Lastly, it's tantamount to success to assign a Process Manager which is someone who:
- Manages process performance
- Ensures the process is documented and reflects actual practice
- Defines performance measures and targets

- Monitors process performance
- Takes action to address process performance

The Process Manager is an individual with accountability and authority for the end-to-end performance of a process. This is a never-ending responsibility and the Process Manager helps create the new process and lives with the results.

6.10 Key Concepts

Process Performance Management - Key Concepts

1. All processes have a metric or measurement associated with the work or output of the process that is performed.
2. There are four fundamental metric dimensions: time, cost, capacity and quality.
3. Effective metrics generally referred to as key performance indicators or KPIs have 12 characteristics:
   a. *Alignment* with corporate strategies and objectives
   b. An owner who has *Accountability* for its outcome
   c. *Predictive* – measures drivers of business value and are leading indicators of desired performance
   d. *Actionable* – provides timely information so users can intervene to improve performance
   e. *Few in number* – Focus users on a few high value activities, or on the overall effectiveness of the process.
   f. *Easy to understand* – straightforward and easily understood.
   g. Provide a *Balanced and linked* view of what is being measured.
   h. *Transformative* –triggers positive changes in the organization
   i. *Standardized* so they can be integrated across dashboards, throughout the organization and used for benchmarking within and across industries.
   j. *Context-driven* – puts performance in context by applying targets and thresholds so users can gauge their progress over time.
   k. *Reinforced* –may be enhanced by attaching compensation or incentives to them.
   l. *Relevant* –must be reviewed and refreshed periodically.
4. Process performance measurements may be captured manually or through the use of sophisticated software including BPM suites.
5. Value Stream Mapping, Activity-based Costing and Statistical Methods are three common methodologies used for performance measurement analysis.
6. The definition of process simulation is the enactment or representation of the behavior or characteristics of a process through the use of another system.
7. Decision support for process owners and managers is essential for continuously monitoring the actual process performance.
8. Business intelligence deals with addressing process performance management and control within an enterprise context. When business intelligence is instituted at an enterprise level, it mines information about specific cross functional processes and the performance of those processes in real-time, displaying the information in a dashboard format
9. Process performance management critical success factors are:
   a. Focus on both PEOPLE and PROCESS
   b. Ensure understanding of the whole process not just individual tasks
   c. Ensure understanding of how the process is tied to operational performance metrics for the company and align compensation to it.
   d. Ensure those who design and approve the activities are the same people who do the activities

7 Process Transformation

7.1 What is process transformation?

Process Transformation is the planned evolution of a business process using a clearly defined methodology and disciplined approach to ensure that the business process continues to meet business objectives. Business processes are affected by many factors both in and out of the Organization's control. Process transformation is enabled by Business Process Management principles and governances adopted by the Organization.

Depending on the process maturity level of the Organization, it will adopt various methods to monitor and respond to these factors in the appropriate manner and timeline to meet each individual situation. This may be achieved through a strategy of continuous improvement or by initiating projects as needed. Some of the more familiar methodologies are discussed here.

7.2 Improvement Methodologies

7.2.1 Six Sigma

The originator of the Six Sigma methodology was Motorola in the mid-80's. It was popularized by GE in the mid-90's when Jack Welch praised the cost savings that the company was able to achieve.

At many organizations, Six Sigma simply means a measure of quality that strives for near perfection. Six Sigma is a disciplined, data-driven approach and methodology for eliminating defects based on statistical data in any process from manufacturing to transactional and from product to service. It drives towards six standard deviations between the mean and the nearest specification limit.

The statistical representation of Six Sigma describes quantitatively how a process is performing. To achieve Six Sigma, a process must not produce more than 3.4 defects per million opportunities. A Six Sigma defect is defined as anything outside of customer specifications. A Six Sigma opportunity is then the total quantity of chances for a defect. Process sigma can easily be calculated using a Six Sigma calculator.

Process analysis can use this set of disciplines in conjunction with modeling current process states, but primarily for process improvement opportunities. Six Sigma does not represent a means of realigning enterprise processes for market differentiation as much as a proven means of driving out costs from existing processes.

7.2.2 Lean

The originator of Lean is Toyota. Lean is synonymous with the Toyota Production System. Toyota has been refining the methodology and tool set post World War Two.

The term Lean was popularized by Daniel Jones and James Womack.[7] It is a management philosophy focusing on reduction of seven wastes (Over-production, Waiting time, Transportation, Processing, Inventory, Motion and Scrap). This philosophy was originated in the early days of the Toyota Production System and, as such, reflects the demands of a small manufacturer entering a mature industry. Through such focused waste reduction Toyota has become a leader in automobile assemblage and quality making it a world leader and world-class manufacturing operation.

Lean thinking brings to bear a set of disciplines which can be very powerful in the realm of operations analysis. Lean thinking is more an operations process improvement instrument rather than a means of reengineering or designing new processes.

Good organizations develop and review checklists to review product designs. Lean thinking is theoretically based and has been practiced in both government and commercial, manufacturing and service sectors.

The key Lean principles are:

- Perfect first-time quality - quest for zero defects, revealing & solving problems at the source
- Waste minimization – eliminating all activities that do not add value and safety nets, maximize use of scarce resources (capital, people and land)
- Continuous improvement – reducing costs, improving quality, increasing productivity and information sharing
- Pull processing: products/services are pulled from the consumer end, not pushed from the production end
- Flexibility – producing different mixes or greater diversity of products quickly, without sacrificing efficiency at lower volumes of production
- Building and maintaining a long term relationship with suppliers through collaborative risk sharing, cost sharing and information sharing arrangements.

Lean is basically all about getting the right things, to the right place, at the right time, in the right quantity while minimizing waste and being flexible and open to change. "Lean is a philosophy which shortens the time between the customer order and the product build/shipment by eliminating sources of waste,"[8]

7.2.3 TQM

Total Quality Management is a set of management practices throughout the organization geared to ensure the organization consistently meets or exceeds customer requirements. TQM places strong focus on process measurement and controls as a means of continuous improvement. Statistical analysis is used to monitor process

---

7   Jones, Daniel and James Womack in their book, The Machine That Changed the World, 1991.

8   Shook, John, Learning to See , 2003

behavior and identify defects and opportunities for improvement. TQM is considered to be a forerunner to Six Sigma.

7.2.4 Activity based costing and activity based management

Activity Based Costing is a methodology that measures the cost and performance of cost objects, activities and resources. Cost objects consume activities and activities consume resources. Resource costs are assigned to activities based on their use of those resources, and activity costs are reassigned to cost objects (outputs) based on the cost objects proportional use of those activities. ABC incorporates causal relationships between cost objects and activities and between activities and resources.

Activity Based Management is a discipline focusing on the management of activities within business processes as the route to continuously improve both the value received by customers and the profit earned in providing that value. ABM uses activity based cost information and performance measurements to influence management action.

7.2.5 Performance improvement model

Developed by Geary Rummler and Alan Brache in the early 1990s this framework aligns processes at three distinct levels: organization, process and job/performer. The framework seeks to align the processes behind the strategy of the organization and the customer's requirements.

The Rummler-Brache[9] methodology is based on what's called "human performance improvement". It can be used to understand the alignment of the human resources central to the performance of one or more value chains. The framework is based on three levels of performance
:
1) an organizational level,
2) a process level, and
3) a job or performer level.

Rummler and Brache then introduced a matrix to provide the means of alignment within the enterprise. Using the three levels mentioned the matrix addresses the nine concerns that anyone trying to change processes in an organization must consider.

	Goals and measures	Design and implementation	Management
Organizational Level	Organizational goals and measures of organizational success	Organizational design and implementation	Organizational management
Process Level	Process goals and measures of process success	Process design and implementation	Process management
Activity or Performance	Activity goals and measures of activity	Activity design and implementation	Activity management

---

[9] Rummler, Geary A. and Alan P. Brache, Improving Performance, Jossey-Bass, 2nd Ed. 1995.

| Level | success | | |

7.3 Redesign

Process redesign is the end-to-end rethinking of what the process is currently doing. It is different from process improvement because it takes a holistic approach to the process rather than identifying and implementing incremental changes. However, although it may lead to significant changes, these changes continue to be based on the fundamental concepts of the existing process. This makes it very different from process reengineering which begins with a "blank slate" and is based on radical change to the process.

7.4 Reengineering

Mike Hammer is credited by many with starting the "process improvement" movement through his book "Reengineering the Corporation" (1993). His premise is one of radical change of process throughout the organization to bring about performance improvements. He describes it as "the fundamental rethinking and radical redesign of business processes to achieve dramatic improvements in critical, contemporary measures of performance, such as cost, quality, service and speed."[10] His methodology is broken up into seven rules or principles of reengineering.

1. Organize around outcomes not tasks. This helps eliminate the need for handoffs and provides a single point of contact for the customer.
2. Have those who use the output of the process perform the process. Those who are closest to the work should do the work.
3. Merge information – processing work into the real work that produces the information. People collecting the work should be responsible for processing the work instead of handing over to some other individual or system.
4. Treat geographically dispersed resources as though they were centralized. Technology advancements make this a reality through combining dispersed systems and teams as though they were a single team.
5. Link parallel activities instead of integration their results. This helps reduce errors at the end of the process.
6. Put the decision point where the work is performed and build control into the process. This empowers the performer of the work to get the resources he needs to get the job done most efficiently.
7. Capture information once – at the source. This eliminates costly mistakes of information not being passed effectively from one handoff to another.[11]

---

10 Hammer, Mike and James Champy, Reengineering the Corporation: A Manifesto for Business Revolution, New York: Harper Business, 1993, p. 30

11 Hammer, Mike, "Reengineering Work: Don't Automate, obliterate," Harvard Business Review 90, no. 4 (July-August 1990), pp 104-12.

7.5 Implementation

Business Process Implementation is the realization of an approved business process design into documented, tested, and operational procedures and workflows. Implementation of new and revised business process policies and procedures is included.

During implementation activities it is assumed that the analysis, modeling, and design stages have created an approved, comprehensive set of specifications so only minor adjustments should occur during implementation.

The scope of implementation activities addresses:

(1) executable primary and support processes,
(2) oversight management processes,
(3) business rules related to all three types of processes, and
(4) relevant and controllable Business Process Management components in the organization's internal environment, e.g., policies, incentives, governance, and leadership style.

This section describes a successful approach to implementing a business process and touches on the implementation of BPM and its components. The scale of implementation varies from limited procedural changes in business processes, business rules, and process management to the transformation of entire enterprise business processes and its BPM governance.

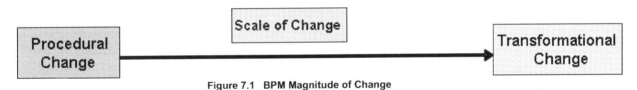

Figure 7.1 BPM Magnitude of Change

A tale of two scenarios will further illustrate the range of BPM changes.

a) Towards the Procedural end point:

- a BPM scenario might be: a business manager may not retain the role of the same process ownership for more than two years, rather than three years. This is a change to how the business process is managed.
- a business process scenario might be: a market research study launch requires authorization by both the Marketing Manager and also now the Sales Manager for that market territory. This is a change to the business process.

b) Towards the Transformational end point:

- A BPM scenario might be: an Enterprise Business Process Council comprised of all process owners, the Chief Operating Officer and the Chief Financial Officer will be created and meet quarterly to evaluate the Business

Process Portfolio performance and proposed major business process improvement projects
- A business process scenario might be: the current evaluation of life insurance applications by a fixed sequence of professional staff groups will be replaced by an application coordinator who will select which professional staff groups need to be involved with a particular application.

The range of BPM changes typically suggests that those towards the procedural end may need less formal (project) management controls. A BPM staff person might need the approval of none or one colleague depending upon the nature and scope of the change. Thus, minimal bureaucracy is involved. In contrast, changes toward the transformational end might require senior management or Process Council approval and a formal program or project management team. Criteria for determining what type of approval and oversight are necessary are part of the BPM governance policy.

There is a distinct difference between implementing a business process and implementing BPM. The first is described at the beginning of this section. Implementation of BPM, on the other hand, deals with setting up the infrastructure for an organization to manage their business processes and defines how they will be managed. It may include governance; tools to develop, maintain and monitor business processes; and a methodology to determine when new processes are required, when changes to existing processes are needed; when a process should be retired and the steps involved in achieving each scenario.

Throughout this chapter, we have attempted to provide a clear delineation between the two. However, the discussion that follows focuses primarily on Business Process rather than Business Process Management implementation.

7.5.1 Implementation phase

As stated earlier, Business Process Implementation is transforming an approved business process design into operational enterprise (or lesser scope) processes and revised BPM policies and procedures that are accepted by the appropriately trained stakeholders. This is where the "rubber hits the road." Indeed, the success of the Implementation effort is dependent significantly on the buy-in and continued visible support by senior management sponsors, process owners, process champions, and process performers (who are responsible for the most critical tasks).

The deliverables of larger-scale Business Process Implementations may include, but are not limited to:
- manual and automated new or revised executable business processes decomposed into detailed workflow scripts including associated business rules and management controls
- BPM metrics and tools to evaluate the performance of the new or revised business processes.

- A new or revised Process Management organization and set of processes for monitoring, controlling, tracking, and assessing process performance and a means to align process performance to strategic goals. Complete and accurate business process and business rules documentation integrated into a business process rules repository.
- As appropriate, installed and tested BPM software and manual activities with related business applications, data sources, and hardware.
- Trained workflow performers and process management support staff
- Users' acceptance of new or revised business tasks through successful change management.
- A plan for the evaluation of the implemented new or modified business processes and continued assessment for improvement.

As the scale and complexity of new or revised workflows, tasks, procedures, business rules, and policies increases, more formal project management and change management oversight will be required.

How do the business process performers, managers, and support staff evaluate the development progress and the post-implementation benefits related to these deliverables? A set of performance metrics is necessary, i.e., "you behave how you are measured." Although there is no universal set of metrics, some guidance is offered in the following table.

	Description	Metric
1	Compare activities to be constructed or modified from the Design Phase with the most recent requirements specification. Are all the requested features addressed? Assessed before Implementation activities are planned.	# of matched activities # of activities specified
2	Obtain a measure of the magnitude of the scope of process changes. Review previous phase metric or develop.	# of (sub)processes to alter # of (sub)processes in relevant domain
3	Assessment of readiness to begin near-term implementation activities	# of resources committed # of resources needed
4	RFP/Q progress by RFP/Q domain, if applicable	# of RFP/Q returned # of RFP/Q issued
5	Testing Progress (manual and automated components)	# of tests passed # of tests executed and # of remediations done # of tests failed
6	Completion progress by stage or cumulative: items	# of components finished # of components to be built
7	Completion progress by stage or cumulative: budget	$ expended $ budgeted

8	Completion progress by stage or cumulative: time	# of hours incurred # of hours budgeted
9	Completion progress by stage or cumulative: on time	# of activities done on time # of activities
10	Training Performance	Average, median and range of training test scores compared to benchmark
11	Business process effectiveness improvement (by sub process)	Actual outcome improvement Expected improvement
12	Business process efficiency improvement (by sub process)	Actual cycle time reduction Expected cycle time reduction

Table 7.1 Business Process Implementation Metrics

One source of additional metrics is A Guide to the Project Management Body of Knowledge Third Edition (PMBOK® Guide).

The Business Process Implementation phase is the critical link between planned process performance, process execution, and business benefit realization. Human and software process components must execute within acceptable tolerances to achieve performance targets. Further, a well-designed process that is poorly implemented will be a failure with both short-term and longer-term consequences. In contrast, a process redesign or improvement effort, regardless of scale, that is well executed will generate expected benefits and sustain the trust of decision makers related to future business process improvement proposals.

The implementation effort includes risk management and consensus-building tasks that could impact the Business Process implementation success or failure. The activities of this implementation phase may vary from a simple, straightforward process-rules change to a major, complex process transformation. Thus, the technological, behavioral, policy, and workflow implementation tasks must be managed carefully.

7.5.2 *Implementation activities*

The orchestration of this multi-thread, multi-stage Business Process Implementation phase presents a significant challenge for larger-scale efforts. All the component tasks described in the prior section must be integrated harmoniously to have a reasonable chance for Business Process project success. The Business Process Implementation tasks are described below in the approximate sequence of execution.

- Review project objectives, deliverables, metrics, and timeline
- BPM and Sr. Business Management decide whether or not to outsource this business process.
- If outsourcing is selected, a set of RFP's are prepared and issued, responses evaluated, and a vendor selected (assuming at least one qualifying response). The contract is negotiated and a transfer of assets occurs. A Business Process Outsourcing (BPO) Relationship Manager reviews installation; test results, and evaluates security at the business process site (including communications channels).

- A decision to purchase or build BPM software is made by the Process Owner, BPM Project Manager, and Application Development Manager
- An Implementation project plan and leadership group are developed including:

    ◊ Tasks in sequence with milestones
    ◊ Assessing and managing project risk
    ◊ Staff resource time and cost requirements estimated
    ◊ Obtaining necessary staff resources—perhaps modifying schedule
    ◊ Revisiting project costs, if revision from Master Budget is required
    ◊ Specify all the relevant BPM components impacted
    ◊ Prepare all the Change Requests for work to be performed and obtain approval
    ◊ Develop, send, and evaluate all RFP's and RFQ's for appropriate items in identified in the prior step.
    ◊ Develop the test plans listed in the prior section
    ◊ Develop the preliminary Business Process documentation and training material.
    ◊ Continue Change Management activities to maintain Business Process owners and performers' "buy-in"
    ◊ Install any scheduled software and hardware; complete any data conversion. Maintain versioning logs.
    ◊ Perform tests of the Business Process and any related new software and hardware as noted the prior section. Resolve exceptions quickly.
    ◊ If outsourcing is selected, perform Acceptance Tests for outsourced business processes; remediate problems
    ◊ Provide training to Business Process owners, performers, and support staff
    ◊ Launch the new or revised Business Processes as executable processes
    ◊ Evaluate performance metrics expected v. actual results (assuming performer learning curve has been satisfied)

For smaller-scale efforts, once the need for an improvement is recognized and appropriate approval is obtained, the streamlined sequence may include:

- Document the improvement
- Test the improvement as needed
- If activity procedures are impacted, document and explain the improvement to the business process performer
- Note the expected performance improvement for the monitoring of the effected business process

Implementation planning

Prior to performing any of the Implementation tasks of larger-scale efforts, the Business Process project manager should re-confirm the commitments from the project sponsors and process owners. Further, the project manager should review with the BPM

Implementation team leaders the previous progress, updated plans, and prepare or review the Implementation Schedule, and required resources.

The following updated project requirements and history are reviewed:

- Business Process project objectives, scope, benefits, and related performance metrics
- BPM project timeline, rationale for major changes and deviations, and expectations for this Implementation phase
- Business process outsourcing considerations
- BPM project budget history and financial targets for the Implementation phase
- BPM project risks: past, current, and anticipated; how these were or could be addressed
- BPM project change management progress including past successes, failures, and next challenges
- BPM introduction/modification rollout scenarios by (1) project objectives' priority, and (2) early, visible benefits

After this review activity, a complete set of BPM Implementation activities can be specified and may be organized using a proven project methodology. These activities may have been done during initial business process project planning, but should be reviewed and potentially modified due to actual changes during prior project phases. Each implementation activity specification should include:

- objectives, performance metrics, and list of deliverables—all related to delivering improved customer value
- risks for completion and how to be minimized
- accountability for completion
- financial, personnel, any IT support, and other resources required
- length of time for completion
- any implementation task cross-functional interdependencies

Smaller-scale efforts may include merely one or two actions with less than one page of specifications.

These individual implementation activities of larger-scale efforts may be configured into a linked network. The specific task interdependencies (e.g. activity start, stop, and parallel execution constraints) are incorporated into the network plan. Given an intended start date for the implementation phase, a complete implementation schedule will be generated. BPM Implementation phase milestones (project progress assessment) should be created, or reviewed and possibly modified. A PERT/CPM [Program Evaluation and Review Technique/Critical Path Method] analysis can be performed for larger scale efforts.

Simply put, the implementation of a large-scale business process initiative should follow a proven project methodology such as A Guide to the Project Management Body of Knowledge Third Edition (PMBOK® Guide).

Specification, review and possible revision of personnel needs (e.g., BPM, IT, business process performers, and any outside consultants) to complete the defined tasks may require revision of the Implementation Schedule (e.g., resource leveling). Internal staff availability and commitments (possibly rates) need to be negotiated within the business process group and other relevant company groups. Gaps in availability and expertise may require contracting with external parties. Smaller-scale efforts may involve only one or two development staff—perhaps just the assigned business process manager or maintenance professional.

The most recent version of the BPM Implementation budget must be reviewed for consistency with revised planned activities and their related costs. Requests for additional funds may require the development and presentation of a well documented justification. Depending upon the amount of funding received, the BPM Implementation plan may require modification. A smaller-scale effort may have been allocated limited funding that includes all the development stages in one small lump sum.

Throughout the Business Process Project, Risk Analysis & Management are performed to improve the chance for a successful outcome. Typically, the major concerns focus on project cost, schedule, and performance. Although BPM project definition, scope, diagnosis, and design risks already have been addressed in prior chapters, the BPM Implementation phase includes significant remaining new and residual risks, e.g.;

- Requirements scope creep can occur if Project Change Requests are not scrutinized carefully (some may be deferred to post-implementation)
- Completion of scheduled activities can be delayed without interim reviews of activity progress and actions to reduce further delay—possibly accelerate appropriate remaining activities
- Intended project outcomes may not fulfill process owner's and performers' expectations if the developed BPM components deviate from the design requirements—incrementally compare requirements to developed manual and automated procedures
- Test procedures may not be consistent with test requirements creating an opportunity for unrecognized defects in manual and automated process activities
- Modifications to Business Process procedures are not updated in the business process and rules repositories
- Cross-functional business process performer harmony may not be stressed during training
- Training programs may not be reinforced with appropriate changes in incentives, culture, and leadership style
- RFP/Q may not have balanced team composition from the performer and supporter/technical groups that could result in purchasing quality BPM technology that does not align with the business objectives.

- Contingency plans and walkthroughs for business or IT interruption have not been documented and tested completely
- Incomplete stress testing of manual and automated business processes may result in an inability to meet increasing business process workflow intensity
- Inadequately prepared Business Process and IT Help Center staff can result in process outcome defects and loss of customer satisfaction, loyalty, and revenue

For any identified risks that have quantifiable threat probabilities and consequences (financial and operational), quantitative risk analysis can be performed with accompanying sensitivity analysis. The usefulness of these analyses is significantly dependent upon the quality and robustness of the risk analysis simulation model inputs.

For identified risks that have insufficient quantifiable threat probabilities and consequences, qualitative scenario analyses can be performed to produce some useful insights and risk-reduction planning. Risk analysis is equally important for efforts that address primary and support (operational) processes as well as management processes. The generation of BPM enterprise value is dependent upon all three of these business process classes to be performing appropriately. Smaller-scale efforts typically do not require a formal risk analysis unless the change or improvement involves a critical component of the organization's value chain.

Risk and issue management

The following guidance has been demonstrated from previous research and consultants' experience to improve the probability of implementation success. Alter (1979) proposed the following recommendations from a study of the implementation of 56 decision support systems. These recommendations are also relevant to Business Process Implementation.

Risk Factor	Problem	BP Relevance
Unwilling user	No commitment to change	Obtain successful BP performer and owner buy-in
Multiple users	Creating a common appeal to create buy-in	Need strong leadership to overcome individual differences, especially cross-functional
Unclear objective(s)	Over promising expected results to users	Create a clear statement of BP project objectives and benefits
Unclear link between task change and benefits	Less commitment to adopt change	Communicate an explicit link between BP change, benefits, and rewards
Loss of budget support	Adoption fails; benefits unrealized	Deliver early benefits to sustain BPM project support
Unfamiliarity with proposed changes	Unrealized expected benefits; loss of support	Obtain consultative help to assure BP success

Table 7.2 BPM Risk Prevention Guidelines

Ginzberg (1979) studied implementation success and failure in 29 management science projects in eleven companies representing nine industries. Kolb and Frohman's (1970) seven-stage organizational development model for consulting was used for the research study. Although the systems were used in all cases, the management scientists (developers) only reported dissatisfaction with project benefits in 4 cases whereas users reported dissatisfaction with project benefits in 8 cases. Potentially, management scientists terminated support (Kolb & Frohman Termination stage; Lewin and Schein Refreezing stage) before the managers (users) had internalized the new behavior.

Formal research on Implementation and consultants' experience provide the following guidance for successful implementation of larger-scale efforts:

- Develop a clear stakeholder cross-functional consensus re: BPM effort objectives and success metrics
- Obtain senior business management visible support initially and continuously throughout the program or project
- Obtain and maintain BPM cross-functional stakeholder support to improve successful adoption and performance enhancement
- Identify and manage BPM project risks
- Protect against project scope creep
- Manage Business Process owners', managers' and performer' expectations carefully to assure that delivered Business Process modifications align with promised deliverables

- Assure that BPM changes are consistent with organization culture, rewards' expectations, and leadership values. If not, seek appropriate resources to modify these elements to maintain BPM-enterprise management alignment.
- Conform to project budget and schedule. Alterations require stakeholder buy-in.
- Deliver demonstrated staged BPM benefits quickly to sustain BPM stakeholder buy-in
- Provide adequate process performer training and assistance during initial experience with BPM modifications
- Completion of the BPM effort is not the end—just continuing the journey for continuous BPM improvement

Implementation "construction"

After preparing the scheduled activities and securing required resources, the construction phase may include both external-oriented and internal activities.

External-oriented activities address procurement of third party resources using Requests for Proposals (RFP's) and Requests for Quotes (RFQ's). Some types of RFP/Q's include: software, hardware, communication services, consulting, and business process outsourcing. Collaboration with Procurement staff, including their approval, is expected. The effectiveness and efficiency of the RFP/Q process significantly are dependent upon the degree of specificity (especially functionality and performance metrics) in the distributed document. The evaluation of responses may be facilitated by overlaying a rating and weighting scheme to the evaluative criteria. Major factors typically include: functional requirements, cost, vendor reputation and support, and time to completion. The results from the RFP/Q evaluations will enable purchase orders to be prepared for approval and distribution. Time is of essence; thus, purchase order fulfillment should be monitored closely. Smaller-scale efforts may include few RFQ's, if any.

IT support resources, e.g., application and system software, hardware, operations personnel may need procurement, upgrading, or reconfiguring depending upon the type and extent of the business process changes. Typically, those components of business processes that are well defined, structured and repetitive can be performed more efficiently by automated means. If IT resource changes are significant, a representative might be a member of the project management team. Some changes may not include information technology change—or at least minor in complexity and scope. Depending upon the specificity of the software development specifications completed in the BPM Design phase, this activity may need to be initiated, reviewed, or outsourced prior to making a determination of how the specifications will be addressed (e.g., purchase an application (extension) or custom coding). Some BP/M changes may not relate to software components at all.

Internal activities include the operational documentation of business processes, business rules, BPM governance and policies, and, as appropriate, interfaces with IT applications, data resources, and networks.

Business Process creation or modification includes the specification of activities' procedures, activity task sequence, decisions with criteria, input content and sources, output content and destinations, activity performer (human or IT application), time for completion, frequency and triggering event for initiation. This may be a manual document, an entry in the business process repository, or input to a BPM suite tool component. As indicated previously, the decision to automate any of the business processes or components thereof is based upon task complexity, degree of structure, and repetitiveness.

Hybrid tasks with manual and automated components may occur. For example, process performers may enter inputs to a production scheduler application, review its output, and conduct further sensitivity analyses. Alternatively, a process performer may conduct a prospective customer credit check. The output is handed over to another process performer who makes the composite judgment to accept or reject a prospective customer. If the credit check is not completed within a specified time interval, the workflow management software sends a "late task" message to the process performer and perhaps the immediate supervisor.

Business Rule creation or modification includes specification of the related business process activity, triggering event, rule content, decision criteria, outcome alternatives, source of the rule, reference to any enterprise, legal, or regulatory requirements. This may be a manual document, an entry in the business process or rule repository, or input to a BPM suite tool component.

BPM governance and polices modifications are entered into a manual or automated content management system for assessing the performance of BPM in the enterprise.

Installation

The conversion and installation of the new or revised business process tasks, BPM activities (including performance sensors), and changes to the business process repository and related business rules may be completed all at once or in stages. Greater resistance to change, project scope, and project complexity all suggest a phased approach. If manual BPM tasks have been automated, both manual and automated components may be executed in parallel for a specified time to check for consistent results. Additionally, applications, middleware, and database software plus any relevant hardware are placed into production. If this business process is outsourced, all the appropriate digital and physical assets should be transferred to the business process outsourcer per the contract. Smaller-scale efforts could be installed rapidly into automated or manual processes—possibly without parallel systems execution.

Training

The business process training program content, schedule, and facilities must be planned. To facilitate this process, a senior trainer should be a member of the BP Implementation leadership team. Program content development can be accelerated if most of the software is "off-the-shelf" vs. custom-developed and manual tasks simulation testing has been completed. Trainers should observe the usability tests (manual and computer-assisted tasks) for guidance in training material preparation. If the prior Change Management tasks have been mostly successful, the training participants should have some insight into the proposed changes and a somewhat favorable (perhaps skeptical) attitude prior to the training sessions.

Process performers should experience the relevant task walkthroughs with training to a defined performance criterion. The walkthroughs will include whatever software (if any) is used in task execution. Process owners also should complete much of the training to understand the tasks being performed and measured within each process.

Some personnel may be transferred internally and require retraining. An outplacement program may be created if business process outsourcing is chosen and results in less than full utilization of existing personnel. Smaller-scale efforts may require little or no training of business and IT staff.

Changes in BPM policies and procedures may only require the distribution of a memo from senior management or a process owner reinforced by an internal webinar.

Orchestrating change

The above phases referred to building the business process platform including specified IT components. Typically, however, the most challenging aspect to a Business Process Implementation is reinforcing and finalizing business process performer and process owner buy-in or acceptance of the changes. Both the continuation of formal change management interventions and training programs are the keys to success.

A major challenge within a BPM project is motivating relevant BPM participants to adopt new behaviors. The intensity of a Change Management activity is dependent upon the complexity and extent of the new or revised business processes. Change Management of BPM participants' behavior is one of the most critical and difficult challenges for achieving BPM project success. A recent survey by Evergreen Systems (Casson, 2006) revealed these business drivers for change management (% respondents supporting the driver):

- Improve service quality (67%)
- Cost reduction (40%)
- Process efficiency (34%)
- Risk reduction (32%)
- IT-Business alignment (30%)
- Regulatory compliance (28%)

The dominance of "improve service quality" is consistent with the major objective of BPM to facilitate an organization's quest to provide superior products and services to customers.

As discussed in the Process Analysis chapter, effective change management activities begin with the project launch and are sustained throughout a project. The remainder of this subsection discusses: (1) targets for organizational change, (2) a change management framework, and (3) guidelines for successful change management.

Smaller-scale changes may be transparent to business process performers. Thus, formal intervention may not be needed.

To be successful, change management needs to address a holistic group of interrelated organizational factors. One source for these factors is McKinsey's 7-S widely recognized organizational alignment and change model based upon their "In Search of Excellence" research augmented by Harvard and Stanford Business Schools' faculty (Bradach, 1996). The seven targets for change are:

- strategy (assure business processes contribute to customer value)
- structure (enables cross-functionality)
- systems—formal processes and procedures including: planning, budgeting, resource allocation, controls and rewards, information, and distribution systems
- leadership style (promotes a collaborative culture)
- staffing (team oriented, open to change)
- personnel skills (cross-activity trained)
- shared values (promoted through culture and performance incentives)

Change management for BPM should directly address the latter five S's aligned with organization strategy, structure, and environment. Thus, to improve organization performance, trained BPM performers and managers must adopt modified tasks in new or revised business processes within shared values nurtured by the leadership. This holistic approach should produce intended, functional consequences and minimize unintended, dysfunctional consequences.

These targets for process change should be pursued within a framework for change management. Many such open and proprietary frameworks have been proposed. One enduring framework is the Lewin-Schein model (Schein, 1987).

This framework contains three stages:

Stage	Name	Content
1	Unfreezing	Creating motivation and readiness to change (or unlearning current task behavior) by: a. communication and acceptance of disconfirming information—admission that something is not working properly—a "burning bridge" b. connecting disconfirming information with a committed personal goal to reduce anxiety or guilt c. create a feeling of "psychological safety" to minimize loss of face or self-esteem
2	Change	Through cognitive restructuring and training, perceive things, judge things, feel things, and do things differently based upon a new perspective by: a. identification with a role model, boss, mentor, trainer or consultant to see things from another's perspective

			b. scanning one's personal environment for information that validates the proposed change(s)
3		Refreezing	Helping to integrate the new point of view and behaviors by:
			a. new perspective and behavior fits with an individual's self-concept and incentives
			b. consistency with relevant others' new behavior and potentially new organization culture

Table 7.3 Lewin-Schein Change Management Model

The essence of this three-stage approach is to activate the process owners and performers for change, provide clear training for new behavior, and support the new behavior until it becomes learned or habitual.

Similar to multiple frameworks and approaches to change management, there are many specific tactics and guidelines for consideration. A set of eight guidelines developed by John Kotter (1996) from extensive industry research is presented here as one example:

- Instill a sense of urgency for change
- Select a good change management team
- Leadership communicates an enterprise vision of change outcome
- Leadership communicates frequently to as many relevant people as possible to sustain change momentum
- Remove obstacles to change
- Plan for early benefits
- Sustain a benefit stream to maintain commitment to change
- Institutionalize changes within the organization culture and rewards

One open source (Harvard Business Review, 2005) provides a set of questionnaires that can be used to assess change management progress from inception through post-implementation evaluation.

Change management is not episodic. An agile organization reacts quickly to changes originating from customer demands, competitor strategies, and regulatory agencies. Some changes are truly transformational, e.g., becoming a digital enterprise. Some changes are of lesser magnitude, but nonetheless provide additional value to customers. Thus, change management should be viewed as a portfolio of tools to be used flexibly for efforts of varying degree. Within a BPM Implementation phase, detailed project changes may occur if project requirements or constraints should alter.

During the Implementation Phase, new Change Requests for business process and business process management activity specifications (e.g.; personnel, IT and financial resources; as well as BPM and Rules repositories) should be prepared and approved consistent with the organization's standard Project Change Management policy and procedures. Sufficient justification for the change request must be included. Even smaller-scale efforts should submit a "short-form" request for review to gain some level of oversight for undertaking any changes to business processes.

7.5.3 Evaluation

Business process post-installation realized benefits (contrasted to expected benefits) are evaluated from assessing the financial and operational performance statistics collected by the BPM performance systems data collection (manual or automated) and Business Process performer interviews. The analysis should include a time series of statistics that has allowed Business Process performers to have mastered the task learning curve. In addition to overall Business Process performance evaluation, the financial and operational performance of the Business Process Implementation phase is evaluated as is the entire Business Process development or improvement project. Smaller-scale efforts may generate limited visible benefits; yet still contribute to process performer productivity, regulatory compliance, or customer value.

7.5.4 Quality control

BPM and IT Quality Control or test plans for new and revised business process components are executed to evaluate the completeness, correctness, consistency, robustness, and usability of both manual and automated tasks. Remediation of errors must be completed.

The first class of tests addresses BPM_(segments) workflow function tests—each manual and automated related new or revised task is independently evaluated. Do the outputs satisfy the requirements? Is expected cycle-time achieved?
The next Integration tests evaluate interoperability between related BPM, especially cross-functional processes' components. One focus is on internal automated and manual business process modules only. A second focus is with external components, e.g., database, another internal business process, and extended enterprise applications such as, shipping or call center. Externally purchased software tests would begin with this "second focus."

Stress Tests are run to assess either persons' or the software's and hardware's ability to complete "transactions" under high volume demands with a typical mix of concurrently executing tasks.

Usability tests are completed by a sample of representative Business Process performers to identify improvements prioritized for the current release and a next release. Are there any suggested efficiency or human factors changes recommended? This class of tests especially is critical to user adoption of the software.

An acceptance test evaluates the operation of all the manual and automated components with typical Business Process user participation. If successful, user management will approve installation/conversion into the production environment.

If this business process is outsourced, some representative from the Business Process Implementation team should observe these tests run at the outsourcer's site.

Dependent upon the scale and visibility of the change and if the process performer would make some judgment or decision based upon the business process component effected, only some of the initial, internal tests may be performed.

7.6 Implementation roles

The team effort may include the roles specified in Chapter 8 and further:

- Business Process (possibly IT) Test Specialists to design, execute, and assess various testing protocols, e.g., process walkthroughs, simulations and controls, software verification as appropriate, and acceptance testing
- BPM Trainers who develop and provide training to business process owners, managers, performers, and support staff for both manual and automated components
- For business processes that include automated components, Application Maintenance, Database, Data Center, and Networking management to assure end-to-end Business Process interoperability
- Organization Development (internal) consultants to continue and accelerate Change Management tasks
- Business Process Repository Manager to implement required business process and business rules modifications
- Technical writers to create or modify user, Business Process, and IT manuals

Depending upon the size of the organization and project, each of the above roles and responsibilities may be independent or combined (e.g., BPM trainers and change facilitators).

7.7 Sustaining the BPM Lifecycle

The BPM Life Cycle is applicable to projects of varying scale from limited procedural changes to large-scale process transformation. Some Life Cycle phases will have more detail; some less—depending upon project complexity and scale.

The conclusion of post-implementation evaluation does not necessarily indicate the end of the BPM Lifecycle (Figure 7.5):

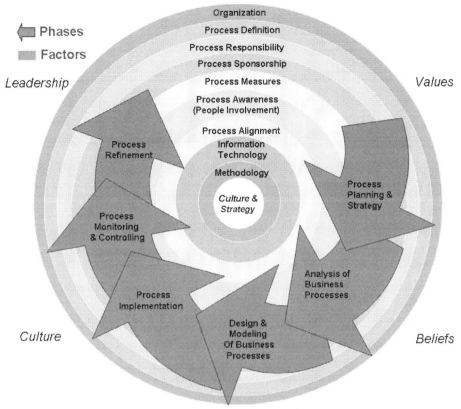

Figure 7.5 BPM Project Lifecycle

Ongoing monitoring of new or revised Business Processes continues to identify both (1) problems to be resolved and (2) further process improvement opportunities to be evaluated. BPM help desk personnel also may uncover or learn about additional Business Process problems and opportunities.

These new or revised manual and automated Business Processes are subject to typical process maintenance activities, e.g.:

1. Business Process enhancements provide new functionality to deliver additional value to business process owners and enterprise customers. The just concluded Business Process project implementation may have requested changes that had to be postponed until post-implementation stability was achieved. Current performers and process owners also may suggest changes for consideration. Potential changes may include:
    a) Modification Business Process functionality
    b) Adding or modifying business process and rule elements or meta-data
    c) Modifying the composition of the BPM Governance Council
2. Experience with Business Process execution may suggest efficiency or productivity opportunities to reduce manual and automated process cycle time as well as operating costs. In turn, this should increase customer satisfaction, loyalty, and revenue.

3. In contrast to the above discretionary changes, regulations and legislation may mandate Business Process changes. Otherwise, penalties may be incurred by the organization.
4. Other changes in the external environment (Fig. 2.3) may also drive business process modifications.

These changes require justification and prioritization. Depending upon the complexity and scale of change, a BPM project management discipline may be introduced as appropriate. Thus, the continuous improvements of business process activities represent business process self-renewal until senior management or the business process owner terminates its operation.

7.8 Organizational Change Management

This section is under development and will be included in a future version.

7.9 Key Concepts

Process Transformation - Key Concepts
1. Business Process implementation must be considered as a critical set of activities even though all the analysis and design has been completed. Execution is the key to successful strategy (Bossidy, et.al. 2002).
2. Perform risk analysis and management to reduce unpleasant surprises and provide business executives and process owners some degree of comfort
3. Continue vigorous change management activities—people, in cross-functional relations, are the weakest link in People, Process and Technology. Use multiple channels to communicate frequently with senior management, process owners, and process performers. Reinforce process/management changes with appropriate modifications to incentives and organizational culture.
4. Business process outsourcing is a challenging process to manage. Appoint trained relationship managers to improve the chance for success.
5. Business Process design changes must be minimized during implementation. Yet, the business environmental factors merit continued scanning for changes that could impact the current Business Process implementation actions.
6. Senior management and business process owners, and business process management must remain active and visible to lead successful change
7. Business Process conversion is meticulous, but an easy trap for implementation failure
8. The scope and rate of Business Process change should not exceed the capacity of business process owners and performers to absorb change
9. Evaluate realized vs. expected benefits. Share the wins. Learn from the losses.
10. Inadequate training will lead to business process/management loss of productivity and probable project failure
11. Choose Business Process implementation techniques to match the scope and complexity of the project requirements

8 Process Organization

The previous chapters have discussed how the introduction of business process management disciplines and enabling technologies can bring new focus on the way organizations perform end-to-end work in order to deliver customer value. A business process management focus may also change the way executives think about and structure their institutions. Historically, most companies have been structured around functional, geographic, or product disciplines. Few companies are structured around their business processes.

This chapter will address some of the organizational changes to consider as businesses introduce and mature in the discipline of managing their business processes. Organizational changes may be challenging and may include changes in work performance processes, organizational structure, roles and responsibilities, performance measures, values and culture. Essentially, everything about the company, perhaps even how it defines itself, is subject to change. Each business is different, and the nature, amount, and pace of change can be dynamic. As institutions reach new levels of process maturity, new skills, management structures, and ways to align, motivate, and reward employees may be introduced. This chapter will help build an understanding of the nature of what these changes may include, so that Business Process Management Professionals can anticipate, plan, prepare, and guide the business through the transition to a process enterprise.

8.1 The Process Enterprise

ABPMP defines the process centric enterprise as an institution that is structured, organized, managed, and measured around its primary business processes. Many companies discover that to be effective in managing their primary business processes, they must assign clearly defined accountability for the design, documentation, maintenance, upkeep, and long term health of these processes. New roles, responsibilities, relationships, and organizational structures may be contemplated. This often results in a significant change in management focus and the way work is performed, evolving from a more traditional structure, focused on a particular resource or business function, to the cross-functional performance of the end-to-end process which delivers value to customers.

Traditional management structures involve hierarchical delegation of responsibility, from one level of management to the next, with ultimate accountability to the organization's shareholders. This delegation is expressed as downward managerial focus on command and control of individual workers with responsibility for a specific set of tasks. In contrast, process organizations include horizontal accountability to the customer for delivery of value across all functions. Process focus involves process design, documentation, measurement, and improvement. Rather than command, process managers may find themselves coaching, advocating for, and supporting a group of professionals who actually perform or execute the process.

It is important to note that a process centric enterprise does not mean that process is the only dimension of management, performance measurement, or organizational structure. Financial, market, and other performance measures remain important, as do functional and product skills. Some organizations may leverage hybrid structures, which include a process dimension, combined with functional, product, market, or geographic dimensions. Others may take a more aggressive leap, structuring themselves almost entirely around processes.

Process Culture

A "process culture" is a concept in which the business' processes are known, agreed on, communicated, and visible to all employees. Characteristics of a process culture include:

- General agreement on what are the business processes
- Understanding how business processes interact and affect each other
- Clear definition of what value each process produces
- Documentation of how each process produces its results
- Understanding of what skills are required for each process
- Understanding of how well each process performs
- Ongoing measurement of process performance
- Management decisions based on process performance knowledge
- Owners of each process having responsibility and accountability for process performance

8.2 Process Management Roles

Managerial structure in a functionally oriented company is typically based on a departmental hierarchy, where managers are responsible for workers performing tasks related to a particular resource or function. Groups of workers are combined into divisions or departments, each adding additional layers of management and control. In large enterprises, these departments are often grouped by product, market, or geography. These silos are represented on a common and familiar organizational chart.

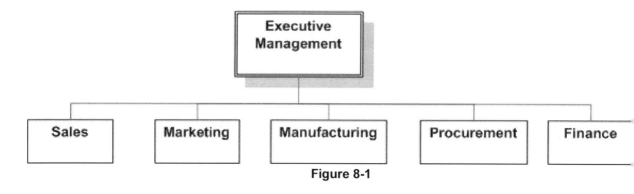

Figure 8-1

Management of a company's core business processes is likely to involve a new, horizontal dimension to the organization structure. This process dimension is commonly identified by the role of process owner.

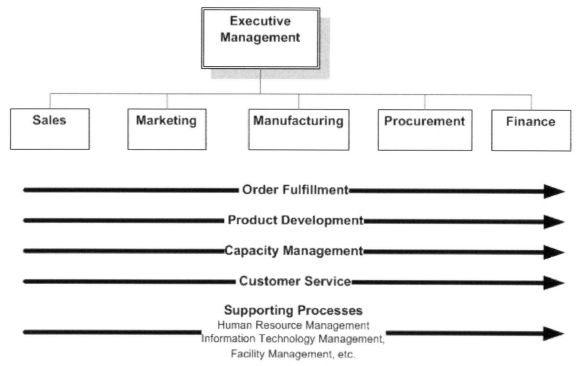

Figure 8-2

8.2.1 Process Owner

The role of the process owner is: an individual or group of individuals with an ongoing responsibility and accountability for the successful design, development, execution, and performance of a complete end-to-end business process.

Some companies may label this role differently. For example, titles such as process leader, process coordinator, process manager, and process steward (see Figure 4) are often used. In addition to the title, the substance of this role may also vary. Process owners may be individuals or a team who share common responsibilities. They may have direct or indirect authority over strategy, budgets, and resources. Their scope of responsibility may vary. They may be business process owners, i.e., those concerned with end-to-end business processes which directly deliver value to the customers of the organization. Or, they may be support process owners who may be concerned with those processes which support the organization's business processes such as human resources, financial, or information technology processes. They may be sub-process owners concerned with sub-components of an overall end-to-end business process.

The Process Owner role may involve other duties such as chairing transformation efforts, integrating process results with those of other process owners, advocating for process priorities, benchmarking process performance, or coaching process performers. Process owners may also have other roles in the organization such as a functional or departmental management. Whatever the title, authority, or scope may be, all process owners share a unique accountability for a business process.

Some common attributes of the process owner include:

Responsibility for process design - Process owners may share decision rights relating to the process design with other managers or participants. However, they are accountable for the overall integrity and integration of the process design. Process design may be iterative, with a goal of continuous improvement involving incremental improvements to tasks and activities, or it may require redesign of the entire end-to-end business process.

Accountability for process performance - Process owners may manage the process, i.e., how work gets done, but not necessarily the people who perform the work. Managing process performance involves developing a strategy for the process, setting performance goals and objectives. It includes insuring that resources and skills are in place, measuring and communicating actual performance against targets, and using this feedback to continuously reset goals and objectives. Process owners initiate process transformation efforts, and define incentives which insure that the process continues to deliver value to its customers.

Advocacy and support - In order to insure that proper resources, training, incentives, and executive attention are allotted, process owners may need to manage communications and advocate for the processes under their care with executive management, customers, suppliers, participants, and other internal and external stakeholders. They may find that they must operate through influence rather than authority. Inevitably even the most professional and successful teams encounter problems, with each other, unanticipated demands, exceptional circumstances, design problems, or changing customer requirements. As process managers continuously monitor results, they must also investigate and resolve problems.

8.2.2 Process Manager

Often, the first version of a process owner is a project manager responsible for a process improvement effort. These individuals typically have responsibility for a project outcome, i.e., improvement to a business process, but lack direct control over resources, policies, budgets, etc. Nonetheless, the project manager is responsible for conjoining many disparate groups within the organization, adhering to the definition of project delivery methodology, designing and implementing the processes, and managing change in order to achieve an overall process improvement. Throughout the project delivery process, project managers may monitor and control process operations in order to ensure that the scope of the project confirms to the project objectives. Projects, however, are temporary endeavors with discrete, finite outcomes and deliverables.

Many companies have begun to realize that process management requires ongoing support, maintenance, and nurturing. The role of the process owner becomes institutionalized as a critical and permanent component of an enterprise's organizational structure.

8.2.3 Process Analyst

Process analysts manage process transformation projects, lead process discovery and design workshops, coach process owners, and measure and report on process performance. Process analysts typically have a great deal of skill in documenting and understanding process design and performance patterns. They provide analysis and assessment of current processes, evaluate alternate process design options, and make recommendations for change based on various frameworks. Their findings provide insight for process integration, design, and structure. This role is often combined with the role of the process designer.

8.2.4 Process Designer

Process designers are individuals with significant process knowledge who design new business processes, transform existing business processes, and implement plans. Designers typically possess analytical and creative skills as well. They use visual and mathematical models to describe each step in a process and the organization of work. A process designer ensures that the process design is in alignment and compliance with the overall business' goals and policies.

8.2.5 Process Architects

Business or process architects may function in a business or technology role. Depending on the orientation, they may be focused on managing business performance or on mapping technology to business operations. Process architects are responsible for developing and maintaining a repository of reference models and standards with regard to a company's products and services, business processes, performance measures, and organization. They are engaged in business process analysis and transformation initiatives. Their involvement may be from a standards and compliance perspective, or as they may serve as subject matter experts to advise the team on the company's process methodology. Through the analysis of business process architecture, companies identify opportunities for market advantage, business integration, and various internal process initiatives.

8.2.6 Other Key Roles

Business Analyst

A common role in process change initiatives is the business analyst (BA). BA's are responsible for analyzing the information and technology needs of their business clients to help propose information and technology solutions. They may facilitate meetings to assist the project team in analyzing current technology mapping or they may be involved with business operations and designing new information and technology functions. Within the systems development life cycle, the BA typically performs a liaison function between the business side of an enterprise and the information technology department or external service providers. Common alternate titles are business systems analyst, systems analyst, and functional analyst.

Subject Matter Experts

Many process improvement projects or process management teams include what is commonly referred to as "subject matter experts." These individuals are typically people who have a deep understanding of the certain business functions or operations, often possessing years of experience as a participant in business operations. They provide input on the current process and assist in designing new processes. They may have institutional knowledge about the rules governing the organization's processes, customer requirements, or the organization's culture. They often validate models and assumptions and are members of implementation teams providing change leadership as trusted stakeholders.

Executive Management and Leadership

The role of executive leadership is critical to business process management. The executive leader(s) set the vision, tone and pace of business process improvement. They determine the direction and strategy of business process management, focusing the enterprise on its larger objectives. They allocate resources and reward success. They may unify the various missions and groups throughout the enterprise, and appoint and empower process owners or other individuals playing key roles in the management of business processes. Executive leaders may even be process owners themselves, owning and institutionalizing the process of process management. They act as champions inspiring the enterprise to change, sometimes by creating a sense of urgency to overcome skepticism and resistance. To do this they must communicate the case for process management and remove obstacles which may impede progress toward the goal. They are responsible for creating the environment for success, sometimes through influence and persuasion, other times by resolving conflict and removing roadblocks.

IT Organization Roles

There are a number of roles within Information Technology groups who may play an important part in business process management including: solution architects, system analysts, BPMS configuration specialists, developers, database administrators, and others. These experts help define supporting technology solutions and may assist in defining new capabilities for business processes based on enabling technology. They assist in process transformation initiatives through the implementation of new technology while ensuring that the company's technical standards are enforced.

Other Roles

Process owners require the support of a team. Supporting roles may include: design, architecture, mapping, modeling, tool management, repository management, change management, or other critical skills. The ABPMP collaborated in a survey which identified over 100 titles and roles introduced by organizations undertaking business process management initiatives (see Table 8-1). Different organizations may use different titles to describe various roles with similar or overlapping responsibilities. Often, a single individual provides the skill and leadership required for two or more of these roles. Several chapters in this Common Body of Knowledge provide additional discussion on some of these roles. For the purposes of simplicity, this section will expand on a small subset of these supporting or stakeholder roles below:

Table 2 - 100 New BPM Job Titles

© 2005 BPM Group - All Rights Reserved

Rank	Job	Rank	Job
1	Business Process Manager	51	Process & Quality Manager
2	Business Process Analyst	52	Process & Organisational Performance Advisor
3	Business Process Consultant	53	Principal, Process and Perf Mgt
4	Business Process Architect	54	National Practice Leader - Business Process Optimization
5	Director Business Process Management	55	Mgr, Business Process Services
6	Business Process Engineer	56	Manager, Continuous Process Improvement
7	Process Engineering Manager	57	Manager, Business Process Analysis
8	Process Owner	58	Manager, BPM Business Programs
9	Business Process Officer	59	Manager, Adaptive Infrastructure BPM
10	BPM Project Leader	60	Manager Process Management Group
11	Process Design Manager	61	Manager Center of Excellence Process Management
12	Process Designer	62	Manager Business Process Engineering
13	Principle Process Consultant	63	Manager Business Process Alignment
14	Business Process Team Leader	64	IT Process/Cost/Metrics Specialist
15	VP, Process Management	65	IT Process Development Analyst
16	Director, Business Process Improvement	66	IT Process Analyst
17	Enterprise Process Architect	67	IT Business Process Architect
18	Business Process Specialist	68	IT Based Business Process Reengineering
19	Business Process Improvement Manager	69	IS Process Consultant
20	Business Process Developer	70	Innovation & Process Manager
21	Process Improvement Consultant	71	Head of Quality & Process, Information Services Division
22	Business Process & Quality Manager	72	Head of Process Improvement
23	BPM Researcher	73	Head of Process Architecture
24	Business Process Administrator	74	Head of Process & Automation
25	VP, Process Engineering	75	Head of Business Process Management
26	VP, Business Process Consulting	76	Head : Business Process and Analysis
27	Sales Process Change Manager	77	Group Manager - Process Management & Improvement
28	Process Strategy Consultant	78	Global Supply Chain Planning Process Leader
29	Process Optimisation Manager	79	Executive Director for Business Process
30	Process Modeller	80	Enterprise Business Process Manager
31	Process Management Specialist	81	e-business Process Manager
32	Process Management Coordinator	82	Director, Business Process Technologies
33	Process Integration Lead	83	Director Process Development and Quality
34	Process Improvement Specialist	84	Director Marketing BPM
35	Process Improvement Officer	85	Director IT & Process Management Europe
36	Process Improvement Manager	86	Director Business Process Change
37	Process Improvement Engineer	87	Delivery Manager : BPM Solutions
38	Process Executive	88	Business Process Quality Manager
39	Process Development Team	89	Business Process Outsourcing
40	Process Development Manager	90	Business Process Optimization
41	Process Development Engineer	91	Business Process Marketing
42	Process Developer/Project Manager	92	Business Process Innovation Manager
43	Process Coordinator	93	Business Process Development Manager
44	Process Consultant	94	Business Process Designer - Project Manager
45	Process Assurance	95	Business Process Design Mgr
46	Process Assistant	96	Business Process Articulation Consultant
47	Process and Process Management Specialist	97	Business Process Arch / Project Manager
48	Process and Change Management	98	BPM Specialist
49	Process Analysis, Education and Communication	99	BPM PreSales
50	Process & Systems Integration Architect - Director	100	BPM Executive

Table 8-1

8.3 Organizational Structures

As organizations have matured in the management of their business processes, issues regarding process integration have arisen, i.e., how various processes must join as a collective whole to ensure a single, coherent organization which consistently delivers value across all of the company's processes. These organizations have identified the need for new mechanisms for planning, budgeting, and allocating resources in order to ensure that their processes are properly resourced, integrated, and aligned with their strategic objectives.

It is critical that organizations have a clear governance structure to provide leadership and clarify decision rights to enable cross-functional and departmental process improvement or management programs to succeed. Often, it is changes in the organizational governance structure that can be the root of resistance to business process management initiatives, sometimes causing them to fail. Individuals who may have had a great deal of power and control over resources based upon organizational functions, product lines, or geographic boundaries may find that their performance measures, authority, and span of control must change in order to successfully implement business process management. The reason for change is simple. Business process management provides an end-to-end perspective of how work is done. This end-to-end perspective crosses traditional organizational boundaries and requires that the mechanisms by which decisions are made and resources are allocated must also be aligned with the end-to-end business process. A sound governance provides a structure of authority and a framework for collaboration. This structure and framework enable proper allocation of resources and efficient coordination of activity control throughout the organization. Traditional managers who are unable to adapt their thinking beyond their organizational silo to end-to-end business process management are likely to resist initiatives which may change their influence in the organization.

8.3.1 Process Governance

There is no single standard governance structure which is widely in use. Organizational focus on process is still emerging and there are a wide variety of governance structures in use and evolving. Issues such as organizational strategy, culture and process maturity, business process outsourcing, and even the nature of individual leaders can cause a significant deviation from any given governance framework. Gartner has suggested four separate frameworks for governance, but goes on to say, "Do not try to fit your [process management] efforts into a 'cookie-cutter' framework. Focus on whether the proper skills, relationships, and mandates for action are available and defined in a clear and powerful governance structure."[12]

---

[12] Melenovsky, M, Hill, J, 2006 "Role Definition and Organizational Structure: Business Process Improvement," Gartner Research Brief.

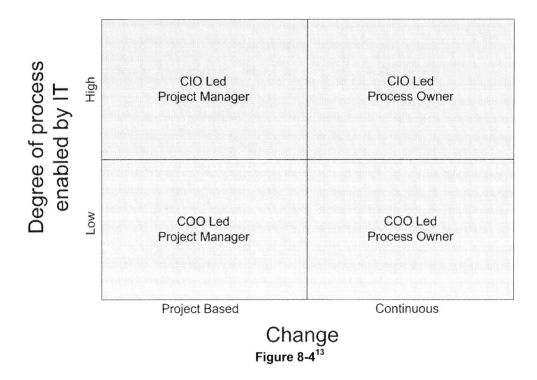

Figure 8-4[13]

8.3.2 Process Council

Organizations undertaking the process journey may want to consider instituting a process council to address these issues. A process council may be made up of a combination of executive leaders, functional or departmental heads, and the process owners of the core cross-functional enterprise processes. Its mission may include the identification and resolution of any cross-process integration issues, conflicts between process and functional (or departmental) ownership, resource allocation, and the development and alignment of the organization's business objectives, goals, and strategy.

---

[13] Ibid.

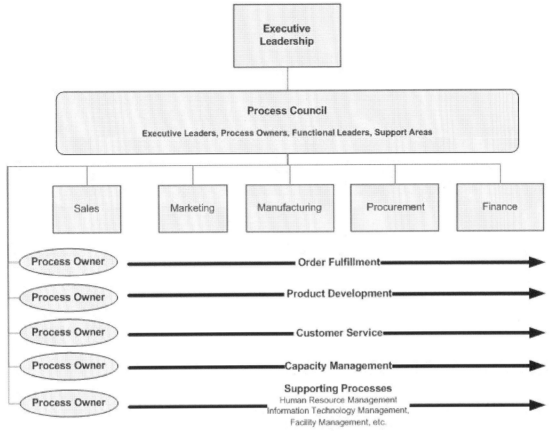

Figure 8-5

8.3.3 BPM Office/BPM Center of Excellence

Some institutions, particularly in government, have created what is referred to as a Business Process Management Office (BPMO) or a BPM Center of Excellence (BPMCOE). Many BPMO's act in a manner similar to that of a project management office, identifying, consolidating and reporting status on various process improvement projects across the enterprise. BPMCOE charters include setting standards, providing common tool and methods, training and education on business process management principles and practices, providing governance on overall process design, and integrating business processes at the enterprise level. BPMO/BPMCOE's play an integral role in prioritizing and allocating scarce resources to business process improvement efforts, as well as tracking and reporting process performance metrics to the respective process owners and executive management. In government, many BPMO's have a role in enterprise architecture efforts as mandated by the Office of Management and Budget (OMB). The OMB Federal Enterprise Architecture Framework (FEAF) requires agencies to maintain models of their key business processes and relate them to other architectural models such as business reference, technology, and performance models. BPMO/BPMCOE's are responsible for maintaining the repository of process models, identifying opportunities for improvement, and working with various stakeholders in the development of business cases for process improvement and transformation efforts.

8.3.4 Functional Centers of Excellence

As businesses mature in implementing process management, assigning accountability for the management of core business processes, and developing mechanisms to integrate and align these processes, they may discover the nature of how work is performed and evolves in the organization. Rather than command and control the performance of individual tasks, process owners find that they need to be supported by cross-functional teams who are also focused on the performance of the overall process. Instead of command and control oversight, these teams may work relatively independently with guidance and support from management.

Companies encounter a need for change in the required skills and culture of their organization as they gain experience in process management. They need to maintain and integrate new skills and professional expertise across all business processes. Specialized skills may have previously resided in a functional group of the enterprise. Best practices groups, sometimes called centers of excellence, provide knowledge, standards, best practices, training, and education. They are responsible for ensuring the proper resources with proper skills are placed and allocated properly throughout the company's business processes.

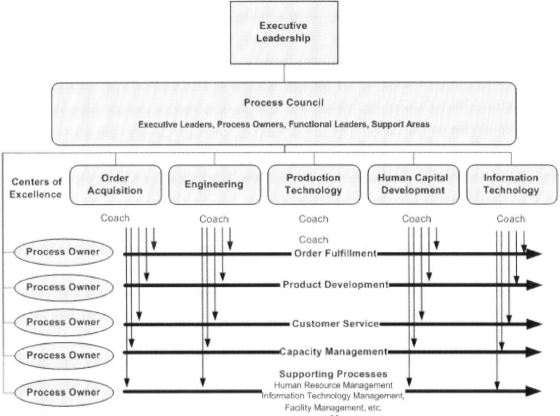

Figure 8-6[14]

Centers of excellence may be virtual organizations (often known as a Community of Interest, or COIN). For example, it may be an email distribution list to connect all engineers, or they may be robust, institutionalized groups with large training facilities. Many centers of excellence are organized around a particular skill or profession: sales, marketing, finance, information technology, etc. Coaches may be assigned to business processes from the centers of excellence with a responsibility for supporting and developing members in order to ensure that the caliber of localized skills are maintained and enhanced. Centers offer training and education programs as well as professional networking for sharing experiences. Some organizations use centers of excellence as an entrée for people, i.e., they are hired by the center and deployed from the centers to process teams.

---

[14] Concept derived from Dr. Michael Hammer's 1997 book "Beyond Reengineering – How the process centered organization is changing our work and our lives" Dr. Hammer discusses several case studies relating to the evolution of the process centered enterprise, including the introduction of centers of excellence.

8.4 Team Based Performance

Companies that manage by business processes recognize that changes must be made in the way performance is measured and how employee performance is recognized and rewarded. In addition to the financial performance of the overall company, consideration may be given to connecting employee compensation to the performance of the process, to the results of the workgroup, and to their individual performance within that group. These measures may be associated more closely to customer satisfaction and the process results such as cycle time, service levels, quality, and value delivered. These changes may also result in a change in culture, with increased individual accountability to the outcome of a process and ultimately the customer.

8.5 Summary/Conclusions

Every enterprise is unique, with its own unique culture, values, incentive systems, business processes, and structure. Today many companies are still structured around a functional hierarchy, with little or no accountability for the end-to-end business processes which deliver customer value across functional silos. As the power and benefit of managing business process becomes more prevalent, organizational focus and structure is likely to evolve to include a process dimension. This evolution may lead to significant change in how work is performed and managed. It may involve new roles and responsibilities, performance measures, and compensation plans. Businesses have found the notion of process ownership is critical to the successful management of their core business processes. Some have also found the need to develop a process council, BPMO, or BPMCOE for the integration and alignment of processes, and a few have identified the need for functional centers of excellence in order to ensure proper skills and best practices are in place across the organization.

There is no single structure, set of tiles, roles or culture that is clearly emerging, but rather each institution appears to be adapting to business process management in their own unique way. Given the uncertainty of how any individual enterprise may adapt to business process management, it is incumbent upon the business process management professional to understand the changes their company may experience, their impact on the business, and the best practices being discovered by companies around the world. This knowledge will serve as a guide, helping address this change in a way that fits each unique situation.

8.6 Key Concepts

Process Organization - Key Concepts

1. An enterprise fosters a process culture when the business' processes are known, agreed upon, communicated, and visible to all employees.
2. As an enterprise matures in managing their business processes, their organizational structure will naturally tend toward change which comprehends a process dimension. Management of work from a downward managerial command and control approach adapts to include a horizontal dimension reflective of end-to-end processes, driving accountability to the customer for delivery of value across functions.
3. An individual or group is assigned the role of process owner for a complete end-to-end business process. This process owner has an ongoing responsibility and accountability for the successful design, development, execution and performance of this process.
4. Successful process management within an enterprise will involve numerous roles in addition to process owner. Some individuals will have responsibility for more than one role. The more common roles include process manager, process analyst, process designer, and process architect, along with business analyst, subject matter expert, and executive management and leadership. There are several supporting roles which play an important part in business process management, from an IT or an administrative standpoint.
5. It is critical that organizations have a clear governance structure to provide leadership and clarify decision rights to enable cross-functional and departmental process improvement or management programs to succeed.
6. While there are many governance structures being proposed and implemented, there is currently no single standard for comprehending an organizational focus on process within an organizational structure.
7. A process council, made up of executive leaders, functional or department heads, and process owners, is one common approach to governance. The process council ensures alignment of business processes with enterprise strategies, goals and objectives, and may have responsibility to identify and resolve cross-process integration issues, conflicts between process and functional ownership. The process council may have responsibility for the allocation of business process management resources.
8. Other organizational approaches to process management include the establishment of a Business Process Management Office (BPMO), a BPM Center of Excellence (BPMCOE), or a functional center of excellence (often known as a Community of Interest, or COIN).
9. The Business Process Management professional must understand the myriad of potential organizational changes which may be brought about through increasing process maturity, so that they can guide the enterprise through the transition.

9 Enterprise Process Management

Process management involves the transition from expressing strategy in general terms or in financial terms to expressing strategy in terms of observable cross-functional activity. This requires both careful thought, a shift in mindset and a new set of leadership behaviors.

The shift in mindset involves a deep appreciation that the financial goals are simply the cumulative outcomes of the activities that the firm executes. Careful thought is necessary to make tough choices on the deployment of limited resources.

It is important to appreciate the following factors, which underlie these decisions:

- a shared understanding of the definition of each enterprise level business process, including details on where the process starts, where it ends, the key steps, and the departments involved
- clarity and agreement on the critical few measures of performance for each process
- acceptance of the estimates of current performance for each process
- agreement on the size of the performance gap that needs to be bridged
- agreement on the top priorities for improvement, allocation of resources, and deep dedication to taking action
- a shared understanding of accountability assignments

Plans cannot be translated into action without a clear, shared understanding of the accountability for improving and managing the firm's major enterprise level business processes. It is worthwhile reiterating that in most firms, no one person has authority or control over the entire set of activities in an end-to-end business process. Hence, the establishment of process governance is of crucial importance to drive customer centricity and collaboration at all management levels.

The final component in this planning stage is a solid communication plan that clearly communicates the enterprise process view, key accountability assignments, and the high level goals and so engages people in the organization.

Process management does not dominate or replace a business unit focus or the need for a functional focus. Instead, it represents an additional and valuable management practice that emphasizes the way in which a company creates value for customers.

9.1 Definition of Enterprise Process Management

Enterprise Process Management [EPM] assures alignment of the portfolio of end-to-end business processes and process architecture with the organization's business strategy and resource allocation. It provides a governance model for the management and evaluation of initiatives.

It involves the deliberate, collaborative and increasingly technology-aided definition, improvement, innovation, and management of end-to-end business processes that drives business agility.

9.2 Benefits of EPM

A firm creates value for its customers via the performance of its large cross-functional business processes. These processes determine the way in which a firm designs, makes, sells, delivers, services its products and performs its services. Enterprise Process Management is the means for the firm's leaders to consciously and collaboratively improve and manage the flow of work in performing for customers.

Of course, there is much more to corporate success than just EPM. But EPM is an essential management practice for the leaders of those firms who wish to satisfy customers and improve performance and provides the means for a firm to better engage its people, shift the organization culture towards more of a performance based model, enables leadership, and facilitates growth. These factors will be discussed further below.

Nor does process management dominate or replace a business unit focus or the need for a functional focus. Instead, it represents an additional and valuable management practice that emphasizes the way in which a company creates value for customers.

It's important to understand that EPM involves a high level, strategic assessment of the organizational process view, and a high level process analysis and performance evaluation and should not be confused with more detailed process analysis and modeling.

The essence of EPM is customer centricity and accountability for the performance of the organizations critical cross-functional processes. This calls for a different way of managing than what has been the norm in many organizations. Invariably, the concept of plan-fully improving and managing a company's large cross-functional processes via a panel or council of executive level business process owners is typically required to operationally deploy EPM.

Why should an organization engage in EPM? Aside from the obvious benefits of managing the firm's value chain, there are also fringe benefits in terms of engagement, leadership and growth.

Process thinking can provide the needed context to engage the entire organization in executing on strategy. Leaders are beginning to recognize that the old worn-out phrases such as 'we are dedicated to growth' and 'we will put customers first' simply do not provide sufficient guidance to employees on what they can do to execute strategy.

The majority of the firm's employees are involved in activities such as developing products or services, selling, delivery, service, etc. These activities are actually performed through collaborative cross-functional activities – or business processes – if you will.

By articulating strategic objectives in terms of the specific improvement needed for these cross-functional activities, firms can better engage and even inspire employees to action.

People have difficulty in identifying their role in delivering on the traditional financial measures of performance such as profit margin, cash flow, and asset intensity. Measuring what counts for customers is the essential ingredient of process management and provides a more relevant mechanism to engage people in the organization and build a culture of discipline.

One of the more common criticisms of leaders by their employees is that they really don't know the business – at least not at the right level of detail. Again, the power of process thinking and through the practice of process management at the enterprise level can enable leadership.

In the book, *Execution: The Discipline of Getting Things Done*, Bossidy and Charan describe seven essential leadership behaviors.

To illustrate the potential that process thinking has for enabling leadership, just consider how process principles and practices can positively influence some of the behaviors cited by Bossidy and Charan.

Knowing the business involves understanding *in detail the work and the roles of key departments and key people across the whole workflow as it* crosses traditional organizational boundaries; only then can executives have sufficient knowledge to deliver best value to customers and shareholders. Many executives do not appreciate the workflow at a sufficient level of detail, and that lack of understanding can detract from how value is created for customers. That is where business process definition and management come into play, for they require this depth of involvement in the workflow.

By looking at the business from the customer's point of view and measuring performance in terms of the timeliness, quality, and cost of products and services provided to customers, executives become better equipped to **insist on realism.** That is precisely what customers care about – a flawless product delivered on time, complete, and defect free; they have no personal interest in how a firm is organized.

The business process view also assists executives in **setting clear and realistic goals and priorities**. People value plain speaking. They appreciate the clear goals and priorities that process thinking enables and provides guidance on their roles within the context of the firm.

Another of the potential benefits of seeing and understanding the business in the context of its cross-functional business processes has to do with **rewarding the doers**.

Expressing priorities in broad, cross-functional process terms can be instrumental in acknowledging the people from different departments who make significant contributions to the creation of value for customers in observable, measurable terms.

A less well-known fact is that process thinking is also essential to growth.

Michael Treacy emphasized in "Double-Digit Growth" that most management teams are adept at meeting cost targets or shaving 10% from the expense base or improving an individual process – but are far less able to plan and execute double-digit growth. Why is that? Treacy argues that firms often lack the tools and management disciplines to tackle growth in a structured, systematic way. And that's part of the answer. But the other part is this: rapid, sustainable growth requires not just a systematic approach but also a systemic view and broad cross-functional collaboration.

A process focus on items such as flawless delivery and "first time right" responsiveness are essential in providing existing products or services to either existing or new markets.

Of course, that is not all there is to fueling growth. A firm can have outstanding performance in terms of delivery and responsiveness and yet fail to grow because the features of its product or service no longer meet customer needs or the offering is priced well above competitive offerings.

In order to achieve flawless delivery and service, firms must measure and manage the performance of the large cross-functional processes that deliver value to customers. For most firms, this involves the definition, improvement, and management of the product or service fulfillment process.

The other half of the growth equation involves the development and introduction of new products or services to either existing or new markets. Here the firm's aptitude in new product/service commercialization comes into play, in addition to flawless delivery and "first time right" responsiveness.

Successful, sustainable growth demands that a firm measure, improve, and manage its performance with respect to at least two key processes; order fulfillment and new product/service development.

9.3 Requirements of EPM

Michael Porter is credited with introducing the concept of interoperability across a company's entire value chain in 1985. This concept is fundamental to EPM. While most firms are structured according to traditional functional departments, EPM demands that the entire value chain involved in providing customers with products and services be defined, improved and managed in an integrated way. This requires a shift in the traditional functional mindset which dominates management thinking in many organizations and the so-called "silo effect" in which each functional unit is only concerned with its processes and coordination is lacking.

Figure 9.1 below illustrates the difference between viewing the firm according to departmental parameters versus in a value chain context.

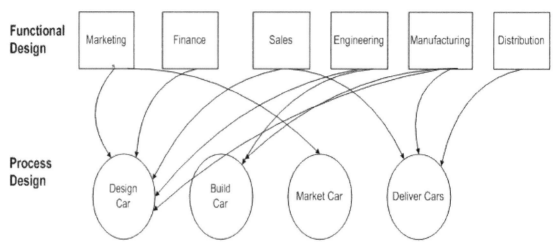

Figure 6.7 ICH Value Chain White Paper Source: www.ichnet.org

The role of measurement is indispensable to maintaining a customer centric focus and assuring accountability for the performance of the firm's large cross functional business processes.

In EPM the focus is on measuring what counts to customers – from the customers' point of view. For most firms this will include metrics of quality, timeliness, completeness, accuracy and responsiveness for the product and services provided.

For example, the Supply Chain Council has defined the concept of 'perfect orders' as performance "in delivering: the correct product, to the correct place, at the correct time, in the correct condition and packaging, in the correct quantity, with the correct documentation, to the correct customer."

The fundamental objectives of developing an enterprise view of process management are then to:

- Define the large cross-functional business processes which deliver customer value
- Articulate the organization's strategy in terms of its cross-functional business processes
- Assign accountability for the improvement and management of the organization's cross-functional processes
- Define the performance measures which matter to customers
- Define the organization's level of performance in terms of these customer centric measures

In order to implement the above there are three essential deliverables; a customer centric measurement framework, an enterprise level process schematic, and an enterprise level process improvement and management plan.

9.3.1 Customer Centric Measurement Framework

A customer centric measurement framework will invariably include aspects relating to new product introduction, product/service delivery and service responsiveness. While the details will vary based on the specifics of the business, there are a number of commonalities presented in Table 9.1 Typical components of an enterprise level measurement framework are shown in the table below:

Process	Output	Metrics	Indicator
Develop New Product or Service	Product or service introduction	Time to market Variance to promise date	TBD
Deliver Product or Service	Product or service to customer	the correct product/service, to the correct place, at the correct time, in the correct condition and packaging, in the correct quantity, with the correct documentation, to the correct customer	TBD
Respond to Customer Inquiry	Solution	First time right responsiveness Variance to promise date	TBD

Table 9.1 Typical components of an enterprise level measurement framework

9.3.2 Process Portfolio Management

Process Portfolio Management is an essential component of governance. It recognizes that the establishment of improvement priorities needs to be viewed on a portfolio basis. Accordingly, it ties the enterprise together from a funding priority and integration perspective. It provides a method to evaluate and manage all enterprise processes in a consolidated view. It provides the framework for process governance with respect to the management and evaluation of initiatives.

9.3.3 Enterprise Process Improvement & Management Planning

For some time now, there has been a debate on what's more important, strategy or execution? More recently, the general view appears to be that 'execution' is more important than 'strategy.'

However, you can't execute flawlessly in the absence of clear strategy. Nor can you do it in the absence of a process view of the business on an end-to-end basis. That is why the creation of process governance at the enterprise level view of business processes is vital.

In spite of a great deal of attention focused on the essence of strategy and execution, relatively little has been written on the benefits of defining and executing strategy in a process context. Yet, many would agree that it is the set of enterprise business processes which defines how work is done and creates value for customers and shareholders.

The combination of a customer centric enterprise level measurement framework and an enterprise level process schematic permits the leadership of organizations to define the size of the gap between current performance and desired performance for its large cross functional processes. Then it is possible to answer the question "Which of our core processes need to be improved by how much in order to achieve strategic goals?" That's what enables execution. It is the answer to this question that pays significant dividends in terms of linking strategy to execution.

Of course, aligning processes with business strategies implies that adequate definitions of the organization's strategies have been developed. This can be problematic.

However, for an organization to take action on the improvement and management of its enterprise level processes it is essential to assign accountability for the performance of these processes. This is a larger challenge than it would seem at first since most companies continue to be structured according to functional or departmental lines.

The two most common methods of establishing process governance via the assignment of accountability for process ownership involve either assigning accountability for the ownership of the process as an additional responsibility to a senior functional manager or creating a staff position as a 'process owner' or 'process steward.'

In both cases, the role of the process owner is to monitor the performance of the enterprise level process and lead efforts in improving and managing the process to deliver value to customers. For many mid-sized and large organizations, the key cross-functional processes are so large that no one executive can have 'control' over all the resources involved in delivering value to customers. That is why the establishment of a process governance structure, often involving a 'panel' or 'council' of executive process owners, tasked with the measurement, improvement and management of the organization's processes is an effective approach in many organizations.

The process owner needs to carry out an assessment of the process in question in much the same way as was done for the set of processes at the enterprise level. Typically, this would include the activities outlined in Table 9.2 below.

Step #	Activity Description
1	Define the critical few measures of performance from a customer's point of view
2	Define the triggering events, inputs, key steps, results and critical metrics for the process
3	Assess the firm's current performance for the process which directly creates value for customers.
4	Determine the level of desired performance for the process by expressing strategic and operating goals in process terms.
5	Assess the size of the performance gap between the firm's current and desired performance for this large cross-functional business process.
6	Develop an improvement and management plan which clearly indicates the desired scope of process improvement, the relative priority, and accountability for action.
7	Communicate the plan, engage and inspire people to take action and conduct training on a common approach.

Table 9.2 Process Owner Initial Activities

Process owners or stewards require some leverage in order to carry out their assignments. Some organizations have assigned the IT budget for the introduction of new technology to the process owner as one means of providing this leverage. In other instances, the discretionary component of executives' and managers' bonuses has been modified in order to allocate 20-30% of that bonus to measurable success in improving the company's business processes.

One of the impacts of globalization has been an increase in the incidence of outsourcing. In some instances, organizations may decide to outsource or offshore an entire business process, such as production. In other cases, a set of activities, or a group of people – such as the call center – might be outsourced or taken offshore.

9.4 *Process Frameworks (Schematics)*

Process frameworks are standards based frameworks used to facilitate process analysis. Frameworks are generally used to provide a *"best practice how-to"* view. As such there are best practices for Supply Chain Management provided by SCOR (Supply Chain Operational Reference model) and others. The following is not an exhaustive summary of such tools but a sampling of the frameworks available. It is important to note, that while these frameworks can be adapted by a number of vertical industries, they have their best fit within a given sector as is the case with Manufacturing and Supply Chain (SCOR) frameworks.

There are at least three important sources of guidance for firms who wish to develop a process view schematic of the firm at the enterprise level; the MIT Process Handbook, the American Productivity and Quality Council's (APQC) process classification framework (PCF) and the Value Chain Group's Value Chain Reference Model (VRM). There are also a number of industry models such as eTOM in the telecommunications and ACORD (www.acord.org) in the insurance sectors that are gaining increasing attention.

It should be noted that while these models are an excellent source of information to stimulate thought, most firms will find it necessary to customize such models to their own organization for optimum use and relevance.

The key aspect of these models is discussed below.

9.4.1 MIT Process Handbook Business Activity Model

The MIT Process Handbook's Business Activity Model (BAM) is a generic business model included in the Process Handbook and attempts to represent a high-level model of everything that goes on in a business. The top level of the model is shown below in figure 9.2. The overall activity in the BAM is called 'Produce as a business', and it includes five basic activities that occur—in some form—in most businesses: 'Buy', 'Make', 'Sell', 'Design', and 'Manage'.

The MIT Process Handbook further breaks down each of these top-level activities, as subparts. For example, 'Buy' includes parts like 'Identify own needs', 'Identify potential sources', and 'Select supplier'. While the handbook specifies that the high level 'Make' activity does not include any subparts because the core "making" activity of a business can vary so widely in different companies and across industries. However, all the other activities cited in BAM appear to be quite general across almost all businesses—large and small, profit and nonprofit—in most industries. The MIT Process Handbook has attempted to use terms and breakdowns that are generic and fundamental and as such it tried to represent a view of the "deep structure" of business.

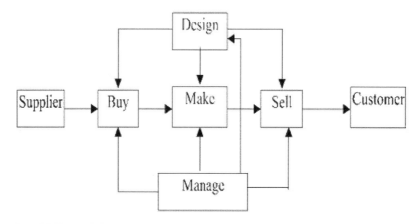

Figure 9.2 MIT Process Handbook's Business Process Activity Model (BAM)

9.4.2 American Productivity and Quality Council (APQC)

Another reference model which firms may find useful to stimulate thought about EPM is the APQC Process Classification Framework (PCF). This is also meant to serve as a high-level, industry-neutral enterprise model that allows organizations to see their activities from a cross-industry process viewpoint.

Originally created in 1992 by APQC and a group of members, the framework has been in use by many organizations on a worldwide basis. The APQC has indicated that the PCF is supported by the Open Standards Benchmarking Collaborative (OSBC) database and is an open standard.

The APQC plans that the PCF will continuously be enhanced as the OSBC database further develops definitions, processes, and measures related to process improvement.

The PCF is available for organizations of all industries and sizes at no charge by visiting www.apqc.org. The PCF is meant to represent a series of interrelated processes that are considered to be business critical.

The PCF can be used to enable organizations to understand their inner workings from a horizontal process viewpoint, rather than a vertical functional viewpoint.

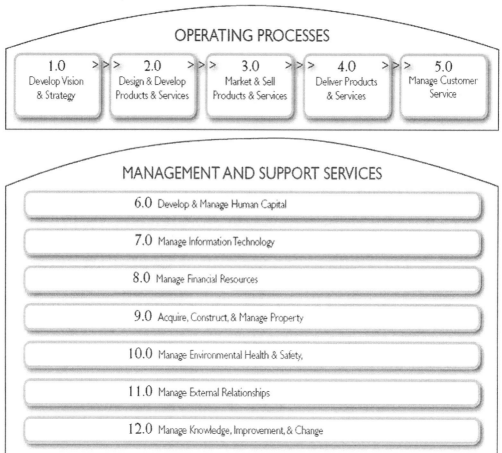

Figure 9.3 APQC PFC (www.apqc.org)

APQC is an international benchmarking clearinghouse who has collaborated with 80 organizations in developing framework for process evaluation. The purpose of this model is to provide a framework for *identifying "high-level, generic enterprise model that encourages businesses and other organizations to see their activities from a cross-industry process viewpoint instead of from a narrow functional viewpoint..*[15]*"* This set of tools provides a beginning for discerning core, support and management processes common between and across industries such as manufacturing and service, health care, government, and education to mention only a few.

The Process Classification Framework provides four phases: **Prepare**, **Plan**, **Implement** and **Transition**.

---

15 "APQC – Process Classification Framework" Retrieved November 8, 2006 from

http://www.apqc.org/portal/apqc/ksn?paf_gear_id=contentgearhome&paf_dm=full&pageselect=detail&docid=121388&topics=%20Measurement%2C%20Performance%20Improvement%20Approaches&process=%20Manage%20Improvement%20and%20Change

Prepare is a strategic phase. It is a comprehensive assessment that focuses on the core processes. During this phase, a business case is identified with opportunities and determines the expected business results.

In the ***Plan*** phase a time-phased approach to implement the changes identified during the assessment is developed. During this phase the process analyst and the analysis team refines, redesigns or reengineers core business processes.

In the ***Implement*** phase the changes are implemented.

The Transition phase is both tactical and strategic. Tactically, employee teams develop process operating procedures and oversee the transition to the new process. Strategically, the organization will repeat the model with other processes based on their business needs and priorities.

9.4.3 Value Chain Group – Value Chain Reference Model (VRM)

A third model worthy of consideration is the Value Chain Operational Reference (VRM) Model. VRM attempts to integrate the three domains of a Value Chain; product, operations, and customer.

The model has 3 levels of detail under one framework. The highest level is called Level 1 – and the Level 1 processes of VRM are: Plan - Govern - Execute

In Level 2 – as the figure below shows, the Level 1 process category Execute is decomposed to the components of Market-Research- Develop-Acquire-Build-Sell-Fulfill-Support process categories.

Level 3, which is not considered here, provides a more complete framework for understanding and control of the extended Value Chain.

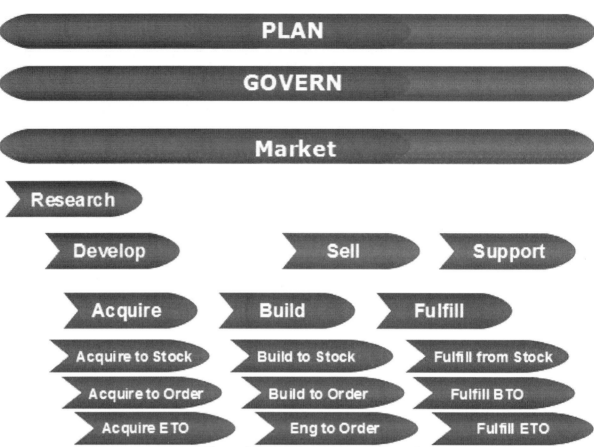

Figure 9.4 VRM Level Two Schematic

The VRM model supports the key issues and the meshing of processes within and between the units of chains (networks) for the benefit of Planning, Governing and Execution (information, financial, physical flows) with the objective to increase the performance of the total chain and support the continuous evolution.

The Value Chain Group describes VRM: as a model that provides *"a common terminology and standard process descriptions to order and understand the activities that make up the value chain."*[16]

Enterprises applying the model are provided with a framework to achieve their goals of both horizontal and vertical collaboration. The VRM model uses a common language while at the same time creating a foundation for the successful Service Oriented Architecture. The VRM framework organizes processes through five levels representing the various layers of the organization. As the processes work the way from the bottom

---

[16] "Value Chain Group – VRM Concepts". Retrieved November 8, 2006 from http://www.value-chain.org/en/cms/?

(actions) through the top to the strategic processes they become more complex and are closer to the realization of the strategic goals.

Strategic Processes
Strategic processes are the top level processes in the value chain. These are the processes specifically designed around the customer needs and the business strategy.

Tactical Processes
Decomposed from strategic processes, tactical processes outline how the goals of the strategic processes will be met.

Operational Processes
Tactical processes are made up from operational processes which are where the work gets done.

Activities
Activities are groups of actions that make up the operational processes.

Actions
Actions are the last group of processes and represent individual items of work that cannot be broken down further.

These processes are further governed by three macro processes that control the enterprise: Govern, Plan and Execute.

9.4.4 SCOR – Supply Chain Operations Reference

The SCOR Model represents a framework which offers a means of facilitating the identification of process models for nearly any and all types of enterprises. This is a holistic end-to-end process inclusive of the supply chain ecosystem. Such a framework is valuable for enhancing enterprise and stakeholder (internal and external) communication for building and sustaining process-centricity into the enterprise.

The Supply Chain Operations Reference-model (SCOR)[17] has been developed and endorsed by the Supply-Chain Council (SCC), an independent not-for-profit corporation, as the cross-industry standard for supply-chain management. Initially this consortium included 69 voluntary member companies interested in advancing state-of-the-art supply-chain management systems and practices. It has since expanding its reach to healthcare, government, education, and many other service-based enterprises.

---

[17] "SCOR-Model" Retrieved November 8, 2006 from http://www.supply-chain.org/page.ww?name=Home&section=root

9.5 Process Repository Management

A Process Repository is a central location for storing information about how an enterprise operates. This information may be contained in various media including paper, film or electronic form with a storage mechanism appropriate to the medium. Electronic repositories range from passive containers which store process artifacts (also referred to as process objects) to sophisticated tools that serve as active participants in monitoring, executing, managing and reporting on business processes. They come in the form of Document Management Systems, Process Modeling Tools and Business Process Management Systems.

Process Repository administration activities includes storing, managing and changing process knowledge (objects, relationships, enablers, attributes, business rules, performance measures and models) for an enterprise. It includes creating the repository structure; defining and maintaining procedures to ensure changes are controlled, validated and approved; mapping processes to applications and data, and providing the required infrastructure to enable effective and consistent use of the models in the repository.

9.5.1 Why is repository administration important to EPM?

A common repository of business processes provides a central reference location to ensure consistent communication of what the process is, how it should be applied, who is responsible for its successful execution, a clear understanding of the inputs or triggers and expected results upon process completion. It maintains information needed to adequately define measure, analyze, improve and control business processes. It helps to promote and support the understanding and acceptance of the cross-functional nature of many of the enterprise's business processes and facilitates collaboration across functional business units by enabling and enforcing a methodology that focuses on the end-to-end process.

A central process repository contributes to the success of the enterprise's business process strategy by providing a blueprint to manage and control how process change is introduced and implemented into the enterprise. It also becomes the system of record for information on process ownership, technological enablers, business rules and controls, both financial and operational. It may serve primarily as documentation about the enterprise's business processes or may be used to simulate various scenarios to (1) evaluate process improvements, and (2) to detect and analyze problems. It can also be used to identify and validate the appropriate solution. Sophisticated repositories can be interfaced with the enterprise's applications to enforce defined business rules.

9.6 Process Management Maturity levels

Many thought leaders have examined the state of business process maturity within organizations (Champlin, 2001; Harmon, 2004; Rosemann & deBruin, 2005; Dwyer, 2004; Delphi, 2003; Sinur, 2004; Fisher, 2004; Rummler-Brache, 2004). Several of the proposed business process maturity models are based on the Capability Maturity Model® (CMM) developed by Carnegie Mellon University's Software Engineering Institute. Similar to the CMM, these process Maturity Models define levels of awareness for business process best practices and automation with some assessing the management of operational processes. In addition to optimizing operational processes, BPM needs to be aligned with the management and stewardship of the process, resulting in distinct but integrated *process maturity* and *process management maturity* where management maturity must precede process operational maturity at each level in order to be successful and sustainable. Figure 9.5 depicts the levels and integration of process and management maturity.

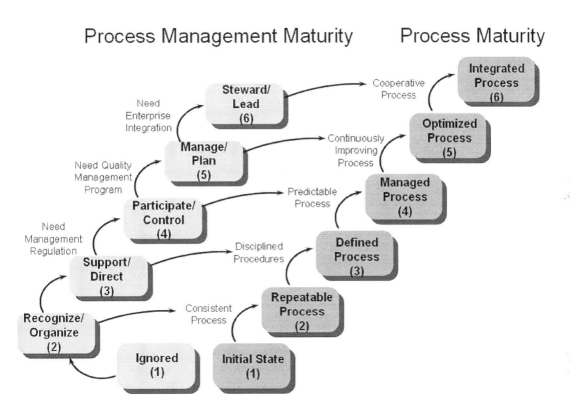

Figure 9.5: Process Management Maturity and Process Maturity levels [Champlin, 2001; extended/adapted from Parker, 1995]

The examination of maturity levels in these models includes the identification of a number of known success factors. Within each of these factors are suggested questions organizations should examine in order to assess their level of business process management maturity. These factors and corresponding questions include:

Organization
- Does your organization have a Process-Centric Approach? Is it customer focused?
- What is the level of process awareness and emphasis; among management?; among stakeholders?; among staff/employees?

- What is your level of process management success?

Process Definition (Organizational Scope)
- Are processes defined? Documented? To what extent?
- Is process success dependent on individuals or teams?
- Are defined processes standardized across the organization?

Process Responsibility (Accountability)
- Have process responsibilities been defined? Who is accountable?

Process Sponsorship
- Who is (are) the primary sponsors of defined processes? Top Management? Middle management? Departmental? IT?

Process Measures
- Have process measures been defined? Used? Planned?

Process Awareness (People Involvement)
- Do your employees, management think in processes?
- What is the level of people involvement in process definition? Analysis? Process improvement?
- What level of change management methods has been deployed?
- Has continuous training been aligned with processes?

Process Alignment
- Are process goals aligned with defined business strategies?
- Are processes aligned with organizational goals?
- Are job descriptions aligned with process definitions?
- Are employee evaluations linked to processes?

Information Technology
- Does IT management use BPM for its processes?
- Are BPM support applications defined and employed in key processes?
- Does management use BPM applications to support performance monitoring?

Methodology
- Are BPM tools, process methodologies or process frameworks used? Successful?

The above list simply represents a sampling of questions organizations may use to begin assessing their business process management maturity. It is proposed that answers to these questions (and those similar to them) provide some guidance on an organization's BPM maturity level. This provides the organization the knowledge of their current business process management maturity and in addition helps in assessing which factors may need improvement or which factors can be leveraged, helping them advance to a higher business process management maturity level.

9.7 EPM "Best Practices"

First, look at the business from the customer's point of view. This will help change the typical inside-out view of the business that the traditional, functional paradigm promotes, and seeing from the customer's point of view will help you identify the critical measures of performance that reflect the customer's particular requirements.

Then, try not to call the end-to-end processes by the same name that you use in describing internal departments. This will assist in shifting the mindset to a process oriented view – new names for seeing things in new ways.

Next, be clear on the definition of each end-to-end process: Clarify where the process starts, the key steps in the process, the departments involved, the output, and the major measures of process performance. It is expedient to assign a group of internal experts to prepare a "draft" schematic for review and refinement by the top team. But assure a high degree of buy-in and ownership at the top team level.

Finally, do it quickly. Don't take weeks or months, hoping to get it perfect. It will never be perfect. A few weeks of data gathering and a couple of days off-site is all that is needed to develop a workable model that will serve as a basis for next steps.

Once the top team has reached a shared understanding on the components of its own enterprise level process model, the next step is to do the same for the firm's current level of performance on a few critical metrics. This typically involves getting real data on a set of measures around the timeliness, quality, and cost of product or service delivery and other key aspects of the firm, such as developing new products or services.

One might think that getting data on the firm's current performance should be easy. In reality, it can be quite problematic. While most companies have a ton of data on revenues, margins, earnings, and cash flow, data on qualitative factors such as on-time delivery, accuracy, responsiveness, and completeness are sometimes difficult to assemble.

The guiding principle of "Do it yourselves and do it quickly" applies here. Sampling is recommended whenever data is not readily available from existing information systems.

There is twofold value in assembling and assessing this type of current performance data. First, it facilitates an objective and shared view of how the firm is performing when set against customer requirements. Second, it sets the baseline for the subsequent assessment of the size of the gap between current level of performance and desired level of performance.

At the top team level, there are several major pitfalls to avoid in reaching a shared understanding of how the firm is performing against customer requirements.

- The first of these is a lack of candor in measuring what customers really want.
- The second pitfall encountered is far subtler and, therefore, more problematic. It often starts when one or several members of the leadership team vehemently challenge the validity of the data on current performance. This lack of buy-in is difficult to assess and even more complex to address. To mitigate this, it is useful for the leader to ask each member of the top team to articulate his or her acceptance of the data on current performance.
- The third pitfall is working at the wrong level of detail. This can occur when some leaders wish to dive into discussion of the as-is conditions vs. optimized/improved processes. This can deter and defer the high level strategic discussions which are vital at this stage.

Once a shared understanding of the definition of the firm's enterprise level business processes and its current performance has been achieved, the top team can then proceed to build a plan that will improve and manage the firm's large, cross-functional business processes.

Such a plan needs to answer two fundamental questions: Which of our business processes need to be improved, and by how much, in order to achieve our strategic objectives? Secondly, who will be held accountable for this planned improvement and management?

9.8 From Planning to Action

The role of process owners or stewards extends far beyond the simple monitoring of business process performance. To convert plans into action, process owners need to collaborate on critical process improvement projects.

The close collaboration of the members of the process 'council' or 'panel' is a critical success factor in the success of large, cross-functional process improvement efforts.

The following table outlines some of the principal leadership behaviors involved in the success of such large, cross-functional process improvement efforts.

Definition	Analysis	Design	Implementation
Agree on process boundaries Set clear improvement goals Appoint the best people Identify realistic constraints Set a clear schedule Charter to	Understand the flow of work in a cross functional context Agree on the size of the performance gap Gain clarity on key issues, disconnects, opportunities Insist on the prioritization of issues based on impact	Probe to test the vision for the new design Understand the cross-functional implications of how business should be conducted in the future Gain clarity on the matrix of performance measures	Process owners chair meetings with process management teams throughout implementation There is increasing conversation and awareness of cross-process dependencies People begin to assign their loyalty as much to process as to function or

| implement, not just to design | Refine working team membership if needed | Constructively challenge the recommendations for change

Assess the business case

Inspect the high level implementation plan | business

People are aware of the progress in closing the gap between current and desired performance

There is a visible improvement in cross-department collaboration |

Table 9.3 Principal leadership behaviors

9.9 Key Concepts

ENTERPRISE PROCESS MANAGEMENT - KEY CONCEPTS
1. Enterprise Process Management [EPM] assures alignment of the portfolio of end-to-end business processes and process architecture with the organization's business strategy and resource allocation. It provides a governance model for the management and evaluation of initiatives.
2. EPM is an essential management practice that provides the means for a company to create value for its customers.
3. The role of measurement is indispensable to maintaining a customer centric focus and assuring accountability for the performance of the firm's large cross functional business processes.
4. EPM has three essential requirements: a customer centric measurement framework, an enterprise level process schematic, and an enterprise level process improvement and management plan.
5. Business processes must be associated to a clear strategy.
6. Successful process governance requires clear ownership and accountability assigned for each process.
7. The role of the Process Owner is to monitor performance and lead the improvement and management of the processes.
8. Process Owners must be given the means necessary to successfully manage the process.
9. EPM can engage the entire organization in executing on strategy by clearly defining and communicating the means to accomplish it.
10. Process principles and practices positively influence leadership behaviors such as knowing the business, insisting on realism, setting clear and realistic goals and priorities, and rewarding the doers.
11. Process thinking is essential to business growth.
12. Each end to end process must be clearly and uniquely defined.
13. Avoid these three pitfalls:
a. a lack of candor in measuring what customers really want
b. members of the leadership team challenging the validity of the data on current performance.
c. working at the wrong level of detail
14. Enterprise Process Management involves the transition from expressing strategy in general terms or in financial terms to expressing strategy in terms of observable cross-functional activity and requires a shift in mindset and a new set of leadership behaviors.

10 BPM Technology

10.1 Why is technology important?

Professionals involved in the various BPM activities discussed in this publication have increasingly turned to computer applications to assist with the analysis, design, implementation, execution, management and monitoring of business processes. The emerging practices in BPM have fostered requirements for new applications and for the convergence of applications developed for specific purposes such as financial analysis, records management, data mining and executive decision making. The purpose of this chapter is to review the features of computer systems that provide support functions for BPM professionals, executives and personnel involved in carrying out process activities as a part of business operations. Business Process Management Systems (BPMS) include a large number of computer applications that continue to evolve as our understanding of business processes matures and requirements for handling complex issues and large volumes of information increase.

The life cycle of developing, implementing, measuring and monitoring processes can involve a number of complicated activities. Computer systems to support these activities have matured in sophistication. All studies of successful BPM programs have found that BPM Systems are important and necessary components of any BPM effort.

Experience shows that the application of technology is effective when the complexity of the process or the amount of information to be processed is too great to manage with manual methods. Automation of processes is increasingly important for medium to large- scale enterprises, especially in attempts to coordinate efforts among members of geographically disperse work groups. The automation of workflow can create remarkable increases in efficiency by reducing the time and costs associated with process activities and the lag times involved between the steps in a process, particularly when compared to paper based methods. As an assistant to human efforts, technology can help people become more efficient by providing memory aids, balancing work loads and making more information available in decision processes.

Some important processes are carried out over a long time period. For example, records retention and destruction processes necessary for legal and regulatory compliance may require the management of records over many years. The limitation of human memory, staff turnover and other factors create compelling reasons to consider the automation of these and similar processes.

Within the context of BPM we can establish performance measures to help us optimize the value of processes and we can access data from process results that support management decisions. When these business performance measures grow in complexity and rely on large amounts of information from a number of sources, then computer support systems are essential.

Technologies applied to the tasks performed by business process management professionals make their efforts more efficient and effective.

10.2 What's involved in BMP technology?

This chapter explores the technology used to support BPM activities. The focus is on software systems that support or automate all or part of:

1. The modeling, analysis and design of processes;
2. Implementation and execution of processes;
3. Management decisions, business performance measures and administrative activities.

Software applications may address specific tasks supporting BPM or software vendors may offer a set of applications covering a number of BPM activities. These related sets of applications are often called software suites or studios. Figure 1 shows the categories of software that may be applied to BPM.

Users of the software are supported by various user interfaces. In addition, there are layers of server-based software behind the facilities seen by users. BPMS tools are developed and implemented with the assistance of standard software languages and supporting platforms. Not all of the development and execution platforms and tools are covered in the diagram and subsequent text, only a sampling of those that are most prevalent and of broad current interest. Some of the details and applicability of the BPMS tools depicted in Figure 1 are discussed throughout the remainder of the chapter.

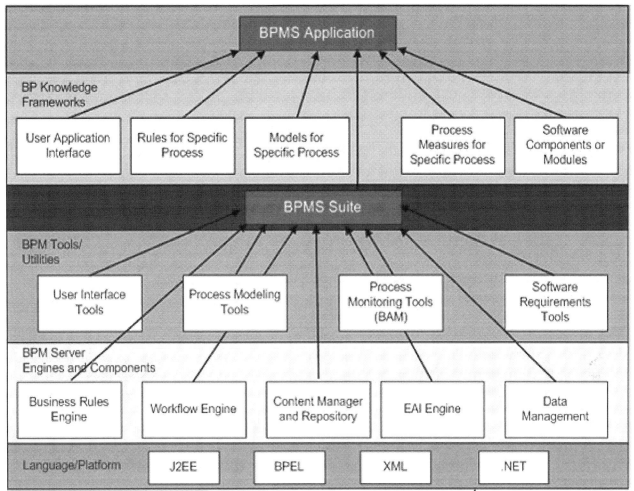

Figure 10.1 – Software Components Supporting BPM Activities[1]

As noted earlier, there are three primary support functions in BPM for technology: 1) modeling, analysis and design; 2) the execution of processes and 3) management activities involving decisions, business performance measures and administrative activities. This section provides a high level description of the functions performed by technology in each of these categories. It is not the intent of this publication to cite particular products but describe the primary features of the types of applications to be considered.

10.3 Modeling, analysis, design

Business Process Modeling and Analysis (BPMA) starts with the initial conception and description of a process. Models of processes are created and various scenarios or alternate processes are constructed in order to analyze the behavior of processes and optimize performance.

The technologies available for BPMA start with applications that support graphical representations of the process and detailed descriptions of the goals and requirements for the process. Drawing a flowchart or map of the activities involved in a process based on the requirements for the process is one of the early steps in process development. The mapping of business processes is an extremely important stage necessary for designing and communicating processes that meet business requirements and are realistic in terms of their use in detailing implementation requirements.

At a fundamental level any graphics application that allows for charting and describing the flow of steps taken to complete a process will be useful. Flowcharts may represent steps with actions as labeled boxes or other symbols, even pictures of objects. Support for annotations describing the requirements and personnel roles at each step in a process is important. Of course, flowcharts may be drawn by hand on a piece of paper but simple computer graphics programs provide better means for editing and electronically distributing the process representation. Available technologies include drawing software, word processors and spreadsheets with drawing capabilities, sophisticated graphics and mapping software and web enabled drawings with links to other information. In addition modeling activities provide documentation on processes useful for communicating processes to management, collaborating team members, process designers and process implementers. Models can create a common language and terminology across functional business units and promote a common base of models to reduce redundancy and incompatibility in disperse process efforts.

Some computer graphics programs treat elements in a diagram as "intelligent" objects such that a mouse click on a step in the process can display underlying data such as a detailed description of actions, sources of information required at a step, rules related to processing information, directions for the routing of output information and metrics used to calculate performance statistics. The underlying information may be stored in a word processor, spreadsheet or database applications linking detailed information to objects in the process map. A number of object oriented modeling tools are available offering sophisticated features for detailing object properties, methods and relationships in a process map.

Efforts to standardize methods for describing processes have resulted in a standard graphical notation called Business Process Management Notation (BPMN). BPMN is particularly useful as a formal system for the precise description of classes, methods and properties of process activities. BPMN is particularly important for the technical design, coding and implementation of business processes using BPMS. Although a complete description of BPMN is beyond the scope of this publication, it is important for BPM professionals involved in formal modeling, design and technical execution of BPM. (See Business Process Modeling Notation – (BPMN) from the Business Process Modeling Initiative (BPMI) by BPMI.org, Version 1.0, May 3, 2004)

Once the process is adequately described, other useful technologies for BPMA may involve process modeling and simulations. Simulation programs will simulate the behaviors of people (or machines) carrying out the activities of a process. Each simulation of a process is an "incident" of the process. For example, the simulation of an Accounts Payable (AP) process will start with the receipt of an invoice and will follow the steps and actions that would be carried out by people or computers in order to pay or reject payment of the invoice. Simulators will simulate the actions taken at each step, simulate the flow of data and other information through the process and execute rules that may change the process flow and dictate additional processes to be initiated such as a process of approvals by a manager when the invoice amount exceeds a certain value.

Metrics developed to measure performance such as the time required to complete a step, the lag time between actions and the cost of resources used will be included in a simulation exercise to measure the effectiveness of the process. Simulations and modeling are iterative activities in that a simulation of a number of incidents will be run by a software program based on a set of assumptions about how the tasks in steps are carried out. During the simulation measures such as total time for completion and costs are recorded to determine points for improvements. Assumptions may be changed and another set of incidents will be simulated to compare the results.

The basic features of a typical modeling and simulation application will include:

1. The ability to graphically represent the process as a map of the steps to be taken;
2. Methods to define the flow of information between steps and conditions under which the flow may change. If the flow of the process can be changed based on events, simulators provide the ability to define the probability distribution of the likelihood of one or more routes through the process.
3. Methods to state assumptions about measurable behaviors in process steps such as the time to complete a task. Such behaviors may be based on a probability distribution. For example, the distribution of task completion times may be defined and each simulation of an incident will use a completion time from that distribution.

10.4 Technologies that support implementation

Once a process has been designed, putting that process into operation may involve a number of information technology support applications. This section covers trends in the use of systems to support the execution of BPM in an organization's internal operations and activities involving interactions with trading partners and customers. The applications listed below are often embedded in integrated/enterprise systems that provide a number of BPM support tools. Some of the most important applications may be considered in the following categories:

1. Electronic Document Management Systems that capture, organize and provide information required for the execution of steps in a process
2. Electronic forms for information capture and distribution
3. Workflow routing and management
4. Workgroup collaboration

Electronic Document Management - Virtually all business processes involve the use of information in documents and data repositories. Fundamental computer support systems are those applications that help us collect and manage this information in electronic formats. A useful definition related to managing information is that of a business record. A business record is any document, data or transaction information that is collected and used in the conduct of business. For years the primary form of records has been paper distributed, stored and organized in file folders. The transformation from paper based processes to electronic based processes has been accelerated by those systems that collect, classify (index), store and retrieve information (records) in electronic formats.

The beginning of electronic systems for managing records and converting from paper to electronic formats is found in imaging applications that scan paper documents into electronic files. Imaging systems grew into Electronic Document Management Systems (EDMS) by adding methods to describe, classify and index documents and facilitate efficient retrieval. As the features of these systems have progressed to include any electronic content whether scanned or created by other applications the term Enterprise Content Management Systems (ECMS) has become popular. The fundamental concept here is that the capture and organization of information contained in documents, databases, transaction information in accounting and ERP systems and other sources are basic requirement for developing BPM systems.

Electronic information in support of processes may be used by people by "pushing" or "pulling" information to support the tasks that are part of the process. "Push" methods involve sending information to a person for initiating and/or accomplishing a task. A very basic form of an information push is sending an email to a person with information for attention. "Pull" methods rely on people finding and pulling information from an information repository in order to accomplish a task. The method of classifying information is important for assisting people find the information they need. Information search applications, including full-text searches are valuable for this purpose.

The reader may have noticed that EDMS applications may also support Process Repository Administration as discussed later in this chapter. The fact that process policies, rules, definitions of authorities and other information may be captured in electronic formats will provide justification for the support offered by document management systems.

Electronic Forms– A great deal of information useful for a business process will be gathered through the use of forms. Most people are familiar with paper forms such as medical information forms filled out in a doctor's office, employment application forms and others.

In computer systems, electronic forms provide a structured method for capturing and presenting information. For example, when one orders products on the Internet they are presented with product information and requested to fill out an electronic form indicating the quantity desired. These forms involve the address for shipping and credit card information. Each piece of information entered is captured in a database when the form is submitted. This data is then used in processes for order fulfillment, shipping and collecting payments.

Most computer applications use forms in one way or another. A user may enter invoice information into a form of an accounting system or fill out a timesheet form for payroll. Further, electronic forms fill many roles in EDMS and BPM systems. Users enter information required to describe and classify documents for search and retrieval, and provide the information required to complete a task in a business process through forms or enter information used to measure activities in a process. The important point is that electronic forms provide an important user interface for capturing, displaying, routing and sharing useful information.

A significant trend in the development of electronic forms that has a great impact on BPM is the standardization of the format of forms and embedded information fields. Efforts to create greater efficiencies in supply chain management led to the development of standards for exchanging information among trading partners. For instance, developing a standard electronic invoice form allows a supplier to transmit invoice data directly to the system of the buyer for electronic processing. The standards developed are the backbone of Electronic Data Interchange (EDI).

Early efforts at EDI were technically difficult and adopted only when extreme volumes of data created a process scenario that justified its use. Many methods for EDI based on a variety of document formatting and transmission have been developed and are used to share information between organizations as trading partners. Today the emergence of Web based forms and applications with standards for form format such as eXtensible Markup Language (XML) have significantly reduced the barriers to automated data sharing in business processes, although many EDI applications are still viable.

Workflow Automation - Once the information involved in a process is captured and stored electronically, the opportunity is presented for using the information with other applications such as workflow automation. Workflow automation involves systems that provide necessary information to each activity in a process and manage the flow of actions and information based on a set of rules. Rules may be as simple as to route the information in an invoice to a manager for payment authorization based on the amount of the invoice.

Many workflow automation applications have been built on top of, or are embedded in EDMS or ECMS systems as a means to push information organized by these systems to workers involved in implementing the actions in a process. In addition, there are standalone workflow applications and workflow features embedded in ERP or other enterprise applications.

The basic features usually found in workflow automation systems will include:

1. A user "inbox" and "outbox" facility. People involved in a process will see tasks to be performed presented in their electronic inbox (or in-basket). When they select a task to be performed all of the relevant information required to perform the task will be presented. Once they have completed the task, the resultant information processes at that step will be placed in an outbox and routed to someone (or possibly a machine) to accomplish the next step in the process. Actions not completed by an expected deadline may trigger an alert to a supervisor to insure timely completion.

Assigning the responsibility and authority for completing an activity in a process will often be determined by assigning roles to individual users or to a group of users. User roles may include data entry, document review, management review authorizations and more. In addition, the assignment of roles to individuals or groups is important for managing information security through access controls based on roles.

2. A facility will be included for establishing the rules to determine the flow of the process, information to be recorded and actions to be performed by users. Such "rules engines" may provide simple routing routines based on specific metrics (such as the amount of an invoice) or they may provide a sophisticated rules "language" that can test for a variety of conditions and execute an algorithm that will dictate the flow/routing of information and tasks.

3. Management, administration, reporting and auditing facilities are often included in varying degrees by workflow automation systems. Basic management and administrative functions may include the ability to change the workflow based on time delays and volumes. If a user becomes involved in a complicated resolution of a task, the workload for that user may pile up in the inbox. In this case, the workflow automation system may generate an alert to an administrator who can reroute some of that load to other users.

Reports may be generated by the system on key performance indicators such as time to complete an incident, time to complete specific tasks, costs associated with parts of a process, resource allocations and more. In addition, the ability to track the actual activities and tasks accomplished by users may be important information for auditing the process for compliance with legal and regulatory requirements. For example, accounting audits may be accomplished more efficiently when the actual activities, controls, information used and final outcomes of transactions can be tracked for activities such as accounts payables, revenue recognition and more. In some applications, users will be presented with a dashboard or information displaying current information from disparate sources of information.

Some of the available BPM systems allow us to graphically map out a process, define the flow and simulate the process, define the metrics and rules that will be used to control the flow at the design phase and then, once the process definition is finalized, the design can be implemented as the production workflow by assigning user roles, responsibilities and authorities. The tasks necessary to implement a production workflow will be dependent on the sophistication of the software applications and the extent to which they may generate executable code based on the design tools. Most applications today provide user interfaces that allow the selection of setup alternatives and execution properties without significant coding. The trend is toward BP systems that may be executed by process owners without intervention by IT technical personnel.

There are a fairly large number of vendors providing workflow products either embedded in applications or as standalone applications that may be applied to any process. The Workflow Management Coalition (WFMC) was founded in 1993 as an organization of adopters, developers, consultants, analysts, university and research groups engaged in workflow and BPM. As stated on the organization's web site "The Coalition has developed a framework for the establishment of workflow standards. This framework includes five categories of interoperability and communication standards that will allow multiple workflow products to coexist and interoperate within a user's environment." This framework of standards is detailed on the web site: www.wfmc.org. The organization also offers standards for workflow versions of XML and a process design format called XPDL.

Business Process Execution Language (BPEL) - A technical trend today is the use of the Business Process Execution Language (BPEL), a programming language optimized for executing process activities. Using BPEL, a programmer formally describes a business process, executes the steps in the process and coordinates information from a variety of sources. BPEL fits into the framework of service oriented architectures and optimizes the use of Web services. Although it is beyond the scope of this publication to delve into the details of BPEL and systems platforms, it is important for BPM professionals to be aware of the main technical trends for executing BPM applications when considering systems.

Workgroup Collaboration - Experience gained from BPM successes and failures shows that one of the most important success factors is the involvement and interaction of management, process designers, people who perform the tasks within processes and representatives of information technology in the analysis, design and implementation of BPM initiatives. Applying BPM systems to poorly designed processes is a sure formula for disappointing results. Truly effective process design is a human intellectual endeavor and is dependent on the skills and experience of groups of individuals. A number of systems applications that can help to support collaborative efforts in the development, execution and management of BPM are grouped under the title of collaborative or groupware systems.

One of the driving forces for consideration of BPM Systems is the geographic dispersion of people involved in various processes. In particular, large enterprises with offices in many locations find that designing and managing processes is particularly challenging. Efforts to analyze and improve complex and sometimes cross-functional processes will often involve the cooperation and collaboration of groups of individuals starting with the analysis, design and modeling of processes and continuing with the implementation and management of process executions.

In general collaboration (also known as workgroup) software applications provide services that integrate work by several users at separated workstations or remote devices. They support communications among groups of people, the sharing of information and triggering tasks that need to be completed. Collaboration software usually includes electronic communication tools, conferencing tools and management tools. Most of the modern collaboration tools take advantage of the Internet by providing web based applications supported by web browsers. Communication tools include e-mail, messaging, faxing and voice mail. Conferencing tools allow interactive information sharing by supporting online meetings and discussions through voice and video conferencing, Internet forums, electronic white boards, chat rooms and Web meeting spaces.

Management tools coordinate and facilitate group activities through a number of application services. Electronic calendars schedule meetings and tasks to be completed. Project management tools schedule, track and diagram the steps in a project such as analysis of current processes.

Collaborative systems can also include workflow systems that manage information and tasks for operations across functional and geographic boundaries. Collaborative workflow systems not only support processes within an organization but may also include collaboration and data sharing with a variety of stakeholders and trading partners such as suppliers, customers and stock-holders.

An emerging method of implementing collaborative systems is through Web Portals. A web portal is simply a location within an organization's web site that provides access to a predefined set of Internet users with a common interest and supplies a variety of services to those users. Those services may include access to specific information as documents and data, support for collaborative forums, calendar of events and alerts for actions to be performed. Portals may be both Intranet applications within an organization and Internet applications providing access by trading partners or other communities of users. Virtually all of the collaborative tools mentioned above may be accessed through a portal and the portal technology allows for the management of information privacy and access controls.

A major endeavor for many organizations is to define the life cycle of records from creation to use and eventual destruction. Such records management is important for legal and regulatory compliance and is also a business process that may be treated as such using the methods discussed in this publication. Some of the vendors offering BPMS suites provide Information Lifecycle Management (ILM) applications that support the management of information sets from creation to archiving and destruction.

10.5 Advantages and risks of process automation

We can summarize the main advantages of BPMS in automating parts or all of a process. First of all, BPMS can produce significant increases in efficiency. Efficiencies may be gained through support of activities such as managing large amounts of documents and data, the geographic distribution of information to workgroup members, reducing the lag time in taking critical actions through workflow and reallocating repetitive, manual processes from people to machines.

Many of the efficiency gains provided by BPMS will also reduce operating costs. In addition, the development of new processes using BPMS tools may be accomplished by line-of-business managers without substantial involvement of technical IT personnel. Development time and costs may be reduced.

A second advantage of BPMS is that it can help in the assurance of compliance for policies necessary for critical legal and regulatory compliance. BPMS can track and audit actions that indicate compliance with controls designed to insure quality in production processes and the veracity of information supplied to regulatory bodies.

BPMS can supply timely information needed for management to measure the performance of business processes and look for areas to improve. Management can develop and access reports summarizing data from many sources to gain new conceptual understanding of interrelated processes across the enterprise. And, BPMS can provide critical points of control to insure that processes are working as intended and exceptions or even dangerous conditions are detected and addressed through intervention.

Although BPM systems may produce significant advantages, they also have risks associated with any systems automation efforts. The most significant risk is that we develop a false sense of security that just because we can automate a process, it is better. As with any systems adoption, automating poor processes will not gain better business practices.

In the implementation of BPMS we must take care to insure that automated processes work properly. The sophistication of some BPMS applications may mask process errors or inefficiencies and careful, detailed understanding of implementations is important. And finally the use of BPMS can increase exposures to information security risks. It is extremely important to understand the technical working of BPMS to insure that vital data is not exposed to individuals that should not see it and we do not open opportunities for systems problems such as viruses and other systems attacks that could bring critical processes to a halt. The very nature of Internet and Web enabled applications is such that systems security measures must be taken when implementing BPMS.

10.6 Types of technologies available

10.6.1 BPMS Suites

Monitoring and Control

Functions for the administration and management of the real-time flow of work are part of most BPM Systems. Administration tools include facilities for changing the flow of processes based on measures of performance, workload balancing requirements and changing worker roles. BPM Systems provide a view of data on the current status of work in a process and detect conditions such as unacceptable delays at a particular step in the process. Such delays may be due to a particularly difficult event to handle on the part of a worker, too many jobs being routed to a particular step, unanticipated exceptions to the tasks to be performed or exceptions to the rules to be followed. In such cases, an administrator will be alerted and may change the flow of work by sending some of the workload to another worker or to a manager for consideration of how to handle an unanticipated event. In many cases the sophistication of the BPMS and rules engines implemented for the process will determine whether some type of automatic intervention will be available or a human supervisor will be required to take action.

Decision Support/ Performance Management

When measurements of process performance have been defined and implemented, the capability to track and report on these critical metrics is available. Management reports may be generated that indicate efficiency data such as the average time to complete a process step, delay times between steps, resource use and costs associated with processes. In addition, process tracking data may tell us what information was accessed to complete a task, who approved actions during a process, when an action was completed and other information that will be useful in auditing how processes and controls were accomplished for compliance monitoring. Reports will be useful for management to continuously look for areas of improvement and to reduce the costs of compliance monitoring. Other reports may be useful to IT managers for managing networks, servers and other systems components.

Performance measurement and management applications have been developed to assist management decision making. Some BPM Systems have integrated these applications into their suite of capabilities. In large enterprises, the data and other information required to make decisions on business performance may be disbursed over a number of different systems and databases. Enterprise Application Integration (EAI) systems have been developed to facilitate accessing and reporting on information from a variety of sources. These systems use a group of application interfaces to pull information and then present summarized information in the form of management reports. Extensions of EAI and Data Warehousing systems called Business Intelligence (BI) systems have sophisticated data mining and management dashboards for presenting process performance data to managers to support decision making.

BI systems are dependent on the creation of metrics for various business performance indicators. The term Business Performance Management has come in use in recent years to refer to efforts to provide management processes taking advantage of sophisticated methods for determining the performance of various aspects of an organization. BPM systems that measure the performance of various aspects of business processes are a part of an overall performance measurement program.

Business Rules Management System (rules engine)

A category of software applications that are related to the monitoring and control of processes are rules engines. In general, a rules engine provides the capability to develop statements that monitor process events and then take specific actions based on an event occurrence. The most common use of rules involve conditional routing where a transition between process activities is based on detecting a particular condition and routing the process to the appropriate employees or to another process action.

Rules are also important to detect business process conditions and identify conditions to determine when further decisions are required. Given the dynamics of business processes it is not always possible to predetermine conditions, and rules engines that allow for exception handling and decision processes are necessary.

Other rules based on data analytics may be used to measure business process performance. We may wish to establish rules that look for events having to do with financial performance, conditions of regulatory compliance or production controls. For example, management may want to be alerted when projected sales of a certain product fall below a certain point so that sales efforts may be adjusted before poor sales performance is a fact. In manufacturing, a rule may be established such that when the inventory of certain parts is below a specified level, then purchase orders are automatically generated by a system.

Basically, most rules engines provide a language for creating rules statements. The most common form of a rule is the "If …Then…." type of statement. Actions supported by the rules engine may include alerts sent to specific individuals to make a decision or take an action or the action may be to execute a set of codes in a software application that would perform a function. Rules engines may be part of a BPM application or may be independent programs that interact with other applications to perform a task.

An emerging class of software is Business Rules Management Systems (BRMS). As management and process designers determine the rules that are applicable to a given process, a somewhat daunting task is to translate the conceptual rules into executable code.

Business Rules Management Systems allow designers to create rules in natural language statements (the If-Then statements). The system then generates the required code for execution. BRMS generally include methods to maintain the repositories of rules, test rules and make changes based on design changes. Therefore, rules management is in the hands of designers without reliance on technical coders. BRMS's are particularly useful for large organizations with complex rules requirements to manage.

Process Repository Management

Process Repository Administration is a critical component of managing business processes that should be taken as seriously as the administration of any other company asset. The Process Repository is the blueprint for process management within the organization, not only as a common frame of reference and method of consistent communication, but it is also the system of record for information on process ownership, technological enablers, business rules and controls, both financial and operational. Effective and consistent administration of this valuable asset is critical to developing and maintaining the holistic nature of the enterprise's processes through promotion and acceptance of their cross-functional nature.

A Process Repository is a central location for storing information about how an enterprise operates. This information may be contained in various media including paper, film or electronic form with a storage mechanism appropriate to the medium. Electronic repositories range from passive containers which store process artifacts (also referred to as process objects) to sophisticated tools that serve as active participants in executing and managing business processes. They come in the form of Document Management Systems, Process Modeling Tools and Business Process Management Systems.

Process Repository administration activities includes storing, managing and changing process knowledge (objects, relationships, enablers, attributes, business rules, performance measures and models) for an enterprise. It includes creating the repository structure; defining and maintaining procedures to ensure changes are controlled, validated and approved; mapping processes to applications and data, and providing the required infrastructure to enable effective and consistent use of the models in the repository.

Process Repository Content

The type of information about a process that should be maintained in a process repository includes:

- Who owns the process
- What the process does
- What technology enablers and controls are used
- What triggers or events initiate the process
- What are the expected results
- When is the process initiated
- Where does the process take place
- How the process interacts or links to other processes
- How the process interacts with those of other business units or external enterprises
- How the results are delivered
- Why it's needed, how the process aligns to strategic goals
- Process metrics such as time to perform, number of resources required, minimum and maximum concurrent executions, direct and indirect cost, etc.
- Business Rules
- Regulatory requirements
- Type and source of data related to the process

Object-based repositories also store information about the individual objects used by the Business. These objects are reused throughout the model providing consistency and simplifying maintenance. Consistent use of common objects avoids redundancy and contradictory information about a business artifact as the object only exists once in the repository but can be visually represented in multiple places. This allows a change to an object to be immediately visible wherever that object has been used.

Examples of these objects are customers, applications, organizations, roles, events, and results. The information kept for each will vary by type but includes such attributes as:

- Name
- Description
- Owner
- Stakeholders

- Associations to other objects or processes
- Value (measurement varies by type of object)
- Importance to the Business
- Technical specifications

Managing and integrating models

Managing models within the enterprise should start with identifying the levels of models that the enterprise will maintain. These range from an enterprise-wide model to temporary working models. While the figure below only shows one level of business unit or project sub-model, there could be additional levels depending on the size and structure of the organization or project. In addition, the granularity of the information contained at each level may vary. For example, the enterprise-level model may contain a few key attributes for each item while a business unit model would contain a more detailed set. However, if the enterprise-level model is a true 'master' then each sub-model will contain a subset of this model and the granularity of information for each item will be the same. Figure 10.2 below shows an example of the relationship between these levels.

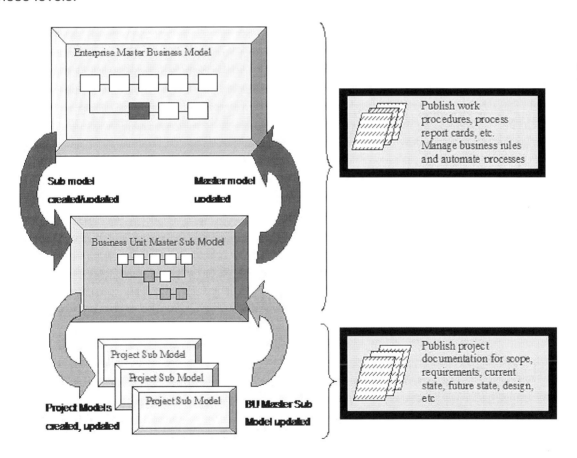

Figure 10.2 - Managing Models

This example starts with the enterprise level model which contains all the processes and related objects for the entire business. Each business unit would own and maintain a business unit master model and the active project models. Note that projects that span business units will also have a project model which may contain components from various business unit master models. The central repository administrator works with the business unit model administrator to identify all the business processes required for the end-to-end execution of the business unit's processes. These should be assigned to a category or subject area. Many of the modeling tools provide this functionality. A modeling tool, should at the minimum, have the ability to maintain an inventory of these groups and the components included.

The business unit master model is a sub-model of the enterprise master model. Formal scheduled synchronizations are performed to maintain the integrity of the information in both models. The next level of model is the project model. For each project, a project sub model is created containing the business processes required for the project. The business processes are checked out of the business unit master and when the updates have been completed and approved, checked back in. A formal change control procedure needs to be in place and adhered to. This procedure must include how to request check-out/check-in, check-in/check-out criteria, approvals required, timelines, and conflict resolution. When any component is checked out, a change freeze must be implemented.

Managing a model should be treated in the same manner as managing databases and source code. There must be regularly scheduled back-ups and full disaster recovery procedures in place.

10.7 Standards

There are a number of technology trends emerging in BPM that suggest standard methods and practices. To claim that there are true standards for BPM technologies is premature. However, methods to design, automate, coordinate and simplify the execution of BPM activities have involved common practices and frameworks for a number of BPM activities and related technologies. Some of these emerging methods include technologies already discussed such as:

- Business Process Modeling Notation (BPMN) used for graphical design of processes
- Business Process Execution Language (BPEL) for coding executable process activities
- eXtensible Markup Language (XML) for sharing data and documents
- eXtensible Process Definition Language (XPDL) is a file format specification compatible with BPMN notation standards and provides a common format for sharing process models between tools

Behind many BPM applications are common industry platforms and technical practices such as object oriented programming, database technologies and operating platforms that could be labeled standards.

10.8 Who participates in BPM technology?

Participants in BPM technology will include three broad classes of people: 1) those BPM professionals who use the tools to analyze existing processes then develop alternatives, parts of which may be automated, 2) those people who use the automated processes in the performance of their jobs and 3) management professionals who use technologies to monitor process performance and analyze data looking for opportunities to improve business processes.

Virtually all categories of BPM professionals will benefit from some of the technology tools. Personnel with responsibilities for any aspect of the BPM life cycle will benefit when their activities are to some extent automated or otherwise supported by the technologies described below.

The participants in BPM technologies may not be limited to personnel within an organization. Processes shared with trading partners, customers and other stakeholders may also benefit from the proper application of technology. The Internet has allowed for sharing information and creating efficiencies in a host of processes. Examples include online catalogs, order forms and order status information to support customer purchases, real-time inventory status and order information necessary to support just-in-time supply purchases and stock-holder communications mechanisms.

From an organizational perspective there must be top management sponsorship and buy-in from process owners. Internal communications and decision processes should include both information systems professionals and BPM professionals when considering what technologies will be used to support BPM.

10.9 Trends and convergence of systems

The history of the development of systems that support BPM activities started with applications designed to handle specific tasks. The need to convert large amounts of paper documents into electronic forms spawned scanning and imaging applications. Requirements to track financial transactions led to the development of accounting and ERP systems. Efforts to gather information from disparate sources for the purpose of analyzing business performance launched EAI systems. And problems associated with managing large repositories of documents led to the development of document management systems.

As the concepts of BPM emerged with the emphasis on analyzing, improving and managing processes, existing application sets were employed and new applications such as workflow, rules engines, and design and simulation tools were added to the systems options. By the mid 1990s a host of applications were available, each with their own features designed to address specific requirements.

A significant problem in the application of these tools to BPM is that the various systems have not been compatible with each other. Systems to design and simulate process flows may not be compatible for implementing workflows in specific document management systems. Workflow applications may have limited capabilities for developing and implementing rules compared to more sophisticated rules applications and the more fully featured rules engines are not compatible with other workflow products. In addition, Business Intelligence and performance measurement applications are useful for defining and measuring business performance but do not automatically plug into workflow applications to monitor the performance of process activities.

Many efforts in applying BPM concepts have started with specific projects based on requirements to improve specific business operations, often at a departmental level. The selection of systems to support these projects has been based on the features of applications targeting the specific requirements. If the main problem is managing large amounts of documents, then a document management system geared to this task may be selected. If workflow is a requirement then a document manager with workflow may be chosen. However, the next project in an organization may have a different set of requirements and the system selected for the first project may not be the optimum solution. Therefore, organizations started to acquire systems for specific functions that represent "islands" of applications and created massive and expensive support requirements.

With a growing recognition of the important elements of the BPM lifecycle from analysis and design to implementation and management, there has been a significant movement among systems vendors to create sets of tools (applications) that address the most important BPM requirements and interoperate with each other. Therefore, we can choose those tools from a set of compatible applications that are important for a particular project with the knowledge that we can add other features from the same vendor for other projects and have a common system architecture to support from an IT perspective.

A family of applications or tools whose goal is to achieve loose coupling among interacting software agents is an architectural style known as a Service Oriented Architecture (SOA). Each application in the family of applications is viewed as a specific service that may be implemented within a common hardware and software architecture. A full suite of applications following a SOA for BPM may include:

- Process mapping, analysis and design tools
- Content management applications
- Workflow execution
- EAI services
- Business Intelligence
- Rules description and execution capabilities
- Process monitoring and control
- Performance management

In addition to the suite of applications offered by single vendors, recent trends in software development have encouraged the interoperability of applications supplied by different vendors. Most vendors have developed Application Program Interfaces (APIs) that provide the ability to share information between applications built on standard software platforms. The emergent standards in software at the operating system level have produced standard software development environments allowing for much greater interoperability of applications using these standards and methods. In particular, standard methods for developing applications taking advantage of the Internet and working as Web enabled applications have enhanced application compatibilities. The primary technology platforms referred to are J2EE and .NET that provide the systems environment to design and execute BP applications.

An additional advantage of current systems is that much of their configuration and the features implemented can be controlled by non technical individuals. Once the software is installed, developing workflow models, specifying rules, developing user interface forms and other functions can be accomplished without computer coding expertise. This allows BPM professionals and managers to develop process applications after training on the features of the software. Should modifications be required in the basic functions of the applications, the development platforms on which these systems are based facilitate rapid changes without extensive coding.

10.10 Implications of BPM Technology

Information systems are an integral part of business processes. The development and deployment of most systems has been based on meeting specific operational requirements, and have been deployed by technical IT experts. A typical problem in many organizations that has been recognized for years is the lack of adequate communication and planning between executive management responsible for the strategic and tactical direction of the organization and the IT management.

With the emerging software capabilities now available, the roles of many professionals are changing. BPM professionals need to understand existing information systems and their functions within business processes. They need to understand the type of information available, its source and its use within existing processes. Efforts to analyze and improve processes will require the examination of software alternatives for integrating information from a variety of sources, determining how to manage and distribute useful information within processes and how to develop improved sources of information.

The enhanced ease of use of BPMS means that BPM professionals will become more involved in configuring these systems to support business needs. With systems that support the design and automation of execution code, the business analyst and BP designer is less dependent on IT technical professionals. The role of IT professionals is also changing because the technical requirements for application development coding are decreasing. The implication is that IT professionals need to become more involved in understanding business strategies and supporting business processes as a part of the BPM team.

Legal and regulatory requirements are forcing executives to pay more attention to internal processes and competitive pressures add to the motivation of executives and board members to understand and improve important processes. The advantages that may accrue from process improvement activities can be substantial and BPM professionals will be at the center of critical changes.

10.11 Key Concepts

BPM TECHNOLOGY - KEY CONCEPTS
1. Information systems are an integral part of business processes. BPM professionals need to understand existing information systems and their functions within business processes.
2. BPM Technologies address the full process management life cycle: process modeling and design, process implementation and execution, process monitoring and control, process performance analysis and assessment.
3. BPM systems and suites (BPMS) may include several of the capabilities of technologies previously designed for specific capabilities such as: imaging, document and content management, collaboration, workflow, work routing and assignment, rules management and execution, metadata management, data warehousing, business intelligence, application integration, communications management and more.
4. Process Repositories are essential components of a full BPMS solution. A Central Process Repository helps to ensure consistent communication about a process including what it is, how it should be applied, who is responsible for its successful execution, and expected results upon process completion.
5. Effective and sustainable business process management cannot be achieved without the integration and deployment of appropriate technologies to support operations, and management decision making.

Appendix A – References

Chapter 1

1. Champlin, Brett (2006) 'Business Process Management Professionals', BPM Strategies, October 2006
2. BPMG. (2005) In Search of BPM Excellence: Straight from the Thought Leaders, Meghan-Kiffer Press.
3. Dephi Group. (2003) "BPM 2003 Market Milestone Report", a Delphi Group Whitepaper, 2003. www.delphigroup.com
4. Fisher, David. (2004). "Optimize Now (or else!): How to Leverage Processes and Information to Achieve Enterprise Optimization", ProcessWorld 2004, BearingPoint Presentation, April 25-28, Miami, Florida, 2004.
5. Harmon, Paul. (2004). "Evaluating an Organization's Business Process Maturity", Business Process Trends, March 2004, Vol. 2, No. 3, pp. 1-11. http://www.caciasl.com/pdf/BPtrendLevelEval1to5.pdf
6. Porter, Michael. (1985), Competitive Advantage, New York: Free Press.
7. Rummler-Brache Group (2004). Business Process Management in U.S. Firms Today. A study commissioned by Rummler-Brache Group. March 2004.
8. Scheer, A.W; Ferri Abolhassan, Wolfram Jost, Mathias Kirchmer (Editors). (2004) Business Process Automation, Springer-Verlag.
9. Sinur, Jim. (2004). "Leveraging the Three Phases of Process Evolution", ProcessWorld 2004, Gartner Research Presentation, April 25-28, Miami, Florida, 2004.
10. zur Muehlen, Michael. (2004). Workflow-based Process Controlling. Foundation, Design, and Application of workflow-driven Process Information Systems. Logos, Berlin.
11. Dephi Group. (2003) "BPM 2003 Market Milestone Report", *A Delphi Group* Whitepaper, 2003. www.delphigroup.com

12. Dwyer, Tom. (2004) "BPMInstitute's State of Business Process Management", *Executive White Paper,* April 2004. www.BPMInstitute.org

13. Fisher, David. (2004). "Optimize Now (or else!): How to Leverage Processes and Information to Achieve Enterprise Optimization", *ProcessWorld 2004,* BearingPoint Presentation, April 25-28, Miami, Florida, 2004.

14. Harmon, Paul. (2004). "Evaluating an Organization's Business Process Maturity", *Business Process Trends,* March 2004, Vol. 2, No. 3, pp. 1-11. http://www.caciasl.com/pdf/BPtrendLevelEval1to5.pdf

15. Parker, Burton G. (1995) "Data Management Maturity Model", MITRE Software Engineering Center, McLean, Virginia, July, 1995.

16. Rosemann, Michael and Tonia deBruin. (2005) "Application of a Holistic Model for Determining BP maturity", *Business Process Trends*, Feb 2005.

17. Rummler-Brache Group (2004). *Business Process Management in U.S. Firms Today*. A study commissioned by Rummler-Brache Group. March 2004.

18. Sinur, Jim. (2004). "Leveraging the Three Phases of Process Evolution", *ProcessWorld 2004,* Gartner Research Presentation, April 25-28, Miami, Florida, 2004.

Chapter 3

1. Bruce Silver (2009). "BPMN Method and Style". Addison-Wesley.

Chapter 4

1. Madison, Daniel J. (2005), Process Mapping, Process Improvement and Process Management, Patton Press

Chapter 7

1. Alter, S., (1979), "Implementation Risk Analysis," in Doktor, R.,et.al. (eds.) The Implementation of Management Science, 13, pp. 103-120.
2. Bossidy, L., et.al. (2002), Execution: The Discipline of Getting Things Done, Crown Books.
3. Bradach, J. (1996), "Organizational Alignment: The 7-S Model," November 19, No. 9-497-045, Harvard Business School.
4. Casson, D. (2006) "Evergreen ITIL and Change Management Survey," Quarter 2, www.evergreensys.com.
5. Ginzburg, M. (1979) "A Study of the Implementation Process," in Doktor, R.,et.al. (eds.) The Implementation of Management Science, 13, pp. 85-102.
6. Harvard Business Review, (2005), The Essentials of Managing Change and Transition: Business Literacy for HR Professionals, Boston MA, Harvard Business School Press and Alexandria VA, Society for Human Resource Management.
7. Kolb, D. and Frohman, A., (1970) "An Organizational Development Approach to Consulting," Sloan Management Review, 12, pp. 51-65.
8. Kotter, J.P. (1996), Leading Change, Boston, MA, Harvard Business School Press.
9. Pro-Sci Change Management Learning Center, http://www.change-management.com/change-management-overview.htm
10. Schein, E.H. (1987). Process Consultation, Vol. II, Reading MA, Addison-Wesley.
11. PMI (2004), A Guide to the Project Management Body of Knowledge, 3rd ed., Newton Square PA, PMI Press.

12. Rudd, C., (2004), "An Introductory Overview of ITIL," <u>IT Service Management Forum</u> (Complimentary Issue) [get URL] <publications site: *www.get-best-practice.co.uk*
13. U.K.OGC (2004), <u>IT Infrastructure Library</u>, 2nd ed., U.K. Office of Government Commerce
14. Waterhouse, P (2006), "State of ITIL Adoption in North America – Survey Results ", webcast available until March 31, 2007, at https://www.cmpnetseminars.com/BTG/default.asp?K=4IK&Q=489

Chapter 8
1. Davenport, Thomas H., PhD. (1992), Process Innovation: Reengineering Work Through Information Technology, Harvard Business School Press, Cambridge, MA.
2. Hammer, Michel, PhD.; Champy, James. (1993 – 2003 addition) Reengineering the Corporation: A Manifesto for Business Revolution. Harper Collins Publishers Inc., NY, NY.
3. Hammer, Michael, PhD. (1996), Beyond Reengineering: How the Process-Centered Organization is Changing Our Work and Our Lives. Harper Collins Publishers Inc., NY, NY.
4. Spanyi, Andrew. (2006), More for Less: The Power of Process Management, Meghan Kiffer Press.
5. Champlin, Brett (2006). Instructional Course - BPM 101, as presented in Chicago, IL at the Brainstorm BPM Institute Conference.
6. BPM Institute. Various conferences and presentations found online at www.bpminstitute.org.

Chapter 9
2. Bossidy, Larry and Ram Charan, Execution: The Discipline of Getting Things Done, Crown Business, 2002.
3. Davenport, Thomas H., Process Innovation, Harvard Business School Press, 1993.
4. Hamel, Gary, Leading the Revolution, Harvard Business School Press, 2000.
5. Hammer, Michael, The Agenda, Crown Business, 2001.
6. Kaplan, Robert S. and David P. Norton, The Balanced Scorecard, Harvard Business School Press, 1996
7. Kaplan, Robert S. and David P. Norton, The Strategy-Focused Organization, Harvard Business School Press, 2001.
8. Kaplan, Robert S. and David P. Norton, "Using the Balanced Scorecard as a Strategic Management System," Harvard Business Review, January-February 1996.
9. Porter, Michael, "What is Strategy?" Harvard Business Review, November-December 1996.
10. Rummler, Geary A. and Alan Brache, Improving Performance: How to Manage the White Space on the Organization Chart, Jossey-Bass, 1995.
11. Smith, Dick and Jerry Blakeslee with Richard Koonce, Strategic Six Sigma; Best Practices from the Executive Suite, Wiley, 2002

12. Smith, Howard and Peter Fingar, Business Process Management: The Third Wave, Meghan-Kiffer Press, 2003.
13. Treacy, Michael and Fred Wiersema, The Discipline of Market Leaders, Addison Wesley, 1995.
14. Treacy, Michael, Double-Digit Growth, Portfolio, 2003

Chapter 10

1. Adapted from Miers, Derek and Harmon, Paul, <u>The 2005 BPM Suites Report</u>, Business Process Trends, p. 14.

2. Sinur, Jim, Hill, Janelle B. and Melenovsky, Michael James, <u>Selection Criteria Details for Business Process Management Suites, 2006</u>,. Gartner Note Number G00134657, November, 18, 2005.

Appendix B - BPM Community

There is a large and growing community of practice and supporting services around Business Process Management. This information is continually changing and requires frequent updating. As such, we cannot maintain a comprehensive current reference in this document.

For current up-to-date information and links to the larger BPM community please see the ABPMP website at www.ABPMP.org. There you will find sections such as BPM Resources, Education, and Events. Some of the listings you will find include:

- A BPM Bibliography with links to the Amazon listings for the books
- Links to BPM Blogs
- Links to BPM content rich websites
- Links to BPM related organizations
- BPM Job Listings
- Academic programs in BPM
- BPM Training Providers
- And more

The ABPMP website also contains links to ABPMP chapters and affiliate organizations, ABPMP programs such as the ongoing maintenance of the BPM CBOK®, our Endorsed Education Provider program, and the Certified Business Process Professional (CBPP™) program. You may join ABPMP online through our website or contact our officers and chapters for more information.

Appendix C-Toward a BPM Model Curriculum

The Need for a BPM Curriculum

As business continues to address globalization and increasing competition, companies are becoming more collaborative and process-centric. This view requires the necessary and needed skills to integrate business processes over different business functions and often disparate information technologies to bring value to the customer. The purpose of this section is to provide a path of educational courses to address this growing need. Most business schools still emphasize a business function perspective. In contrast, those who complete the required program will have the knowledge to manage business processes by leveraging the people and technology to meet the changing needs of the business environment. Successful completion of a BPM degree or concentration will prepare the graduate for meaningful participation in the employer's BPM activities. The suggested curriculum allows for an undergraduate major in BPM and a Masters in Science in BPM. In addition, the modular format can be adapted to a specialized certificate program in BPM. The suggested coursework consists of five core BPM courses that range from a general introduction of BPM and continues throughout the process lifecycle of modeling, analysis, design, and implementation. In addition, three elective courses allows for a more in-depth exploration of BPM followed by a capstone course on Business Process Strategy.

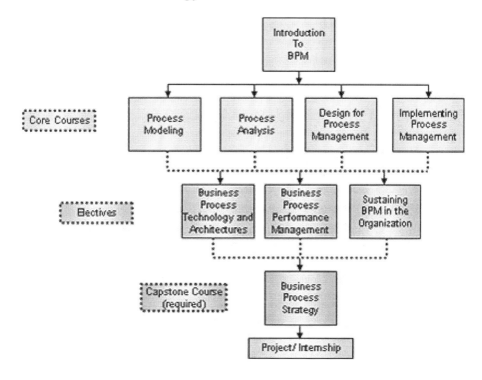

Figure C.1 - General Course Sequence

Business Process Management [BPM] introduces a change in organizational focus from functional silos to integrated business processes. Driven by the need to compete in a fast-paced, real-time economy, organizations are beginning to recognize the need to achieve a process-centric organization. This not only requires an understanding and deployment of successful process management principles, but also the understanding and ability to improve end-to-end processes enabled by appropriate business process management systems and technologies.

As organizations are beginning to realize the need to increase business process related skills, the interest and need has arisen for a common BPM educational curriculum outline that leads toward a BPM certification. In addition, colleges and universities must also provide a learning environment that embraces the business process management practices of the new process-centric organization.

Since BPM involves several organizational dimensions such as culture, governance, organizational issues, process, and technology, a BPM curriculum needs to be well rounded, containing courses in both organizational and technical related areas. At present time, there are very few dedicated BPM programs in colleges and universities worldwide. Those that do exist vary in focus and coverage. In addition, organizations in need of trained graduates in the BPM arena know little about the existing programs. This model curriculum aims to create a template for addressing both the needs of industry and the education institutions' services to industry.

Contributors

The authors of this Model Curriculum represent the academic and practitioner communities. Indeed, all the contributors to this section have some degree of both BPM practical and teaching experience.

Intended Users

Faculty can adopt all or part of the model curriculum to promote a process-centric emphasis that meets the changing needs of for-profit and not-for-profit organizations. Industry can assess this model curriculum and propose modifications and extensions to maintain shared expectations for graduates. A BPM model curriculum is relevant to more than a business school, e.g., an information sciences, information studies school, a health sciences school, and an industrial psychology program in a psychology department. Students within any relevant academic unit can assess an education institution's commitment to a process-centric approach by comparing the school curriculum to the model curriculum.

Who would the curriculum benefit?

Ultimately the organization will benefit from an educated and trained staff that both understand and have deployment knowledge for improving business processes. Individuals from both business and technical sides of the organization will benefit from an understanding of the BPM body of knowledge and learning to share a common set of procedures and practices.

Colleges and Universities will benefit from a BPM curriculum framework to help them remain competitive. Students graduating from this program will obtain desirable skills and knowledge.

What type of programs would be beneficial?

Various educational opportunities have emerged that focus on BPM. They include professional seminars, university certificate and degreed programs. Certificate programs (e.g., four courses) permit currently employed individuals to apply BPM skills quickly in the workplace. While many of these have merit, a comprehensive BPM curriculum that concentrates on *an* established Guide to a BPM Common Body of Knowledge surrounding defined Knowledge Areas is the goal of this Appendix.

The role of the model curriculum

This model curriculum will be reviewed for endorsement by the ABPMP Board of Directors, ABPMP Advisory Board, and Education Committee. It represents authoritative guidance for educational institutions' planning to incorporate a business process focus to their educational programs at the undergraduate and graduate levels. Feedback from both industry and educational institutions will modify the model curriculum content and thus maintain its currency and value.

Model Curricula

Undergraduate BPM Program

Goals

The Undergraduate BPM major student will acquire the knowledge and skills initially to model, analyze, design and implement business processes working with an experienced BP developer. If sufficient computer technology courses also have been taken, the graduate could work with the BP suite support services. One intent of the model curriculum is for every student to understand the value of a process-centric organization design, appropriate metrics, and how business processes execute in contrast to a functional structure approach.

Student Background Profile

Students should have mastered an understanding of economics, organizational strategy and design, use of information technology in business, and the basic business functional areas. This knowledge may have been obtained as a business school undergraduate or having completed a four or more course minor in business.

Career Opportunities and Paths for Graduates

Undergraduates may seek BPM entry-level positions as jr. analysts, BPM software maintainers, BPM junior consultants, or junior administrators of business processes or rules repositories. With experience, individuals can increase their seniority in current areas or move into other BPM areas, e.g., design, implementation, performance evaluation.

Curriculum Overview

Type	Course Title	Sample Content
core	Introduction to BPM	To overview the BOK material, BPM and related topics. BPM Lifecycle. Why process management What is involved in BPM Business Architectures. Explore BPM career paths.
core	Process Modeling	Modeling and simulation Business and operational modeling Modeling end-to-end processes to task level models Simulation / optimizing Activity-Based Costing simulation BPMN Event driven models
core	Process Analysis	Business Analysis techniques Process analysis techniques Applied and descriptive statistics Assessment methods: BPM maturity assessment Analysis of support; skill sets; Change management...
core	Design for Process Management	Operational design Design principles Techniques and methods of successful process designs What drives process design?
core	Implementing Process Management	Project management for Process Implementing Process change Project management and change management
core	Business Process Technology and Architectures	BPMS BPM Repository Technologies SOA
elective	Business Process Performance Management	Monitoring, controlling, refining processes KPIs; metrics

Type	Course Title	Sample Content
		How to map performance Data Warehousing Business Analysis and Intelligence
Capstone (required)	Business Process Strategy	Enterprise Process management BPM Organization Process portfolio Leading by metrics How to sustain BPM initiatives Engaging process owners for the long term Establishing the process oriented customer focus cases
elective	Internship/ Project	Analyze current situation Design BP improvement and implementation plan Presentation and report to client

Master's Degree in BPM Program

Goals

The Graduate Masters Degree in BPM student has a more advanced depth of knowledge for developing, evaluating, and managing business processes. This graduate should be prepared to assume greater responsibility for an initial job position than an undergraduate. The MS program graduate initially may be responsible for evaluating, perhaps managing a business process that is not an enterprise end-to-end process .If sufficient technical courses were taken, the graduate could work with Business Process and Business Rules repositories in addition to business process development.

Student Background Profile

Students may enter this graduate curriculum with a business or non-business undergraduate degree. Ideally, the student will have at least 2-4 years experience in for-profit, not-for-profit, or government positions. The student's primary asset is an understanding of how an organization operates for planning, execution and control. The design and improvement of collaborative business processes requires an understanding of each of the major organization functional areas. Use of information technology in organizations also will be helpful.

Career Opportunities and Paths for Graduates

Depending upon the student's prior work experience, the BPM graduate may begin as a junior or senior business analyst or designer, a BPM consultant, a business process performance evaluator, a BPMS junior or senior support staff, a junior repository administrator, or controls evaluator. These examples are not exhaustive.

Curriculum Overview

Type	Course Title	Sample Content	BPM Program
core	Introduction to BPM	<ul><li>General overview of BPM</li><li>How people, process & technology are involved in BPM</li><li>Overview of Business Architectures</li><li>BPM Lifecycle</li><li>Explore BPM career paths</li></ul>	x
core	Process Modeling	<ul><li>Business and operational modeling</li><li>Modeling end-to-end processes to task level models</li><li>BPMN</li><li>Event driven models</li><li>Introduction to Simulation</li></ul>	x
core	Process Analysis	<ul><li>Business & Process Analysis techniques</li><li>Applied and descriptive statistics</li><li>Assessment methods and metrics</li><li>Simulation / optimizing</li><li>Analysis of support; skill sets; change management…</li></ul>	x
core	Design for Process Management	<ul><li>Operational design</li><li>Design principles</li><li>Techniques and methods of successful process designs</li><li>What drives process design?</li><li>Simulation testing of process design</li></ul>	x
core	Implementing Process Management	<ul><li>Improvement methodologies</li><li>Implementing Process change</li><li>Project management for Process Implementation</li><li>Organizational change management</li></ul>	x

Type	Course Title	Sample Content	BPM Program
		• Process evaluation and quality control	
core	Business Process Technology and Architectures	• BP Application Integration • BPM Suites • BPM & BRM Repositories • SOA and web services • Business and IT architectures	x
elective	Advanced Business Process Technology	• TPS and BI support • Enterprise Content Mgmt • XML, SOA, BPN and BPEL • Network Support • BPM Server Configuration	
Elective	Business Process and Rules Repository	• Workflow Engine • Rules Engine • BP Collaboration Support • Repository Mgmt & Maintenance • Repository Integrity & Security	
elective	Business Process Performance Management	• BP and Enterprise Performance • Monitoring & controlling processes • Metrics—KPIs. CSFs • Measurement Methods • Measurement Frameworks	x
Capstone (required)	Business Process Strategy	• Leveraging the BPM Organization • Managing the Process portfolio and leading by metrics • How to sustain BPM initiatives • Strategies for managing BP for the long-term • cases	x
elective	Internship/ Project	• Identify the BP problem root cause or opportunity • Scope the BP improvement including politics • Analyze current situation • Design BP improvement and implementation plans • Presentation and report to client	x

Introduction to BPM is suggested as the first course a student should be required to complete, and should be the pre-requisite for all other courses. The modeling, analysis, design, and implementation of business processes are considered the core of BPM. The understanding and ability to develop a business process strategy is key to BPM success, and as a result, recommended as a capstone course. Several electives are suggested for programs that do not have the liberty of a full 10 course sequence.

MBA Concentration in BPM

Goals

The MBA BPM concentration student initially should be prepared to manage a BP segment (less complexity) and participate in the development and evaluation of business processes along with an experienced BPM practitioner.

Student Background Profile

Students should have mastered an understanding of economics, organizational strategy and design, statistics, use of information technology in business, and the basic business functional areas. . Ideally, the student will have at least 2-4 years experience in for-profit, not-for-profit, or government positions. The undergraduate degree need not be in business or computer science.

Career Opportunities and Paths for Graduates

Depending upon the student's prior work experience, the BPM graduate may begin as a jr. or. sr. business analyst or designer, a BPM consultant, a business process performance evaluator, a jr. repository administrator, or controls evaluator.

Curriculum Overview

Type	Course Title	Sample Content	BPM Program
core	Introduction to BPM	<ul><li>General overview of BPM</li><li>How people, process & technology are involved in BPM</li><li>Overview of Business Architectures</li><li>BPM Lifecycle</li><li>Explore BPM career paths</li></ul>	x
core	Process Analysis and Design	<ul><li>Business & Process Analysis techniques</li><li>Applied and descriptive statistics</li><li>Assessment methods and metrics</li><li>Simulation / optimizing</li><li>Analysis of support; skill sets; change management…</li><li>Design principles</li><li>Techniques and methods of successful</li></ul>	x

Type	Course Title	Sample Content	BPM Program
		process designs	
elective	Business Process Technology and Architectures	<ul><li>BP Application Integration</li><li>BPM Suites</li><li>BPM & BRM Repositories</li><li>SOA and web services</li><li>Business and IT architectures</li></ul>	x
elective	Business Process Performance Management	<ul><li>BP and Enterprise Performance</li><li>Monitoring & controlling processes</li><li>Metrics—KPIs. CSFs</li><li>Measurement Methods</li><li>Measurement Frameworks</li></ul>	x
Capstone (required)	Business Process Strategy	<ul><li>Leveraging the BPM Organization</li><li>Managing the Process portfolio and leading by metrics</li><li>How to sustain BPM initiatives</li><li>Strategies for managing BP for the long-term</li><li>cases</li></ul>	x

The number of BPM courses will vary by MBA program and whether courses are quarter or semester length. In addition, several MBA programs already have courses that could be enhanced with BPM cases and required for the student interested in a BPM track; courses such as Change Management and Project Management.

Student backgrounds

A BPM curriculum *may appeal* to students from varied disciplines. Since BPM merges *organization* and technology concepts, the curriculum is appropriate to students of *organizations* and those focused in technology. Students from all business disciplines (accounting, information systems, marketing, management, operations, etc) can benefit from a BPM curriculum. Likewise, technology based disciplines such as those based in the computer science and schools of information are also appropriate.

Common Business Process Management Courses

The proposed COMMON Business Process Management curriculum is primarily designed for a University at both the Graduate (both a masters and MBA emphasis) and Undergraduate Levels. A feasible major for BPM would most likely reside in the graduate level, but a less rigorous approach in the same courses could also be placed at the undergraduate level. While a business school would be the most appropriate place for a BPM curriculum, other academic units with specialized degrees can adapt portions of this curriculum as appropriate. In addition there are several types of specialty programs that the proposed business process management curriculum could be adapted for such as executive education and BPM certification programs.

Course Descriptions

Course	Description
Introduction to BPM	An introduction to concepts and strategies required to successfully manage your business processes from a holistic end-to-end perspective.
Process Modeling	In order to have effective and efficient repeatable end-to-end processes, an organization must understand existing processes and use appropriate techniques to model and design improved processes. This course overviews various process modeling methods for all levels of the organization. Appropriate process modeling techniques are explained and aligned with process analyses and process design. Learn use of process modeling tools.
Process Analysis	In order to have effective and efficient repeatable end-to-end processes, an organization must understand existing processes and use appropriate techniques to model and represent those processes. This course overviews various process analysis methods for all levels of the organization. Appropriate process modeling techniques are aligned with process analyses.
Design for Process Management	The design of business processes needs to consider results from a process analysis and then utilize process modeling techniques to develop an improved process design. Process design should occur at various stages of the BPM practice cycle and also at various levels of detail. This course introduces current process design techniques practiced today. Appropriate process modeling techniques are applied to the design of a renewed process.
Process Transformation	Business Process implementation is the bridge between design and execution. This course examines the steps required to transform the approved process design into a set of documented, tested, and operational sub-processes and workflows that are accepted by the appropriately trained stakeholders.
Business Process Technology and Architectures	Several BPM Technologies, systems, and tools have emerged into the market in recent years. This course examines the functional contributions from these various BPM technologies, systems, and tools.
Advanced Business Process Technology	An in-depth examination of BPM technologies, systems and tools. The emphasis is on technical specifications, current vendor offerings, and actual use of selected tools.
Business Process And Rules Repository	How to design and implement business process and rules repositories including relevant metadata. Interfaces with manual and computer-based tasks are considered. Performance metrics, regulatory compliance, and current vendor offerings are discussed. Limited scale repositories will be constructed.
Business Process Performance Management	The success of BPM requires a set of meaningful outcome and execution performance metrics that convey the value added to business operations and strategy for assessment by senior executives, process owners, and process staff. An integrated network of performance metrics spanning customer

Course	Description
	requirements through fulfillment and cash inflow is needed to deliver this information to appropriate stakeholders. Performance metrics for extended enterprise business processes must be included to enable an end-end complete evaluation. Both business-oriented and technology-oriented metrics will be addressed. Criteria for generating reports will be discussed, e.g., events, user queries, or date. Class examples and cases will be used to illustrate how to develop an effective BPM performance evaluation system.
Sustaining Business Process Management In the Organization	The benefits from BPM are harvested from a long-term commitment, not as a short-term burst of productivity. Thus, BPM benefits' sustainability follows from a transformation to a process-centric culture by all relevant organization stakeholders. Without successful change management, BPM cannot deliver continual, perhaps radical improvement benefits. An effective program for sustaining BPM value will be discussed including senior executive support, incentives consistent with BPM improvement, and creating BPM innovation focus groups. Successful implementation of BPM improvements must be celebrated openly and enthusiastically to maintain a commitment to BPM improvements. Industry examples and cases will enable discussion of implementing a BPM sustainability plan.
Business Process Strategy	Alignment between Business process objectives and enterprise strategy is essential to harvest BPM benefits. Efficiency without effectiveness will not accomplish institutional objectives. Customer requirements must shape business strategy, objectives, metrics and organization. This thrust must continue to shape BPM objectives, strategy and metrics. Clear delineation of end-to-end (cross functional) business processes with process owners should include extended business processes and more detailed business sub-processes. Given finite enterprise resources, the proposed business process investments must be analyzed within the context of the current business process portfolio. For BPM to be successful, clear accountability from the business process owner through business sub-processes' owners must be established in conjunction with appropriate metrics.

Table C.1: General Course Descriptions

Detailed Course Descriptions

The previous material contained course content highlights and summaries. In contrast, this section provides greater descriptive depth, i.e., course title, course description, course objectives, course topics, and any pertinent discussion. This content should help instructors create detailed syllabi for their BPM courses. This content will change as industry and the CBOK change.

Introduction to Business Process Management

Course Description:
An introduction to concepts and strategies required to successfully manage your business processes from a holistic end-to-end perspective.

Course Objectives:
The objective of this course is to provide a general overview and understanding of all of the concepts and strategies related to business process management. This course is a high level course designed for managers, business leaders and anyone else looking for an understanding of business process management concepts.

Major Topics:
The following topics will be covered in this class.
- Management discipline for continuous process management
    - Monitoring and measuring process performance
    - Customer focus in process management
- Structure and organization of process management within the enterprise
    - Skills required for business process management
    - Roles involved in BPM
    - Role of technology in BPM
- Definitions of BPM concepts and terminologies
    - Processes
    - Process types
    - Activities
    - Analysis
    - Design
    - Modeling
- Technologies used in process management
    - Modeling
    - Process monitoring
    - Process integration
- BPM Lifecycle
- BPM industry (providers, outsourcers)
- Critical success factors

Discussion:
The approach to this course is to provide a broad and general overview of the concepts relating to BPM. This includes an understanding of business architectures and the relationship of people, process, and technology involved in BPM. Different BPM career paths are also explored. The audience for this core course includes business users and others interested in learning about BPM.

Process Modeling

Course Description:
In order to have effective and efficient repeatable end-to-end processes, an organization must understand existing processes and use appropriate techniques to model and design improved processes. This course overviews various process modeling methods for all levels of the organization. Appropriate process modeling techniques are explained and aligned with process analyses and process design as well as learning how to use process modeling tools available.

Course Objectives:
At the end of this course the student will have obtained proficiency in the following learning objectives.

- Purpose of modeling
- Process modeling techniques and standards
- Modeling and analyzing business processes for various end to end processes and task level models
- Introduction to business process simulation

Major Topics:
The following topics will be analyzed during this course.
- Process modeling
    - Purpose of process modeling
    - Definition and scope of modeling
    - Process modeling standards, techniques and methodology
        - Notation techniques
        - Perspectives (domain, enterprise, technology, data)
        - Charts, swim lanes
        - BPMN
        - Personnel
    - Process modeling technologies
        - Technical tools
        - Manual tools
    - Introduction to Business Process Simulation

Discussion:
The approach to this course is to learn how to model end to end processes and to learn how to use the process modeling tools available. The audience for this core course includes business users and others not familiar with BPM modeling.

Process Analysis

Course Description:
In order to have effective and efficient repeatable end-to-end processes, an organization must understand existing processes and use appropriate techniques to

model and represent those processes. This course overviews various process analysis methods for all levels of the organization. Appropriate process modeling techniques are aligned with process analyses.

Course Objectives:
At the end of this course the student will have obtained proficiency in the following learning objectives.

- Purpose of process analysis
    - Efficiency of process
    - Effectiveness of process
    - Impact of process
- Business process analysis techniques
- Analyzing business processes through the application of assessment methods and metrics

Major Topics:
The following topics will be analyzed during this course.
- Process Analysis
    - Purpose of process analysis
        - Effectiveness of process
        - Efficiency of process
        - Decisions made through process
    - When to perform process analysis
        - Continuous monitoring
        - Event triggered
        - Performance
    - Defining process analysis
        - Customer Interactions
        - Performance Metrics and benchmarks
        - Process Controls
        - Process Attributes
    - Preparing process analysis
        - Scope of analysis
        - Choosing analysis resources / roles of analysis
        - Researching data for analysis
    - Analysis Process
        - Business Environment
        - Culture
        - Customer interactions
        - Critical business goals
    - Analysis models
        - Business environment
        - Performance metrics
        - Customer interactions

- Business rules
- Process capacity
- Process controls
- Process resources (human and technology)
    - Analysis tools, techniques and frameworks
    - Simulation and optimization
- Critical success factors

Discussion:
The approach to this course is an understanding of the different analysis methods of business processes. This includes both applied and descriptive statistics, simulation and optimization techniques, and process metrics and benchmarks. The audience for this core course includes business users and business process analysts/designers.

Design for Process Management

Course Description:
The design of business processes needs to consider results from a process analysis and then utilize process modeling techniques to develop an improved process design. Process design should occur at various stages of the BPM practice cycle and also at various levels of detail. This course introduces current process design techniques practiced today. Appropriate process modeling techniques are applied to the design of a renewed process.

Course Objectives:
At the end of this course students should have learned the following objectives:
- Business Process Design Principles
- Techniques and methods of process designs
- Simulation testing of process design

Major Topics:
The following topics will be analyzed during this course.

- Understanding Process Modeling techniques for design and Implementation
- Designing and modeling the renewed process (TO-BE)
- Simulation testing of the renewed process (TO-BE)

Discussion:
The approach to this course is to provide an understanding of process design as well as the simulation and testing of process design. The audience for this core course includes business users, business process analysts/designers, and BPM technologists.

Process Transformation

Course Description:
Business Process implementation is the bridge between design and execution. This course examines the steps required to transform the approved process design into a set of documented, tested, and operational sub-processes and workflows that are accepted by the appropriately trained stakeholders.

Course Objectives:
At the end of this course the student will have obtained proficiency in the following learning objectives.

- How to implement and manage process change
- Process evaluation and quality control

Major Topics:
- Understanding the Implementation phase
- Deploying BPM
- Process Automation
- Understand BPM best practices and methodologies
- BPM Reporting and Monitoring
- Preparing for Business Testing
- Developing Rollout Plans
- Implementing Changes
- Managing Business Process and Organizational Change
- Project management for BPM

Discussion:
The approach to this course is to understand how to implement and manage change at the process level.

The audience for this core course includes business users, business process analysts/designers, and BPM technologists

Business Process Technology and Architectures

Course Description:
Tasks within business processes are executed manually and/or by computer-based applications. For the latter, source data and an IT platform are necessary. This course will address how a business architecture (business process content) is translated into an IT architecture (hardware and system software)—that is those components of an IT architecture relevant to BPM support. The functionality provided by BPM suites and their toolsets will be discussed. Languages and notations for representing business processes will be examined. The role of web services and services Oriented Architecture for enabling business process agility will be explored. Exercises with BPM tools will be included.

Course Objectives:
At the end of this course the student will have obtained proficiency in the following learning objectives.

- Transform business architecture requirements into a BPM subset of an IT architecture
- Specify the BPM technology functionality necessary to execute computer-based execution of business processes and supporting manual tasks
- Prepare and evaluate RFP for BPM technology
- Understand the role of web services and SOA for supporting BPM

Topics:
- Evaluating BPM Software and BPM Suites
- BPM Solution Architectures
- Business Process Modeling Notation (BPMN)
- The Business Process Modeling Language (BPEL)
- BPM Framework
- Business Activity Monitoring (BAM)
- BPM Tools and trends

Discussion:
The approach to this course is to provide a functional understanding of the BPM platform with sufficient examples of BPM technology to participate in BPM software and hardware procurement requirements and evaluations. The audience for this core course includes business users, business process analysts/designers, and BPM technologists.

Advanced Business Process Technology

Course Description:
Building upon the Business Processing & Technology architecture (what is) prerequisite course, this course presents in-depth analyses (how to) of BPM support technology. Thus, the content is more appropriate for individuals pursuing a technical career interest. All the components in the technology chain from business processes through Internets and Intranets to applications and data supported by a SOA platform will be addressed. Exercises will provide an opportunity to experience basic functions of leading BPM software.

Course Objectives:
- To understand the interoperability among BPM relevant applications, data sources, networking, system software, and hardware
- To specify the technical requirements to execute a typical BPM suite
- To design content management system functions for capturing business process documents

Major Topics:
- BPMS configuration management
- Defining and selecting industry standard or vendor specific interfaces between BPMS both related software applications and data sources
- Preparing and evaluating RFP's for BPMS
- BP languages, e.g., BPEL (execution) and XPDL (extensible process description)
- Security for (1) protecting the integrity of BP software, workflows and data and (2) permitting BP software to execute by whom or what application
- Coordinating with operative business processes in extended enterprise entities
- Linking business activity monitoring to business process performance management
- Creating collaborative tools and common workspaces to facilitate BP execution productivity

Discussion:
Much of the value from this course will be the students' experience using leading software for designing and executing selected business processes within an integrated platform configuration.

Business Process and Rules Repositories

Course Description:
To promote business process effectiveness, efficiency and regulatory compliance, the business processes should be clearly and completely documented and automated to the greatest extent feasible. The design, deployment and evaluation of business process and rules repositories will be studied at both the functional and technical levels. Both these repositories represent the knowledge bases for successful business process engine execution. Policies for administering these repositories will be examined. Leading vendor product functionalities will be compared. Actual experience using these repositories will be included.

Course Objectives:
- Define the role of business and rule repositories for delivering value to enterprise customers and other supply chain stakeholders
- Describe the functional components or business process and rules repositories
- Define the policy, governance, and performance requirements
- Understand the contribution of business process and rules repositories to the flow of business process execution
- Compare the leading repository vendors' product offerings

Major Topics:
- Business process and rules repositories functional and technical components
- How business process and rules repositories operate [active or passive]

- Development and maintenance of process and rules repositories including version control
- Content of process and rules repositories including ownership
- Integrity and security for repositories
- Performance metrics and evaluation
- Regulatory compliance and records retention

Discussion:
Whether active or passive, the information resident in these repositories is critical to the effective and compliant execution of business processes and rules.

Business Process Performance Management

Course Description:
The success of BPM requires a set of meaningful outcome and execution performance metrics that convey the value added to business operations and strategy for assessment by senior executives, process owners, and process staff. An integrated network of performance metrics spanning customer requirements through fulfillment and cash inflow is needed to deliver this information to appropriate stakeholders. Performance metrics for extended enterprise business processes must be included to enable an end-end complete evaluation. Both business-oriented and technology-oriented metrics will be addressed. Criteria for generating reports will be discussed, e.g., events, user queries, or date. Class examples and cases will be used to illustrate how to develop an effective BPM performance evaluation system.

Course Objectives:
- To develop BPM metrics that improve alignment between business strategy and business process services
- To identify key business process activities and outcomes that should be evaluated
- To develop valid and reliable key performance metrics for both business and technology activities
- To specify the manual and computer-based components of an effective BPM assessment system.
- To gain experience in building and assessing business processes through in-class exercises

Major Topics:
- Relationship between BPM performance and enterprise performance management,
- Specifying types of BP metrics (outcomes, operations, and development) for relevant classes of stakeholders
- How to develop valid and reliable BPM metrics.
- How to develop valid and reliable BRM metrics.

- How to assure that BPM/BRM metrics continue to be aligned with enterprise strategy, customer requirements and environmental influences (e.g., industry competition, regulatory agencies, and technological change)
- Sources and validity of data captured for BPM/BRM metrics
- Types of analysis and alerting reports based upon specified classes of triggers
- Building a BPM performance repository for longitudinal analysis
- Developing criteria for deciding whether a BPM performance gap requires remediation
- Using cases to evaluate the appropriateness and quality of BPM metrics

Discussion:
Suggested pre-requisites are: Intro to BPM, Process Modeling, Process Analysis (metrics), and Business Process strategy (align BPM metrics with enterprise metrics)—perhaps Business Process Technology & Architectures to obtain a comprehensive viewpoint? Some lecture is needed to create a foundation for metrics development, but the majority of the content should emphasize real examples, cases and exercises to cement the concepts. If feasible, business process performance software and dashboard building software, should be used (at least a demo) to create an implementation experience (but not at the cost of diminishing the learning of foundation material. If the set of courses in a particular program variation has not included experience with BPM simulations to analyze the impacts of changing process components to assess performance improvements—include an exercise in this course. You can't construct metrics until you experience them. This is a MUST course for any full curriculum or certificate subset. For the latter, perhaps it is a significant module in a certificate or executive course.

Sustaining Business Process Management in the Organization
Course Description:
The benefits from BPM are harvested from a long-term commitment, not as a short-term burst of productivity. Thus, BPM benefits' sustainability follows from a transformation to a process-centric culture by all relevant organization stakeholders. Without successful change management, BPM cannot deliver continual, perhaps radical improvement benefits. An effective program for sustaining BPM value will be discussed including senior executive support, incentives consistent with BPM improvement, and creating BPM innovation focus groups. Successful implementation of BPM improvements must be celebrated openly and enthusiastically to maintain a commitment to BPM improvements. Industry examples and cases will enable discussion of implementing a BPM sustainability plan.

Course Objectives:
- To understand the sustainability movement and its application to BPM
- To develop BPM sustainability objectives and benefits
- To create a plan for institutionalizing BPM as a normal way of conducting business
- To develop metrics for assessing the effectiveness of a BPM Sustainability Plan

- To evaluate the types of BPM sustainability in relation to the complexity and dynamics of the organization's market space

Course Topics:
- Sustainability programs and practices in the for-profit and not-for-profit sectors globally
- What are sustainable business processes?
- How can sustainable business processes facilitate enterprise sustainability?
- How to get sustainable BPM jump-started in your organization
- What are meaningful metrics of BPM Sustainability?
- What is the relationship of BPM sustainability with enterprise agility?
- What organizations have adopted BPM Sustainability in practice?

Discussion:
Course Pre-requisites: BP Performance Management, Business Process Strategy. Since sustainability has many interpretations, numerous examples to make the BPM sustainability clear will be important. The challenge of attaining BPM sustainability in relation to industry competition, customer requirements predictability, technological change, and regulatory mandates needs clarification. Senior executives must be seen as continuous advocates of a process centric organization despite strategic uncertainties.

Business Process Strategy
Course Description:
Alignment between Business process objectives and enterprise strategy is essential to harvest BPM benefits. Efficiency without effectiveness will not accomplish institutional objectives. Customer requirements must shape business strategy, objectives, metrics and organization. This thrust must continue to shape BPM objectives, strategy and metrics. Clear delineation of end-to-end (cross functional) business processes with process owners should include extended business processes and more detailed business sub-processes. Given finite enterprise resources, the proposed business process investments must be analyzed within the context of the current business process portfolio. For BPM to be successful, clear accountability from the business process owner through business sub-processes' owners must be established in conjunction with appropriate metrics.

Course Objectives:
- To stress the importance of alignment between enterprise and business process management strategies.
- To create BPM objectives consistent with providing customer value
- To develop a business process organization with business process and sub-process owners to establish clear accountability.
- To develop end –to-end business processes that promote collaborative cross-functionality
- To analyze new business process investments' risks and rewards in the context of limited resources and an existing business process portfolio

- To understand the benefits from establishing a Process Project Management Office and a Process Council.

Course Topics:
- Enterprise and BPM strategy alignment
- Application of business strategy models to BPM strategy
- Creating end-to-end, cross-functional business processes including the extended enterprise
- Developing appropriate business process metrics consistent with the enterprise strategy
- Building a Business Process Organization with clear business process and sub-process accountability
- Developing BPM metrics at each level to evaluate the contribution towards generating business value
- To apply portfolio theory to the evaluation of current and proposed BPM investments
- To understand the potential benefits from establishing a Center for Process Excellence, and a Business Process Project Office.

Discussion:
None

Internship/Project
Course Description:
Course prerequisites include Introduction to BPM, Process Modeling, and Business Process Performance. After examining business strategy frameworks and models, use cases and field projects to analyze BPM strategy, structure, and performance. Experience the analysis, development and improvement of existing or new business processes in real or simulated environments.

Course Objectives:
- Synthesize and apply the knowledge from prior BPM courses
- Learn effective consultant's skills
- Analyze a business process improvement opportunity
- Use previously discussed and piloted BPM software in more complex situations

Major Topics:
- Business process current status discovery techniques
- Successful consulting skills
- Surfacing root causes from apparent symptoms
- Effective written and oral communication

Discussion:
Concrete experience has no substitute. The internship can be a gateway to employment after graduation.

KEY CONCEPTS

1. A model curriculum guides the education of new and experienced BPM professionals
2. Curriculum content will vary in scope and depth by type of constituency, e.g., undergraduate or graduate students
3. Model curriculum content is a joint effort of educators and practitioners
4. The model curriculum content must reflect changes in practices, concepts, regulations, and technology
5. Value of the model curriculum is a function of the extent of adoption by educational institutions

Appendix D - Certification Program

The Education Committee of ABPMP is currently engaged in developing a professional certification program for BPM Professionals. The Certified Business Process Professional (CBPP™) program will evaluate an individual's knowledge and experience based on a rigorous examination and an assessment of work history and education.

The first version of our certification program will be an assessment of general knowledge and skill in practicing Business Process Management. Future options may recognize discipline specialties such as specific experience with BPM technologies, Process Transformation Design, performing the Process Manager role, Process Modeling, etc.

For current information on the status of the CBPP™ program, see the ABPMP website at www.abpmp.org

Program Components and Qualifications

Experience

A candidate must have 4 years or 5,000 hours of professional experience performing BPM related work. A candidate may substitute up to 2,500 hours total experiential credit for the following:

- **Education**
    - Formal
      1,000 hours for a Bachelor degree in relevant field
      1,000 hours for an advanced degree in a relevant field
    - Training
      up to 500 hours each for completion of ABPM endorsed education programs

- **Related Certifications**
    - 500 hours each for relevant recognized professional certifications such as: PMP, CBA, CBIP

Examination

Candidates must take and pass the CBPP examination. The CBPP examination is under development and is expected to be available to the public by April 2009

Professional Code of Ethics and Good Conduct

Candidates must sign and adhere to the ABPMP Code of Ethics and Good Conduct

Recertification

Candidates must commit to a program of continuing professional education. Recertification is required every three years in order to continue to use the designation. A minimum of 120 hours of continuing professional education and development in each recertification period is required.

Continuing Education Activities

- College/University Credit Courses, 1 recertification hour per contact hour
- College/University non-credit course, 1 recertification hour per CEU or classroom hour
- Seminar, tutorial or training, 1 recertification hour per CEU or classroom/instructional hour
- Conference/Symposium with Educational Content, 1 recertification hour per session hour attended
- Company Education Courses (CEUs or contact hours)
- Teaching/Lecturing/Presentations (development and initial presentation), up to 60 hours per recertification period
- Self Study up to 60 hours per recertification period
- Published Articles/Books/White Papers/Blogs, 1 recertification hour per 100 words, up to 60 hours per recertification period
- Other certification, 40 recertification hours
- Professional Society Programs, 1 recertification hour per activity hour
- Leadership Role in Professional Society, 20 recertification hour hours per year up to 60 hours per recertification period
- Other professional continuing education activities may be submitted subject to approval by certification committee, generally 1 recertification hour per hour of activity

Appendix E – Maintenance of the BPM CBOK®

Managing Future Releases and Versions

With the release of this second version of the ABPMP Guide to the Business Process Management Common Body of Knowledge (CBOK®) we welcome the feedback of BPM practitioners so that we can make sure that this publication meets your Business Process Management needs and expectations. To this end, we established a CBOK® Maintenance Sub-Committee to evaluate feedback and manage changes to be included in future versions. This publication is the result of that effort by a core team of dedicated BPM Practitioners.

ABPMP is pleased to announce that we have signed an agreement with the International Association of Business Process Management (IABPM). IABPM is a group of legally independent national associations and societies dedicated to the promotion of Business Process Management (BPM). It is headquartered in Europe. This partnership is exciting for BPM practitioners around the world for obvious reasons. However, two noteworthy efforts currently underway are the translation of the CBOK® into French and German and the merging of IABPM's Body of Knowledge with this work. ABPMP would like to welcome all the IABPM affiliates and their members to this joint effort in promoting Business Process Management to the business community worldwide. IABPM will be represented by Goetz Schmidt, IABPM Chairman and Martin Pfaendler, IABPM Vice Chairman.

Background

A presentation was made to the ABPMP Education Committee on May 14, 2007 outlining the proposed structure and mandate of the sub-committee. The Education Committee approved the proposal and it was sent to the ABPMP Board of Directors and approved. A summary of the proposal follows.

Sub-Committee Structure:

- Committee should have representation from the following groups: practitioners, academics, and the Certification Committee
- Training Providers should not be members of the Committee

Sub-Committee Mandate

- Maintain a publication schedule of interim releases
- Compile and publish minor changes to the CBOK® as interim releases
- Recommend major changes for approval by the Education Committee and possibly the Board depending on the scope of the change.
- Provide a method to gather feedback once CBOK® is released
- Analyze feedback and determine course of action which may include
    - Doing and/or coordinating research of proposed change
    - Making minor changes
    - Recommending major changes

- Ensure new versions of the CBOK® remain in alignment with Certification requirements and study guides.
    - advance notice to Training Providers
    - planning updates for certification exam
- Determine a method for tracking downloads of CBOK® to maintain distribution list for updates.

Change Categories

Major changes would include

- Changes to scope
- Changes to definition of key items
- Adding or Removing Chapters
- Adding or Removing sub-disciplines
- Restructuring of the document
- Changes that change past decisions on content or scope of the CBOK®
- Major changes would result in a major release, i.e. V2.0

Minor changes would include

- Wording clarifications
- Minor editing: grammar, spelling, punctuation
- New graphics that add clarity
- Minor changes would result in interim releases, i.e. V1.1, 1.2, etc.
- Minor releases would be quarterly

Handling Feedback

- Provide a formal forum including transaction # to track change requests, analysis and actions (implement or decline)
- Create a Blog for informal discussions but formal requests must go through the formal forum.
- Create a formal request form for submission to the Maintenance Committee

For this version of the CBOK® feedback can be sent by completing the CBOK® Feedback form located in the Members Area at **www.abpmp.org**. All feedback will be acknowledged and suggested changes will be will be assigned a tracking number and be reviewed by members of the Maintenance Sub-Committee. They will be categorized as outlined in the Sub-Committee Mandate above. Suggestions that fit into the Major Change category will be evaluated by members of the BPM Community. This may be in the form of a request to ABPMP members for their comments, having a recognized BPM Contributor review or establishing a short-term work group to research.

We are excited to be launching this publication and our hope and, indeed, our expectation is that with your help it will evolve into a truly relevant and effective resource that will become a recognized authority on Business Process Management.

Appendix F – Contributors

ABPMP is deeply grateful to the following contributors for their many hours of writing, reviewing, editing, and other efforts. These are the people who directly contributed to the development of this volume. There are many others who indirectly contributed thoughts, comments, and morale support to these contributors while they worked on this and to them we extend our heartfelt thanks as well.

Professor Yvonne Lederer Antonucci, Ph.D.
Yvonne Lederer Antonucci is an Associate Professor in the Department of MIS and Decision Sciences at Widener University in Chester, PA where she is also the SAP alliance coordinator and the director of the Business Process Innovation Center of Excellence. Yvonne has been an invited speaker at several international BPM conferences and has published in numerous international journals and conferences in the area of information technology including business process management, and enterprise systems. She has been involved in various information technology consulting activities including workflow management systems and BPM projects. Yvonne has developed and teaches courses on process analysis, process modeling, and process automation for over ten years. In addition she has received several industry grants related to Business Process Management, process analysis and business-to-business collaboration. Yvonne is a member of the ABPMP Education Committee and Philadelphia chapter in which she is Vice President, Information Systems.

Professor Martin Bariff, Ph.D., C.P.A.
Martin Bariff, Ph.D., C.P.A. is an Associate Professor of Information Management and Director, e-Business Certificate Program at the Stuart School of Business, Illinois Institute of Technology. He has taught BPM within MBA courses, e.g., Strategic Management of IT, for more than ten years. Martin has published research on information management, including BPM, in leading academic journals. He a member of the ABPMP Education Committee and Vice President of Finance and IS in the Chicago chapter. Martin participated in the development of the initial ISACA CBOK® and CISA program. He is or has held leadership positions in ACM SIGs, INFORMS Colleges, and the Chicago chapters of IIA and SIM. Martin is a member the BTM Academic Council of the BTM Institute. He has consulted with organizations in industry and government.

Tony Benedict, MBA, CPIM
Tony Benedict, MBA, CPIM is the Vice-President and Director of Relationships for the Association for Business Process Management Professionals (ABPMP.org). Currently, he is a Senior Manager in the Global Supply Chain Practice with Tata Consultancy Services. Previously, he was a Manager in the Business Architecture Office in the Information Technology Group at Intel Corporation. Tony has led business process improvement projects for the last 8 years in the high tech industry. Tony has been a Best Practices Lecturer in Decision Technologies at the Katz Graduate School of Business at the University of Pittsburgh for the last 3 years. He also has spoken at

Brainstorm's BPM conferences on Enterprise Blueprinting for BPM and Enterprise BPM and Strategic Alignment. Tony has been an instructor for Intel's university for the past 7 years and has taught business process improvement, web programming and design, and SAP materials management and production planning. He has a Bachelor of Science degree in Psycho-Biology and an MBA in Finance and Operations. Tony is also APICS Certified in Production and Inventory Control (CPIM).

Brett Champlin, MBA, CSP, CCP, CDMP

Brett Champlin, MBA, CSP, CCP, CDMP is the President of the Association for Business Process Management Professionals (ABPMP.org) and a Manager in the Business Performance Improvement group with a Fortune 100 insurance company. He has led business process transformation projects for the last 15 years, and has over 25 years of experience working in Information Systems Management. Brett is a member of the adjunct faculty at the University of Chicago where he teaches a course on BPM in the Strategic Process Improvement program. He has served on the board of directors of the Data Management Association and the Institute for the Certification of Computing Professionals. He is an occasional contributor to BPM Strategies and various trade publications and has been a popular speaker at international conferences and professional associations for over 10 years. Brett is a member of the ABPMP Education Committee and ABPMP Chicago chapter.

Bruce D. Downing, Ph.D.

Bruce D. Downing, Ph.D. is the president of Provisory Services, Inc. a business management and Information Systems consulting firm focusing on business process management, work flow and records management systems. The services offered by Provisory include analysis, design, implementation and systems support for business processes. Mr. Downing's experience in BPM includes projects in insurance claims processing, machine manufacturing, parts management and the development of web-based procurement and ecommerce processes for the U.S. Department of Defense. He also offers business seminars in BPM approaches to internal controls and records management for legal and regulatory compliance. Bruce is a member of the ABPMP Ed Committee and the Philadelphia Chapter.

Jason Franzen, MBA

Jason Franzen is a principal in Adnovus Consulting and provides audit performance management consulting and training to internal audit departments in Fortune 500 companies and government agencies. Mr. Franzen is an MBA graduate of Purdue University's Krannert School of Business and also holds degrees from the University of Colorado and San Jose State University. He has served as an adjunct faculty member at several local universities and community colleges where he teaches classes and seminars on business strategy, execution, and process management. He is also a highly praised facilitator at global business forums. Jason is a member of the ABPMP Education Committee and an at-large member of ABPMP.

Daniel J. Madison, MBA, CFA
Daniel J. Madison, MBA, CFA, Lean Office Certificate is a principal in Value Creation Partners, an organizational consulting and training firm. For the past 19 years, he has helped clients increase value through process mapping and improvement, organizational redesign, and lean six sigma techniques. Dan regularly teaches courses on Analyzing and Improving Operations, Streamlining Office and Service Operations with Lean, and Process Mapping and Process Improvement through several universities, e.g., the University of Chicago and University of Pittsburgh. In addition he teaches "Analyzing the "As Is" Process and Creating the "To Be" Process" through the Business Process Management Institute. His book titled Process Mapping, Process Improvement, and Process Management continues to be #1 on Amazon in the areas of process mapping and improvement. Dan is a member of the Consortium of Advanced Management-International and the Association of Business Process Management Professionals. Dan is a member of the ABPMP Education Committee and an at-large member of ABPMP.

Sandra Lusk, PMP
Sandra Lusk has over twenty-five years experience in system and process design and development working with utility, transportation, logistics, insurance and banking organizations in the US, Canada, Australia, New Zealand and Wales, UK. She has taught at Algonquin College in Ontario and at the Saskatchewan Institute of Applied Science and Technology. As a Senior Business Process Management Consultant, her responsibilities included development of a BPM Governance, training, mentoring and support of business improvement initiatives. In addition to being a frequent speaker and course leader at national conferences, Sandra has published a number of BPM articles. A graduate in Computer Science from the University of Regina, she is a certified Project Management Professional (PMP) and is currently President of the Association for Business Process Management Professionals, Portland Chapter.

Andrew Spanyi, MBA
Andrew Spanyi is the founder and Managing Director of Spanyi International Inc.
Andrew has nearly two decades of consulting experience including assignments as a Principal of the Rummler-Brache Group, and a Practice Manager with Kepner-Tregoe Inc. His management experience includes assignments with SCONA as a senior Vice President and with Xerox Learning Systems as a Director of Marketing and Business Development. He has managed over 100 major performance improvement projects and has taken part in the development of dozens of sales and management training programs. Andrew has authored two books, More for Less: The Power of Process Management and Business Process Management is a Team Sport. He holds a Bachelor of Arts (Economics), and earned his MBA in Marketing/Finance from York University, Toronto, Ontario, Canada. Andrew was Vice President for Education and chaired the Education Committee of the ABPMP. He is an at large member of the ABPMP.

Mark Treat

Mark Treat has extensive experience in designing and evaluating business processes. Presently, Mark is a BPM practice lead with Science Applications International Corporation (SAIC). Previous he held a variety of positions with the state of Rhode Island. Mark was chairman of the Information Technology team in the Governor's Program Office. He also founded the first Program Management Office within the State and developed an enterprise architecture all of which improved services with lower costs. Prior to these positions, Mark was Director of strategy and Planning for Commerce One Global Services. He received a B.S. in Finance from Babson College and completed additional coursework in e-business strategy, enterprise architecture, and project management. Mark has been a featured speaker at national conferences and published BPM articles. Within ABPMP, Mark is a Corporate Director, chair of the Education committee, and both manages and contributes to the first Common Body of Knowledge project.

Professor J. Leon Zhao, Ph.D.

J. Leon Zhao is Eller Professor in the Eller College of Management, University of Arizona. He holds Ph.D. from the Haas School of Business, UC Berkeley. He received an IBM Faculty Award in 2005 for his contributions in business process management and services computing. He developed one of the first courses in Workflow Management in 2001 and has taught it many times to both undergraduate and graduate students. His research focuses on database and workflow technologies and their applications in business. Leon has been an associate editor of seven academic journals and has co-edited nine special issues in various journals and chaired numerous academic conferences including the Workshop on E-Business (2003), the Workshop on Information Technology and Systems (2005), the IEEE Conference on Services Computing (2006), and the China Summer Workshop on Information Management (2007). More information is found at www.u.arizona.edu/~jlzhao.

Robyn L. Raschke, Ph.D., C.P.A.

Robyn is an Assistant Professor at the University of Nevada Las Vegas and teaches undergraduate and graduate accounting information systems courses. Robyn has published her research in academic journals and presented her BPM research to national and international academic conferences. She is an at-large member of the ABPMP and has consulted in industry.

One of the benefits of the partnership between ABPMP and IABPM is that we will begin incorporating the IABPM Body of Knowledge into the next version of this work. A significant effort has gone into the development of the IABPM Body of Knowledge and we would like to acknowledge those who have contributed to that effort.

Contributors to the IABPM Body of Knowledge

Hartmut F. Binner

Since 1978 Hartmut Binner has given lectures at the University of Applied Sciences in Hannover, Germany as an associate professor. Currently he is the CEO of the Professor Binner Academy, which is a training provider based in Hannover offering a wide range of management seminars. He is a frequent author of publications on organizational research in the most well known German professional journals on process and project management, BPM and integrated process management systems.

From 1999 to 2003 Mr. Binner was the Chairman of the German *REFA*-Association, a federal authority on work design, method and process studies. Moreover, he is the Chairman of the board of the "Gesellschaft für Organisation" *gfo*, the association for business organization and management in Germany.

Kai Krings, Ph.D

Kai Krings is the head of a subject matter expert circle in BPM sponsored by the German association for business organization and management (gfo).

During his 18-year career he has gained a great deal of experience with business transformation projects. He started his career with MRP-implementation projects in small and medium sized companies. Thereafter, he implemented team structures in the automotive supply industry and continued his career with the responsibility for the organizational development of a major player in the international glass-manufacturing industry based in Germany.

During the last few years he has implemented business process management as a guiding management principle in a service and media company of a leading group in the financial industry in Germany. During this time he also conducted various business seminars in process and change management. Kai Krings is a member of the board of directors of gfo, the established association for business organization and management in Germany.

Horst Ellringmann

Horst Ellringmann is the senior partner of M&E Consulting based in Cologne, Germany. After completion of his academic degree in Electrical Engineering, he held various positions in manufacturing and service companies including positions in top management. After his corporate career of about 15 years he built a consulting firm that is specializing in the field of environmental and quality management. In the mid-nineties he concentrated his consulting activities on business process management and process reengineering. Horst Ellringmann has published several books and numerous publications on the subject of business management and organization.

Wolfgang Buchholz

Wolfgang Buchholz is a professor for Organization and Logistics at the University of Applied Sciences in Münster, Germany. After earning his Diploma in Business Administration at the "Justus-Liebig-Universität" in Gießen, he received his PhD in organization and strategic management.

Prior to his promotion to professor of the University of Münster he was co-founder and managing director of the consulting company Eic-Partner. He worked for several years in the chemical industry for Hoechst AG and as a management consultant for CSC.

Mr. Buchholz has published several books on innovation management, supply chain management, management of value nets and supplier relationship management as well as articles on strategy and organization in a number of relevant professional journals, such as DBW, ZfbF or ZFO.

Jakob Freund

Jakob Freund has a Master of Sciences in Business Computing. He is a general manager of the company camunda GmbH. The company develops and sells Software for BPM applications. Camunda provides a web-based BPM-Platform for process hosting that is called "process as a service". Jakob Freund is the founder and chief analyst of BPM-Guide.de, and is also running BPM-Netzwerk.de the largest BPM Web community in Germany, Austria and Switzerland combined with over 3,000 members as of February 2008.

Jakob Freund gives lectures on BPM at the University of Applied Sciences in Berlin, Germany, and the Business School PHW in Zurich, Switzerland. He has published several articles and white papers on BPM and is currently working on a book on BPM. He is the conference manager of the annual "process solutions day", and is also a regular speaker on BPM-related conferences and fairs in Germany such as the Cebit. Jakob Freund has participated in many BPM and SOA projects as a member as well as a project manager. His main competences are process automation including real-time monitoring, SOA, BPMN, BPEL and process simulation.

Appendix G - Summary of Changes

Version 2 – Released February 2009
1. Added Section 1.5.6 Summary of Process Performance Measurement.
2. Chapter 4 – Process Analysis has been completely rewritten based on feedback received from members of the BPM Community.
3. Chapter 5 – Process Design has been updated based on feedback received from members of the BPM Community.
4. Chapter 6 – Process Performance Measurement – New in version 2
5. Appendix C – BPM Model Curriculum has been expanded and updated.
6. Appendix D – Certification has been updated to show current status.
7. Addition of Appendix G – Summary of Changes
8. Minor edits of content, spelling, grammar and formatting have been made throughout.

Note: While many of the feed back items received have been addressed in this version, there are still outstanding items to be considered. These will be reviewed with any additional feedback received for release of Version 2.

Made in the USA
Lexington, KY
20 December 2009